W9-COT-937

Quantitative Risk Assessment in Regulation

Studies in the Regulation of Economic Activity

TITLES PUBLISHED

The Dilemma of Freight Transport Regulation
Ann F. Friedlaender

Technological Change in Regulated Industries
William M. Capron, Editor

Reforming Regulation: An Evaluation of the Ash Council Proposals
Roger G. Noll

International Diffusion of Technology: The Case of Semiconductors
John E. Tilton

Public Policy toward General Aviation
Jeremy J. Warford

The Local Service Airline Experiment
George C. Eads

Economic Aspects of Television Regulation
Roger G. Noll, Merton J. Peck, and John J. McGowan

Government and the Sports Business
Roger G. Noll, Editor

Energy Regulation by the Federal Power Commission
Stephen G. Breyer and Paul W. MacAvoy

Economic Regulation of Domestic Air Transport: Theory and Policy
George W. Douglas and James C. Miller III (out of print)

Social Responsibility and the Business Predicament
James W. McKie, Editor

Bread upon the Waters: Federal Aids to the Maritime Industries
Gerald R. Jantscher

Promoting Competition in Regulated Markets
Almarin Phillips, Editor

Transition to a Free Market: Deregulation of the Air Cargo Industry
Andrew S. Carron

The Strategy of Social Regulation: Decision Frameworks for Policy
Lester B. Lave

The Scientific Basis of Health and Safety Regulation
Robert W. Crandall and Lester B. Lave, Editors

Clearing the Air: Reforming the Clean Air Act
Lester B. Lave and Gilbert S. Omenn

The Plight of the Thrift Institutions
Andrew S. Carron

Quantitative Risk Assessment in Regulation
Lester B. Lave, Editor

Studies in the Regulation of Economic Activity

Quantitative Risk Assessment in Regulation

LESTER B. LAVE, Editor

The Brookings Institution / Washington, D.C.

Library of Congress Cataloging in Publication data:

Main entry under title:

Quantitative risk assessment in regulation.

(Studies in the regulation of economic activity)
Bibliography: p.
Includes index.
1. Environmental health—Government policy—United States—Decision-making. 2. Environmental health—United States—Evaluation. 3. Pollution—Toxicology. 4. Toxicity testing. 5. Environmental law—United States. I. Lave, Lester B. II. Series.
RA566.3.Q36 1982 363.1′76 82-22603
ISBN 0-8157-5164-8
ISBN 0-8157-5163-X (pbk.)

9 8 7 6 5 4 3 2 1

THE BROOKINGS INSTITUTION is an independent organization devoted to nonpartisan research, education, and publication in economics, government, foreign policy, and the social sciences generally. Its principal purposes are to aid in the development of sound public policies and to promote public understanding of issues of national importance.

The Institution was founded on December 8, 1927, to merge the activities of the Institute for Government Research, founded in 1916, the Institute of Economics, founded in 1922, and the Robert Brookings Graduate School of Economics and Government, founded in 1924.

The Board of Trustees is responsible for the general administration of the Institution, while the immediate direction of the policies, program, and staff is vested in the President, assisted by an advisory committee of the officers and staff. The by-laws of the Institution state: "It is the function of the Trustees to make possible the conduct of scientific research, and publication, under the most favorable conditions, and to safeguard the independence of the research staff in the pursuit of their studies and in the publication of the results of such studies. It is not a part of their function to determine, control, or influence the conduct of particular investigations or the conclusions reached."

The President bears final responsibility for the decision to publish a manuscript as a Brookings book. In reaching his judgment on the competence, accuracy, and objectivity of each study, the President is advised by the director of the appropriate research program and weighs the views of a panel of expert outside readers who report to him in confidence on the quality of the work. Publication of a work signifies that it is deemed a competent treatment worthy of public consideration but does not imply endorsement of conclusions or recommendations.

The Institution maintains its position of neutrality on issues of public policy in order to safeguard the intellectual freedom of the staff. Hence interpretations or conclusions in Brookings publications should be understood to be solely those of the authors and should not be attributed to the Institution, to its trustees, officers, or other staff members, or to the organizations that support its research.

Foreword

GOVERNMENT regulation of health risks has proven controversial and costly. A more systematic approach than that followed hitherto is likely to make better use of available scientific data and prompt future investigations that might lead to better decisions. The theme of this book is that *quantitative* risk assessment can greatly improve regulatory decisionmaking. Without it, different health risks cannot be as easily compared, nor can the degree of protection afforded by the regulatory process be estimated with any precision. Yet the technique is new, and some of the issues to which it must be applied lie on the frontiers of scientific investigation. It raises questions that cannot be answered with confidence—about, for example, the health risk to the general public of low doses of a chemical known to be toxic to rodents in high doses.

The authors of this book describe the current methods and uncertainties of quantitative risk assessment and present six case studies of recent regulatory decisions. The studies show that risks cannot be assessed by rote procedure and that uncertainties, always unavoidable, will often dominate the estimates. Even so, it is clear that such assessments provide valuable insights and are essential to sensible regulation.

The research upon which this book is based was carried out under a contract between Carnegie-Mellon University and the American Petroleum Institute and was directed by Lester B. Lave, then a senior fellow in the Brookings Economic Studies program. The resulting report became the background material for a conference on risk assessment held in May 1981 at Brookings under the joint sponsorship of Brookings, Carnegie-Mellon University, and the American Petroleum Institute. The papers in this volume, whose publication was financed in part by a grant from the American Petroleum Institute, are revisions of those presented at the conference.

Lave, who returned to Carnegie-Mellon University as professor of economics in September 1982, has written extensively on the regulation of risks. He is the author of *The Strategy of Social Regulation: Decision Frameworks for Policy* and coeditor (with Robert W. Crandall) of *The Scientific Basis of Health and Safety Regulation,* both published by Brookings in 1981. Thomas R. Bartman is a clerk for three judges in the U.S. District Court for the Eastern District of Virginia. Dwight D. Briggs is an engineer with Schlumberger Ltd. Ronald J. Marnicio is a graduate student in the Department of Engineering and Public Policy at Carnegie-Mellon University. Christopher H. Marraro is a staff attorney for the American Petroleum Institute.

The work was guided by an advisory committee consisting of Morton Corn, Bernard Goldstein, and Richard Merrill, all of whom offered many useful comments on the manuscript. Howard Runion and Steven Swanson did much to keep the project on track and to clear away obstacles, as did Martha Bradford. Helpful comments and encouragement were also received from John A. Budny, Salvatore Casamassima, Vojin Joksimovic, Norton Nelson, Michael Norvell, Frank Parker, Barbara Price, M. B. Slomka, Curtis Smith, E. W. Starke, Mary Jane Von Allmen, Chi-pang Wen, John Wheeler, D. C. Wobster, and Donald Womacks.

Tadd Fisher and Nancy Davidson edited the book. Penelope S. Harpold verified its factual content and Susan Woollen typed the manuscript; both contributed to the initial rewriting. Kathleen Heffernan gave research assistance; and Diana Regenthal prepared the index.

This is the nineteenth publication in the Brookings series of Studies in the Regulation of Economic Activity. The series is devoted to presenting the results of research focused on public policies toward business. The project was financially supported by grants for the Brookings regulatory program from the Alfred P. Sloan Foundation and the Andrew W. Mellon Foundation, as well as the American Petroleum Institute.

The views expressed in this volume are those of the contributors and should not be ascribed to the foundations whose assistance is acknowledged above, the American Petroleum Institute, Carnegie-Mellon University, or to the trustees, officers, or other staff members of the Brookings Institution.

BRUCE K. MACLAURY
President

November 1982
Washington, D.C.

Contents

Tables

Figures

CHAPTER ONE

Introduction

LESTER B. LAVE

In the past decade the United States has created many agencies to regulate health and safety. These agencies have promulgated myriad regulations, some of which have helped decrease risk, but many have also increased bureaucracy, private-sector costs, and litigation; slowed or impeded productivity; and generally increased conflict. Despite both positive and negative outcomes, the public's demands for increased health and safety have not abated. The issue at hand is to translate these demands into workable goals and then to attain the goals efficiently.

Improving regulatory decisions will not be simple, because the processes required to carry out those decisions are complex, costly, and often grounded in scientific uncertainty. Indeed, regulatory decisions have been treated far too casually; guesses are often substituted for observable facts, and litigation frequently is used simply to cause delay. Even minor improvements in the scientific bases of the regulatory decisions could have saved society far more than it would have cost to provide the additional information.

A careful review of scientific evidence and a quantitative risk assessment should be the basis of regulatory decisions. Regulation without these elements is uninformed, arbitrary, and unlikely to withstand litigation, induce cooperation from those being regulated, or produce the results desired. Scientific analysis has not been emphasized in most rule making; rather, many hold the cynical view that regulation is power politics, with the winners imposing their will on the losers. A change in administration should not be used to extend this cynicism; it is quite possible for an administration to demonstrate that society's health and safety goals can be reconciled with a healthy industrial economy and can be implemented efficiently, making greater use of scientific data and analysis.

Quantitative risk assessment is not a panacea. A primary limitation is that such an assessment is concerned only with what can be measured and quantified. In practice, scientists tend to focus on the measurable aspects of most health and safety issues and neglect the areas that are more difficult to analyze. If the risk assessment is to be interpreted correctly, however, and if it is to be useful, both decisionmakers and scientists must keep the goals and general picture in mind.

Despite its limitations, quantitative risk assessment has no logical alternative. With the exception of a policy of no risk, which is impossible to implement in a modern industrial society, risk assessment is the only systematic tool for analyzing various regulatory approaches to health and safety. All other frameworks involve some sort of intuitive balancing that is inappropriate where quantitative analysis is possible and where the stakes are high.

A Conference on Risk Assessment

At a Brookings conference in May 1981, participants reviewed methods for and limitations of quantitative risk assessment and analyzed four major and two minor case studies of the role of risk assessment in recent regulatory decisions. One part of the conference discussion emphasized the advances in method that will resolve the uncertainty of risk assessment over the next several years. Another emphasized that risk assessment is done routinely in several agencies and that the resulting risk estimates affect agency decisions. Much of the discussion focused on how to conduct an assessment on a highly politicized issue and how to interpret scientific uncertainties. While the shortcomings of quantitative risk assessment were evident, there appeared to be a consensus that it provides both a valuable framework for structuring the problem and insights into better solutions. Emphasis also was placed, however, on the possible misuses of risk assessment when there are major uncertainties and a politicized environment.

Although important problems characterize current agency regulation of health and safety, solutions need not require either years of waiting or new legislation. Much can be done in the short term to improve the process with existing resources.

The case studies in chapters 3 through 8 are revised versions of the conference papers and provide data on the process of analysis and evaluation used in each case. Sufficient data were available in all six cases to carry out some sort of quantitative risk assessment. While no analysis reached a unique answer or would garner unanimous support, all provided important insights into the regulatory process.

The numerous current inadequacies in data and analysis will be repaired only when risk analysis occupies a more central role in decisionmaking. Agencies allocate their resources to the inputs most crucial to their decisions; the result is that data collection and analysis have generally been reduced as funding is cut. In short, regulatory agency officials should emphasize the importance of science in identifying and studying problems and in seeking solutions.

Most scientists and voters believe that regulatory decisions are, or at least should be, based in scientific fact and that value conflicts are resolved through Congress and thus indirectly by citizens. Yet many scientists inject their personal values into the regulatory analysis. Blatant intrusion comes when "prudent" assumptions rather than best judgments are incorporated into these analyses. The resulting estimates and interpretations, while intellectually interesting, contain so many hidden assumptions that often they provide no useful information.

Perhaps the most surprising result of the case study analyses was the discovery that the agencies frequently fail to engage in a careful, systematic review of the available scientific evidence to determine which conclusions are appropriate. Confounding this sloppiness is the tendency to regard the risk analysis as an advocacy document that must be shaped to support an agency decision, even if that decision is reached by political judgment without regard to science. Rather than attempting to determine the most probable estimate of risk and the range of uncertainty, the risk assessment generally has been structured to be arbitrarily conservative.

The type of careful review advocated here need not be time consuming or expensive. Each agency routinely devotes much more professional effort to its studies than the authors of the papers in this book have done, and yet the results are often less scientifically satisfying.

The emphasis on quantitative risk assessment is not meant to indicate there is some rule for decisionmaking that antiseptically converts scientific data into finished regulations. The scientific analysis contains many uncertainties that require educated judgment in light of the partial information that is available. Political judgments are required as well. The objective of risk assessment is not to eliminate judgment but to inform it.

No one should be under the illusion that quantitative risk assessment has a pro-industry or anti-environmental bias. The result of clarifying scientific evidence and its implications would not be to insulate industry from regulations. Properly applied risk assessments should produce fewer inadequate regulations and fewer neglected areas; efforts would not be squandered in the wrong places and on the wrong methods.

The stress on careful review and on quantitative risk assessment brings with it ancillary benefits. This more analytic, less frenetic approach clarifies the implications of decisions, helps achieve goals at lower cost, identifies alternatives and eliminates bad ones, and generally makes clear that not all goals can be or need be achieved. Indeed, a regulatory agency must explicitly recognize conflicts among goals if it is to be successful in achieving its mission. Analysis is needed to identify high-risk groups and to set priorities for action. Perhaps most important is the fact that regulations are made in a world experiencing rapid change in social goals, economic structure, and science and technology. Uninformed guesses are likely to be irrelevant or pernicious in the four to ten years required to investigate and establish a regulation. Careful thought and good science are important contributions to effective regulation.

The six cases in this book reveal a lack of communication between the agency professionals and their counterparts in the regulated companies. These professionals need not discuss policy, and in this setting should not; but they can clarify methods and results and explore common technical problems. The goal of both groups should be the resolution of most scientific issues with accuracy and a minimum of conflict.

The major case studies identify a need for the clarification of the goals of an agency and its legislation. As agencies formulated their regulations, goals were a major subject of debate, which often led to litigation. Since the goals or purposes of a law can be clarified only by Congress, steps need to be taken in these areas, or the courts will be defining legislative goals by their decisions.

Risk Assessment's Potential Role in Regulation

The United States, like other developed countries, has exhibited increasing concerns for risks affecting health. While the magnitude of these risks evidently has declined, the nature of the threat has also changed. Risks from infectious diseases and disabling accidents have been reduced substantially or in some cases eliminated. They have been replaced by fears of chronic disease, particularly of cancer, although there is little evidence that these risks have been increasing (after adjusting for age), except for lung cancer due predominantly to cigarette smoking.

This widespread concern for lowering risks to health resulted in major new legislation in the 1970s and more stringent standards for activities already regulated (for example, a miner's exposure to coal dust). This legislation can be divided into two basic types. The first requires the regulators to lower risks from a substance to zero or negligible levels without concern for the resulting costs; technological feasibility is the only constraint. The second requires the regulators to balance some measure of the benefits from lowering the risk against the costs of doing so. I have shown elsewhere that the first framework is self-contradictory.[1] In each regulatory action there is at least an implicit weighing of costs and benefits; the second type of legislation differs from the first only by making the balancing explicit.

Whether the balancing is implicit or explicit, crucial pieces of information are the magnitude of risk and how risk will change with alternative regulations. Without being able to measure risks quantitatively and to estimate the effects of proposed standards, regulation is reduced to guesses based on what are called prudent judgments. These guesses uncover and exacerbate value conflicts between those who are opting for greater safety, and are thus willing to accept less consumption, and those who are not. Without estimates of risk, guesses or value judgments are the only devices for setting standards, and the inherent differences in values inevitably lead to maximal conflict.

The conceptual steps in discovering and regulating risks are shown in the middle column of figure 1-1. The data needed to support each decision are shown in the left-hand column; the right-hand column shows the judgments or expert opinions required for each stage. The process cannot begin until a possible hazard is identified.

Scientific evidence is usually the primary input in deciding if possible hazards are worth further regulatory consideration. Those warranting further attention must be subject, at least implicitly, to risk assessment. Data are needed on exposure patterns and interacting substances; a judgment is needed about whether the observed association is causal or

1. Lester B. Lave, *The Strategy of Social Regulation: Decision Frameworks for Policy*.

Figure 1-1. Hazard Management

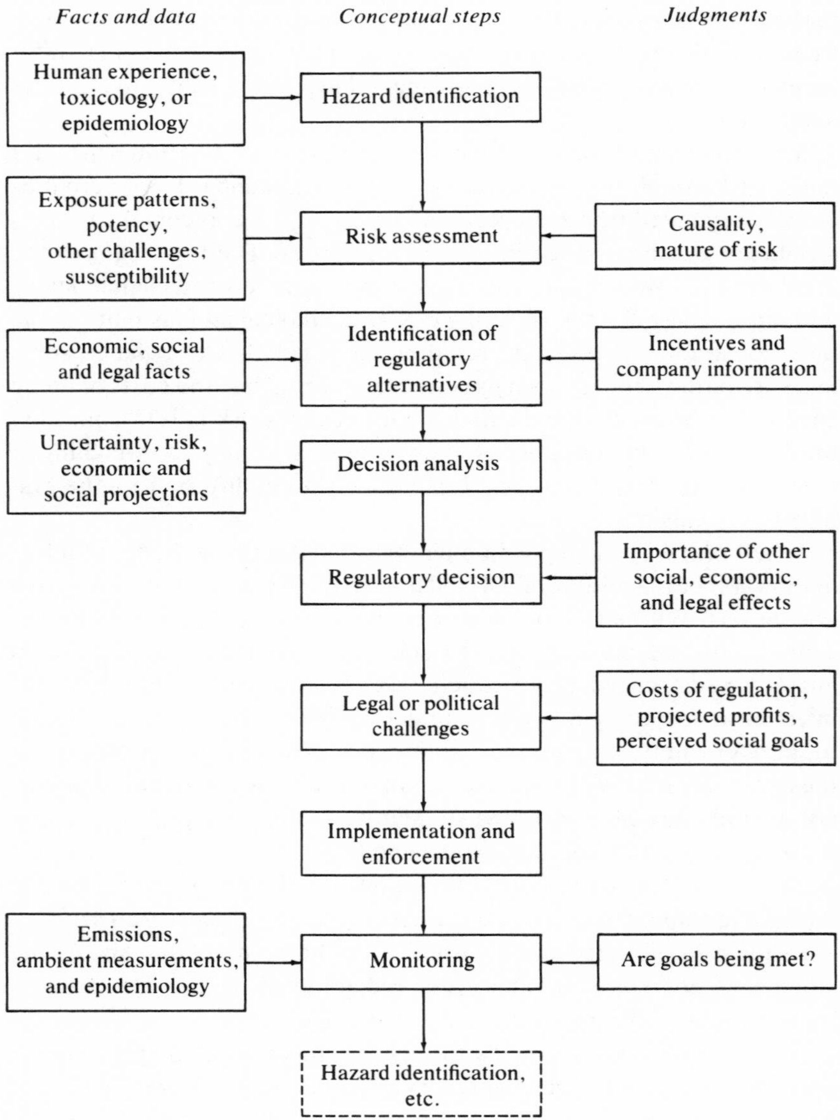

simply a spurious correlation. If the risk appears to warrant some action, the next step is to identify the conceptual range of regulatory alternatives, from complete reliance on the marketplace to developing and disseminating information, assessing effluent fees, or promulgating formal regulations. In analyzing the alternatives, it is important to develop information on such issues as incentives for currently employed workers, those seeking jobs, or companies involved. In addition, it is essential to assess the current level of information. These alternatives are then analyzed in an attempt to specify the consequences of each alternative in terms of various benefits and costs and current and future uncertainties. A regulatory decision must then be made among the alternatives, based on the information and judgments concerning the importance of unquantified effects. As a virtual certainty, legal or political challenges will occur, influenced by private judgments about the costs of litigation and the value and probability of success, or at least of delay.

A large step in hazard management is in implementing and enforcing the decision regarding alternatives; surprisingly little research has been done to clarify this step, although evidence shows that many regulations are modified significantly at this stage. The final stage, monitoring to ensure compliance, is not addressed here.

The flow shown in the figure progresses from top to bottom in a multistage but orderly fashion. Regulatory processes are anything but orderly, however, since a fact or judgment at one stage can cause the process to begin over again, set it back several stages, or stall it indefinitely. In particular, monitoring often identifies additional hazards, thus initiating the process again. Implicit in the figure is the decision at each stage to stop if the hazard is judged insufficient to warrant proceeding or the cost too high to justify action.

The focus of this book is on the first two stages, hazard identification and risk assessment, although the case studies attempt to examine each step. It is evident that the entire process of regulating risks is difficult. Many scientists argue that knowledge is so rudimentary that this process is, and can only be, a judgmental one in which the media, public opinion, and real or imagined disasters, such as occupational exposure to vinyl chloride or public exposure to toxic wastes from the Love Canal, all play roles.

Certainly there are major uncertainties. However, there are also powerful reasons for not surrendering to ad hoc decisionmaking. Past regulatory controversies and ineffectiveness, as well as a growing mistrust of government, have led to low confidence in current institutions. It is difficult to resist cynicism when regulations involving billions of dollars and hundreds of lives are based on arbitrary guesses in which politics rather than science has the primary role. Both industry and government must find more efficient ways to identify the most important risks and to accomplish the social objective of reducing these risks. While there is a strong short-term incentive for assuming an adversarial role of deprecating the facts, analysis, and motivation of the opposite party, the costs to society of such an approach have grown to the point where neither government nor industry is seen as working for the public interest or as worthy of public trust. No one is surprised at value conflicts, but often these are cloaked in spurious disagreement about the science involved. Value conflicts and scientific uncertainties will persist, but scientific issues must be separated from social values as clearly as possible.

Despite the difficulties, quantitative risk assessment has a central role in reforming regulation. If risk assessment were deemed impossible for judging the risks associated with individual materials, then all toxic substances, or at least broad groups such as carcinogens, would have to be treated similarly. In an industrial society it is impossible to ban all carcinogens or even to apply a technology-based standard such as the "best available control technology" required in the Clean Air Amendments of 1970;[2] either would shut down the economy with a negligible decrease in risk. If Congress writes such rigid frameworks into law, inevitably a few substances will arbitrarily be selected for special treatment, while the rest will languish until some real or imagined disaster elevates them to the spotlight. When the public has sufficient experience with a suspected carcinogen, such as saccharin, it has dismissed bald assertions about the disastrous potential of allowing exposure; however, lack of familiarity can lead to irrational concern and unnecessary alarms. Common sense tells us that some substances are more toxic than others, that some are more useful than others, and that regulations must take account of these differences. Without a scientific basis for measuring risk and usefulness, opposing experts are plunged into disagreements that confuse rather than enlighten and cloud rather than clarify the issues.

2. 84 Stat. 1676. Various versions of technology-based standards have been defined by Congress and the Environmental Protection Agency.

Quantitative Risk Assessment Methods

Few scientists would disagree in principle with the value of quantitative risk estimates. However, some would argue that such an assessment is impossible given the current state of knowledge because of ignorance about many of the underlying biomedical mechanisms involving health hazards, necessitating crude guesses at each stage of the analysis. Doing an assessment requires knowing (1) the health effects from exposure, (2) the dose-response relationship, (3) the population at risk, (4) the distribution of doses of the toxic substance, and (5) exposure to and the effects of confounding substances. Each item has its own major difficulties, both conceptually and empirically. While admittedly a demanding framework, quantitative risk assessment is nevertheless necessary to set priorities and to help choose among alternative solutions, as well as to provide evidence that health regulation is working.

Determining the health effects from exposure to a new chemical is complicated by the types of problems that might arise, including cancer, acute or chronic disease, genetic change, and birth defects. The initial indication of toxicity is rarely more than suggestive: an increased level of disease in some population or suggestive effects observed in a laboratory test. Even when more systematic efforts are devoted to exploring toxicity, the results are often inconclusive. A positive result in an epidemiological study or animal bioassay could be due to a statistical fluke or some failure in method; a negative result could indicate the same or that the toxicity was not great enough to be significant under the test conditions. Highly toxic substances can be discovered easily, but a small increase in the incidence of a chronic disease is extremely difficult, often impossible, to detect. Unfortunately neither animal bioassays nor epidemiological studies are powerful methods for investigating toxicity unless they are testing specific narrow hypotheses about effects, for example, that vinyl chloride causes liver cancer. In addition, a substance cannot be proved to be safe; testing can only indicate whether exposure to a substance significantly increases the incidence of some condition. Thus testing a new substance is painstaking, expensive, and often inconclusive.

The fact that scientists are unable to show that a substance is safe, but can only show that it is not significantly harmful in particular settings, leads to a confusion of the interpretation of the science and of resulting policy. Policymakers cannot conclude that a substance is safe because it failed to cause significant problems in one test or that it is necessarily unsafe if positive results are obtained. Unfortunately, instead of presenting the data and direct interpretation, scientists often give policy advice by interpreting insignificant positive results as more important than significant findings of no effect. This muddles the scientific evidence and its interpretation.

The inherent difficulty of not being able to prove the safety of a substance is confounded by the expense and time required for each test and the difficulties of interpreting results. For example, the Ames test is quick and inexpensive, but its results are given little weight;[3] animal bioassays take two to five years for lifetime studies and are easily marred by defects in design and interpretation; epidemiological studies are time consuming, expensive, and inevitably controversial; even the qualitative results of simply identifying a substance as carcinogenic are usually disputed. Quantitative risk analysis, however, requires a more controversial estimate—the quantitative relationship between risk and response, known as the dose-response curve.

The dose-response relationship is inescapably tied to the mechanisms by which the substance causes damage. The mechanisms are almost entirely unknown, however, and there is no basis for choosing among a large number of alternative functional forms in the statistical estimation. The result is a large difference between the amounts of damage that would be estimated using different, equally plausible, dose-response curves. Usually a procedure is chosen that gives high estimates of damage or perhaps the highest estimated damage. Such a method for dealing with uncertainty suppresses information and obscures crucial questions concerning what substances should be regulated first and at what level standards should be set.

Estimating risk requires knowing how many people are exposed to a substance and the dose each receives. Generally there are only gross data concerning who is exposed and little more than guesses concerning the dose. These data are not conceptually difficult to gather nor do they

3. The Ames test is a revertant salmonella mutagenicity test, which rapidly indicates whether the substance being tested causes mutations in a one-celled organism. Obviously, the results of such a test would be extremely weak predictors for potential human health effects.

generally require elaborate, complicated methods. But they do require painstaking, often costly collection and attention to detail.

For epidemiological studies and even for animal bioassays, the difficulty in identifying the effects of a substance is augmented by the presence of other substances. For example, the conclusion that cyclamate is carcinogenic may have been due to contamination by saccharin in the animal experiments. For experiments, much of this difficulty can be eliminated by going to elaborate lengths to purify air, food, and water and to keep the animals in a sterile environment. However, the resulting sterile conditions are unrepresentative of those facing humans. Such artificiality can lead to overestimating or underestimating risks if, for example, the sterile conditions prevent manifestation of a decrease in resistance to disease or if the artificial surroundings cause animals to be more susceptible to the substance. Epidemiological studies are filled with confounding factors, and it is impossible to control for all such factors.

No one should underestimate the difficulties and uncertainties of quantitative risk assessment. The set of methods discussed here provides controversial, generally ambiguous results. At best, much uncertainty will surround the quantitative estimates of risk. In practice, uncertainty is much greater because critical experiments were not done, crucial information on the population at risk and dose are missing, an animal bioassay was marred by a flaw in experimental design, or an epidemiological study was weakened by failure to collect information regarding a critical variable such as cigarette-smoking habits.

While most of the difficulties cited above stem from the current state of biomedical knowledge, many result from sloppy research or inadequate analysis. Flaws in experimental design can and must be found before half a million dollars are invested in an animal bioassay. Whatever the state of the input data, the task of the analysis is to determine what can be concluded despite the weaknesses or defects.

The risk assessment is of little use unless attention is given to the sources of uncertainty and the effects each have on the resulting estimates. Each source of uncertainty must be specified and related to the final estimates. For example, when the functional form of the dose-response relationship is unknown, reasonable high and low estimates must be calculated in addition to a best-guess estimate and this range of estimates must be carried through the analysis. Often the resulting range will be so large that uncertainty dominates and risk assessment is of no direct help, even though it is of immense help in sorting out the issues and structuring the analysis. Where the issue is inherent randomness, such as the genetic susceptibility of the population to a substance, high and low estimates can be carried through the analysis. Where the issue is some question of fact, such as whether the substance causes a particular kind of cancer, the analysis can carry through twin calculations showing the implications of each assumption.

All the uncertainty must be described and displayed in the final estimates of risk. By doing this decisionmakers can decide how prudent they would like to be. Furthermore, this procedure identifies the most important uncertainties, providing a focus for future research and indicating how new results can be integrated into existing evidence.

Although the array of difficulties is formidable, many can be avoided by better experimental design and analysis. It is not evident that a marked increase in research funds would be required, since the greatest need is for more careful design and execution. Improvements in method offer the hope of quicker, cheaper results. Finally, improved analysis can do much to put current results into perspective and provide better inputs for future decisions.

The difficulties of quantitative risk assessment may qualify the results, but they do not preclude its use. Whatever the difficulties, risk assessment must be used until it is replaced by something better. Its appeal is not its ease of use or its elegance, such as that of abstract mathematics. Rather, risk assessment is used because no other tool is currently available that can produce the information necessary for intelligent regulation.

The Brookings conference included a lively discussion of the process of regulating health risks and of the role of risk analysis. Several inherent difficulties were raised, such as the contradiction between the need of the administrative-legal process for well-defined procedures and its reliance on previous conclusions and the process of scientific research. Certainly every issue cannot be examined anew in each case, but there must be room for changes in scientific knowledge and judgments. Another difficulty is that there is more agreement on best estimates than on confidence intervals or extreme estimates. That is, there is much more agreement on the proportion of the population that would show various symptoms when exposed to 0.25 part per million (ppm) of ozone than on what level of ozone would be innocuous to even the most susceptible group.

General concern was expressed about the extent to which quantitative risk assessment would slow the already cumbersome regulatory process and open it to further legal challenge. The discussion did not resolve the polar views; some argued that risk assessment would result in a vast slowdown, increased litigation, and perhaps a greater number of agency regulations being vacated. Another group felt that risk assessment would speed the process and lessen litigation by clarifying the facts and providing better justification for the regulations and a more systematic process. Perhaps the one point of agreement, as one participant put it, is that further enriching lawyers seems an idle threat.

Somewhat surprisingly, no one objected to the use of risk assessment or even to the necessity of doing it. The uncertainties and limitations of past analyses and the difficulties to be faced in future analyses were spelled out at great length. The difficulties are dishearteningly large. But what is the alternative? Everyone rejected the alternative of being more casual or intuitive; everyone supported the notion that all that could be gotten from science should be extracted. The decisions are too important and too difficult for intuition.

The discussion turned to how to introduce quantitative risk assessment formally into the regulatory process without requiring vast additional resources and time. In terms of resources, one scientist remarked that devoting one-tenth of the cost of litigation in the benzene case to clarifying the science would have resolved much of the uncertainty (see chapter 4). In terms of delay, the ultimate reversal of the benzene decision dramatically illustrated that formulating better regulations and getting better justification for them can do much to shorten the delay before they become effective.

The Case Studies

The four major case studies discussed at the conference and presented here examined risk assessments of photochemical oxidants, benzene, coke oven emissions, and ionizing radiation; two less extensive studies, also covered in this book, examined the regulation of the pesticide chlorobenzilate and that of food additives. These case studies are formidable in technical complexity, involving scientific results and judgments in the areas of cancer research, statistics, epidemiology, toxicology, atmospheric chemistry and physics, and pharmacology as well as human factors.

A central fact in regulating risks of toxic substances is the incredible ability to measure minute amounts of such substances. Often one part per billion can be reliably detected, a feat equivalent to finding one person in a country four times as populous as the United States. Scientists can detect substances at concentrations so small that they have no idea whether exposure would have any adverse consequences. Thus regulators must confront the decision of what levels of substances such as arsenic or dioxin to permit.

The reader of these case studies cannot escape the impression that each of the regulatory decisions is complicated, involving questions at or beyond the current frontiers of science; each involves areas where measurement is difficult, theory is incomplete, and judgment is required for answering many, if not most, of the scientific questions. In many cases the perceived inability of scientists to answer all questions has led to a feeling that science will provide none of the answers, that answers can come only from yet more careful exegesis of the statutes and legislative history, from sampling public opinion and the media, or from political compromise. Yet in each of the cases the scientific investigation in general and the quantitative risk assessment in particular played a crucial role in shaping the regulatory decision, its speed of implementation, or its form as actually implemented.

In some cases, unfortunately, the regulatory agency selected its policy and made its regulatory decision before the results of a scientific investigation were completed or even made. This premature action sometimes necessitated an embarrassing change in policy. The agency might have progressed faster toward its regulatory goals if it had put time and resources into scientific investigation and risk assessment rather than into trying to push ahead quickly in the absence of facts. More information and analysis would most likely have (1) made the hearings smoother and spared all parties the embarrassment of revealing major flaws in the agency proposals; (2) avoided reproposals; and (3) resulted, presumably, in more sensible standards. These improvements, together with the better scientific support, might have convinced companies and public interest groups not to challenge the regulations, caused the courts to sustain the agency proposals if they were challenged, resulted in faster implementation of the standards by those being regulated, and provided protection from risk at an earlier date. While many of these statements are presumptions, some can be documented. If an agency can position itself so that dissatisfaction is over conflicts in value rather than over conflicts in science, it is more likely to prevail.

Photochemical Oxidants

Perhaps the most striking result of the photochemical oxidant case study is the paucity of epidemiological research regarding the effects of this pollutant on health. Only a handful of small clinical investigations and no new epidemiological studies have been published since the standard was initially set in 1971. It is natural that an agency finds itself on the defensive when forced to rely on studies whose flaws have been recognized for more than a decade. In recognition of this fact, the Environmental Protection Agency (EPA) proposed a slight relaxation of the standard. While some evidence has been gathered on acute reactions to ozone among both healthy and asthmatic volunteers, there is virtually no evidence on long-term exposures, particularly the effects on chronic disease, on the developing lung in children, or on possible cytogenic effects. The emphasis on acute effects is particularly unfortunate since this work does not provide justification for a standard close to the 1971 standard; indeed, the new evidence on acute effects suggests that ozone is less of a threat than had been feared in 1971. However, more recent investigations have not explored the chronic effects that now seem of greater concern than the acute effects. Even with almost a decade of lead time, the EPA failed to act to establish a scientific basis for its regulation. This is particularly difficult to understand since from early 1976 it was clear that the EPA would be required by Congress to review all of its air pollution standards.

A second point, in addition to the paucity of scientific data about ozone's health effects, is the sloppiness of the EPA's examination of each study involving ozone. The agency does not appear to have asked whether the methods, analysis of each study, and corroborating studies were sufficient to support the conclusions. Scientific review accepts results only when the underlying methods are worthy of confidence and there is corroborative evidence. Many of the studies had major flaws in apparatus design and use, measurement of levels, and the failure to consider the interaction of ozone with other pollutants; such flaws destroy confidence in the results. A careful review of each study is necessary in order to identify which conclusions are proved, which are good conjectures, and which are unlikely to be true.

A third point is that the scientific analysis and risk assessment seem to have been designed to support a standard arrived at by other means rather than to answer the question of what standard best fulfills the legislative requirement. Thus the scientific analysis and assessment had at most a secondary role in the determination of the standard.

The fourth point stems from the third. In groping for supporting evidence, the EPA cited the results of a highly preliminary exploration. The experts whose opinions were cited disavowed the EPA's use of the study when such use came under attack; the agency was forced to back off and claim that it had never relied on the study. While the method used in the study is interesting and worthy of the further exploration it is receiving, no preliminary explorative study should be used as a basis for supporting a major regulation.

The fifth point focuses on what constitutes an adverse health effect and how far society should go to avoid it. The new studies involving ozone (discussed in chapter 3) concerned acute respiratory problems (due to heavy exercise) that were reversed quickly after the experiment ended. People limit their activities due to a variety of weather conditions, such as extreme heat or cold, precipitation, or humidity, or because they are not feeling well. Limiting their activities once or twice a year because of air pollution seems a small problem compared to the other limitations. When the social dislocations required for controlling air pollution are great and the effects of exposure are reversible, there is little need to set a standard more stringent than the level at which stress was experienced under moderate exercise. If, however, stress occurs at lower concentrations for more sensitive people or is not always reversible, or social dislocations caused by pollution control are small, then more stringent standards might be warranted. The experiments shed no light on these possibilities. If effects on chronic disease or on the developing lung occur at lower concentrations, there is reason for a more stringent standard, but again there is no evidence.

The sixth point is that most of the epidemiological studies and many of the clinical studies are marred by not accounting for the presence of other air pollutants. If these other pollutants are the true cause or even a partial or contributing cause of any observed effects of ill health or stress, ozone is being blamed incorrectly. There is some indication of a positive interaction effect (synergism) between ozone and sulfur oxides.

This point is a subtle one because elevated levels of ozone are nearly always associated with elevated levels of other pollutants. The concentration of ozone that will cause a given physiological response will be lower in the presence of other pollutants. The synergism among pollutants argues for joint standards rather than a stringent ozone standard. Rather than finding an excuse for exonerating ozone, it is desirable to learn the source of any health problem so that regulation can focus on the precise problem and design a strategy that mitigates effects at least cost.

The seventh and final point is that EPA procedures did not permit a full and explicit discussion of biological mechanisms and analogies by which photochemical oxidants might harm health. The focus was on evidence regarding somatic damage. Somehow, the EPA seems to have placed a narrow interpretation on what constitutes evidence regarding health effects. Insofar as evidence exists concerning physiological mechanisms, air chemistry and physics, or animal bioassays that would help with the interpretation of current clinical and epidemiological studies, a forum should be provided for displaying and discussing both this evidence and its implications.

Benzene

The set of generalizations made regarding ozone applies to many of the other case studies and thus their summaries will be briefer. The Occupational Safety and Health Administration (OSHA) took a strong position that a quantitative risk assessment for benzene could not be done, or at least not with sufficient confidence to warrant the effort. This position was taken despite analyses introduced at the hearings by the EPA and a nonagency expert. Having neither dramatic epidemiological evidence nor a risk assessment, OSHA was unable to show that the existing standard permitted an appreciable risk to health. This led the Supreme Court to set aside the agency's standard. Apparently the agency had feared that a risk analysis would expose the standard to court challenges and increase the likelihood of it being reversed. The Supreme Court's opinions, however, seem to indicate that it was aware of the inherent uncertainties in such an analysis and that it would have given the agency deference to encourage greater effort to get at the scientific implications.

The benzene case is complicated because the epidemiological studies were of poor quality. The doses actually received by exposed workers were so uncertain that leukemias observed could have been caused by exposure to less than 10 ppm or several hundred ppm of benzene, or perhaps exposure to some other chemicals. The level of exposure of these workers makes quite a difference for the construction of estimated dose-response curves and the implied risks at 10 ppm.

The exclusive attention given to leukemia by the agency seems to ignore "better" evidence concerning benzene levels that cause other blood disorders. Certainly this information could have been used to clarify the nature of effects and the dose at which effects might be expected.

The benzene case is a classic illustration of the cost of being unprepared. Three years after promulgating the standard, OSHA was reversed. Agency morale and credibility were injured and three years were lost in the battle to regulate benzene to lower concentrations. More careful analysis initially could have produced better scientific evidence and a better regulation that would have been sustained. This case shows the unfortunate consequences of a decision to base a health standard on political grounds without careful analysis of the scientific support for such action.

Coke Ovens

OSHA's regulation of exposure to coke oven emissions was a more dramatic case than that of benzene, since an American epidemiological study showed topside coke oven workers to be at extraordinary risk of lung cancer. The health problem was evident, but the issue was how much exposure had to be decreased in order to eliminate or at least reduce the excess risk.

In this case again, the epidemiology generated dispute since a study of British coke oven workers found no excess risk. However, a careful comparison of the two studies showed the American one to be superior and its conclusions more worthy of confidence. As with benzene, it was nearly impossible to get exact corroboration from animal data because coke emission substances cannot yet be produced in laboratory inhalation chambers. Animal studies had to rely on testing only constituents of the emitted mixture; they did find these materials to be highly carcinogenic. In addition, these constituents were known to be carcinogenic in humans. Even with the difficulties in using these constituent studies, however, the scientific basis for concluding that coke oven emissions are carcinogenic was stronger than for benzene. It is evident that current levels of exposure to coke oven emissions posed an appreciable risk to workers.

The greatest source of uncertainty in the coke oven case was the dose-response relationship, particularly what level of exposure would produce little or no excess risk. The dose that workers received was not known with accuracy, nor was there evidence concerning contributing factors such as cigarette smoking. Finally, the lag between when the dose was received and when lung cancer was detected was extremely important in estimating the health risks of lower doses. Although not totally clear, the evidence was sufficiently detailed to permit quantifying the implications of various assumptions about exposure, cigarette smoking, the latency period, and the form of the dose-response relationship. Although uncertainty remains, the analysis is sufficiently complete to enable exploration of the implications of each assumption and identification of the place where additional research could make the greatest contribution.

Ionizing Radiation

Regulation of exposures of the general population to ionizing radiation from the nuclear fuel cycle is the most thoroughly researched subject of the cases studied. Large amounts of resources have been devoted to estimating the effects of exposure to ionizing radiation, and a good deal is known about the dose-response relationship for various types of radiation, at least at moderate and high levels of exposure. For long-term exposure to very low levels of radiation, however, little is known, and little can be deduced empirically from epidemiological studies. If the answers exist, they must come from understanding the mechanisms by which low doses of radiation produce cancer or other effects.

The case study shows a vast effort at attempting to characterize radionuclide emissions at each stage of the nuclear fuel cycle. It traces the emitted radionuclides through the environment to human exposure and estimates the resulting radiation exposure levels and health effects. While it is difficult to conceive of a more complete investigation, it is also evident that no investigation could conceivably provide precise answers to all the questions. Any investigation will be characterized by areas in which data could be more complete and additional analysis could be done. Presumably the investigation should be stopped at the point where additional data collection and analysis add only another digit, possibly of spurious accuracy, to the calculation.

Following such a careful investigation, it is disheartening to see that the regulatory goals were set so arbitrarily. Numbers were pulled out of the air in defining the acceptable level of exposure and the required safety factor. These numbers could easily have varied by a factor of five or ten, based on the data. Since at the end of the calculation small changes in emission levels imply large changes in cost, a mechanism is needed for feeding back the final calculations to the initial estimation. Somewhat arbitrary initial goals must be matched with their implications, and where a small change in the assumptions would have no discernible effect on health but a large effect on costs, the assumptions should be modified.

The level of effort expended in the scientific analysis for ionizing radiation is so great that it is instructive to examine what was gained from the process. The analysis does pinpoint facilities that were causing the most population exposure and show how that exposure could be averted relatively inexpensively. However, it often gets bogged down in useless detail, as in calculating pathways of secondary importance. Finally, the analysis cannot provide full and complete answers; an element of judgment is required. The purpose of the scientific analysis is to identify and isolate those areas where judgment is needed and to ensure that the result is informed judgment.

Conclusions from Case Studies

A few conclusions from the case studies are worth repeating. In none of the cases was the risk assessment sufficiently complete to provide an automatic mechanism for making decisions. Each case contained important scientific uncertainty and needed informed judgment. Quantitative risk assessment is not the universal remedy for current regulatory problems, but it can be a helpful tool, contributing to the improvement of the regulatory decisionmaking process.

Emphasizing risk assessment would have pushed each agency away from frenetic, crisis-oriented action into behavior more appropriate to the long-term study of the nature of risk. Worker and general population risks could have been reduced more quickly by a more thoughtful approach that developed the risk and cost information and attempted to convince on the basis of data and analysis rather than immediately trying to compel.

While the regulatory and court hearings generated useful information, their adversarial nature tended to obscure legitimate criticisms, suggestions for change, and the meaning and implications of different scientific viewpoints. The process would have proceeded more quickly and smoothly had an initial attempt been made in a nonadversarial setting to discover areas of scientific agreement and to identify the extent of and reasons for disagreement. In particular, it would have been helpful to the process to have had communication among experts in the academic, business, and government communities.

In the four major case studies, the quality of information supplied to regulators, and presumably the resulting regulatory decisions, would have been improved markedly by better analysis. Despite the ambiguous goals provided by Congress and the uncertainty and often poor quality of biomedical evidence, quantitative risk assessment could have improved estimation of the risks associated with each substance and could have helped the agency to design better standards. The case studies indicate that better scientific studies and more precise clarification of goals by Congress would be invaluable and that careful analysis of risks and costs can do much to improve the regulatory decisionmaking process at little additional expense.

CHAPTER TWO

Methods of Risk Assessment

LESTER B. LAVE

THE DESIRES of the public for health, safety, and an unpolluted environment led to a wave of legislation in the 1970s that created new regulatory agencies and thousands of new regulations.[1] After a decade the environment is still polluted, and occupational disease and accidents have not been eradicated. To be sure, progress has been made in many areas, but ground has been lost in some others.[2] The failures, together with large estimates of the cost of regulation, have created widespread discontent with the current institutions.[3]

Regulatory Decisionmaking

Improving regulatory decisions requires four steps. The first is to clarify the agency's goals. Underlying statutes are generally so unclear that a large range of alternative outcomes would appear to satisfy them equally well. The second is to improve scientific information relevant to the decision. Often one can design research to add precision to previous results or raise new doubts without providing data relevant to the decision. The third is to structure the decision process so that data are

1. Lester B. Lave, *The Strategy of Social Regulation: Decision Frameworks for Policy*.

2. Lester B. Lave and Gilbert S. Omenn, *Clearing the Air: Reforming the Clean Air Act;* and Richard Zeckhauser and Albert Nichols, "The Occupational Safety and Health Administration—An Overview."

3. See, for example, Murray L. Weidenbaum, *Costs of Regulation and Benefits of Reform;* The Business Roundtable, *Cost of Government Regulation Study: Executive Study;* and James L. Sundquist, "The Crisis of Competence in Government."

interpreted correctly and their degree of accuracy is neither underestimated nor overestimated as they are incorporated into decisions. Steps two and three present formidable difficulties that have tended to make regulators cynical about the value of supporting research.

Even with currently available data, more could be done in examining the implications of alternative decisions and the methods of implementing a decision, a fourth step in the decision process. A broad set of alternative decisions must be examined carefully; otherwise the somewhat arbitrary selection is likely to be inefficient. One corollary to considering an array of alternatives is to encourage those being regulated to find the cheaper solutions. For example, performance standards, which specify the desired outcome (such as lowered employee exposure to a carcinogen), are superior to design standards, which specify the control device to be added. Furthermore, imaginative alternatives must be explored to the current legal framework for stating standards and enforcing them with civil or criminal penalties.

A major problem is the failure of Congress to give the agencies clear goals. The legislation generally contains a preamble declaring the agency should stop at nothing to clean the environment or protect workers; it later has qualifying words like *feasible* or *practicable*. Often an agency finds itself sued simultaneously by those who charge it is too lenient and those who claim it is too strict in promulgating a new regulation.

Another problem with regulation has been the incompleteness of scientific evidence.[4] Regulations rest on a foundation of judgments more than on facts.[5] In part, this is inevitable. Science grinds slowly, while regulatory concerns arise quickly and decisions must be made quickly. Long lead times are required to obtain scientific answers, and the regulatory process does not provide the time and often not the resources to obtain comprehensive answers. Analysis can be initiated of which the results will appear only after the regulatory decision is made. Society is characterized by inertia; once a regulatory decision is made and is in the process of implementation, it is extremely difficult to change its speed, much less its direction. To admit that the initial decision was wrong and that vast resources were wasted is difficult, though possible. For exam-

4. M. Granger Morgan, "Bad Science and Good Policy Analysis"; and Victor J. Kimm, Arnold M. Kuzmack and David W. Schnare, "Waterborne Carcinogens: A Regulator's View."

5. Robert W. Crandall and Lester B. Lave, eds., *The Scientific Basis of Health and Safety Regulation*.

ple, the Food and Drug Administration banned saccharin, but Congress intervened to prohibit the FDA from enforcing the ban. Each regulatory agency is confronted with dilemmas and contradictions. On the one hand, a timely decision must be made despite the lack of data; on the other hand, mistakes, especially initial mistakes, are costly. The agency must initiate research and analysis that could lead to a different decision in the future, while at the same time it must convince those affected that the decision is sound and will be enforced.

Regulatory decisions are complicated by the necessity of estimating future technological progress in control techniques and various future scientific, economic, and technological events. How rapidly will abatement technology improve? Will there still be a demand for this product in ten years? How will goals change?

A force for change is the contradiction among executive, congressional, and public desires. Regulatory agencies are willing to weaken goals in order to minimize conflicts. Congress swings from making statements of high purpose to seeking to protect constituents. Public desires cover a vast range; rarely are more than a few special interest groups involved. All three institutions are volatile, and constant change seems inevitable.

The regulatory agencies are in the unenviable position of facing trial by media, congressional oversight, and legal challenges of virtually all decisions. The atmosphere is often so chaotic that compromises to minimize conflict produce the best results.

The regulatory environment puts a premium on quick solutions that can be defended in court, and on satisfying the most pressing immediate needs. Much of the behavior of regulatory agencies follows from these pressures and any proposed solution must recognize their nature and conflicts.

Discretion under Current Statutes

Since time and resources are limited, agencies must avoid alternatives that seem unproductive or politically infeasible. Thus a favorite phrase is "our hands are tied"; that is, agencies are required by the statute to do precisely what they have done and are prohibited from doing anything else. In reality, however, the policies and goals of each agency have changed with personnel, with new directives from the president or Congress, and with court rulings. These changes demonstrate a wide range of discretion for the agencies. Their hands are not tied by the current interpretation of the statutes or even by strict language and dates built into the statutes. The Environmental Protection Agency had a statutory deadline for achieving reductions in emissions into the air and water and creating a system of regulating toxic substances; it failed to meet the deadline and had to reinterpret quite specific statutory language. The EPA is singled out as an obvious case since Congress imposed time deadlines, but every agency has given a broad interpretation to its statute. Even the inflexible language of the Delaney clause in the 1958 amendments to the Federal Food, Drug, and Cosmetic Act of 1938 has been treated flexibly by the FDA.[6] For example, the FDA must decide whether a substance is to be classified as an additive or natural constituent (the former is subject to the Delaney clause while the latter is treated more permissively). Although agency discretion is often subtle, it is important.

Setting Priorities

In such a high-pressure environment it is imperative for regulators to set priorities and use them to govern the allocation of the agency's scarce staff time and resources.[7] The ability of an agency to control its agenda and allocate staff time is limited because agencies generally must react to issues raised by others rather than being able to initiate action. Other agencies, Congress, pressure groups, and the media make requests that must be accommodated. Rarely does an agency have the luxury of adequate time and resources to develop and implement a comprehensive plan. Nonetheless, it is important to not simply react to recurring crises.

An agency can accomplish little without a plan and priorities. These begin with developing a set of working goals that can be used to structure priorities. Goals and priorities must be communicated to the public, Congress, and those being regulated. Developing these goals can promote helpful debate about what the public and Congress desire from the

6. Richard A. Merrill, "Regulation of Toxic Chemicals." The Delaney clause, named after its sponsor, James Delaney, forbids the addition of carcinogens to food. See also chapter 8 of this book.

7. Testimony of Roy E. Albert of New York University for the U.S. Department of Labor, Occupational Safety and Health Administration, June 7, 1978, OSHA Docket No. H-090; and Donald Kennedy, commissioner of the Food and Drug Administration, "Statement before the U.S. Department of Labor, Occupational Safety and Health Administration," April 4, 1978.

agency; it isolates conflicts and specifies a set of goals by which the agency can be evaluated. Debate over these goals can focus general attention on an agency and perhaps inhibit the efforts of special groups to capture it.

Unfortunately Congress rarely gives the agencies clear instructions regarding goals and constraints. Instead, the legislation contains bold statements of goals such as "it is the national goal that the discharge of pollutants into the navigable waterways [of the United States] be eliminated by 1985."[8] Generally congressional debate raises the crucial issues, but the legislation rarely resolves them. Instead, Congress identifies a problem and then delegates it to an agency. Seemingly Congress does not know what it wants, but will know if it likes what the agency does. If congressional review were rapid and if it cost society little to have the agency's decisions overturned by Congress, this would be a good solution. Unfortunately by the time Congress examines a decision, there has been considerable cost and delay. If the process is to improve, Congress must specify working goals for the agencies.

For example, Congress instructed the National Highway Traffic Safety Administration (NHTSA) to lower the toll of injury and death on highways. To ensure that all occupants buckled their seat belts, 1974 model vehicles had an interlock device.[9] Reacting to complaints, Congress then prohibited the NHTSA from requiring the interlock.[10] A fiasco costing hundreds of millions of dollars could have been avoided had Congress clarified the trade-offs among injury reduction, cost, and personal convenience. The debate has surfaced again with the controversial requirement that all automobiles have passive restraints.

Data Collection and Analysis

Health, safety, and environmental regulations are much too costly for uninformed regulatory guesses. One can defend hasty actions in response to a crisis or a perceived crisis; one cannot defend the failure to collect data and perform analysis that would correct that decision once the crisis had passed.

The costs of current regulatory decisions are large. Furthermore, those costs would change significantly if there were minute changes in

8. 86 Stat. 816, Federal Water Pollution Control Act Amendments of 1972.
9. 39 Fed. Reg. 2610 (1974).
10. 88 Stat. 1477, Motor Vehicle and Schoolbus Safety Amendments of 1974.

regulations such as the emissions standards for automobiles.[11] In comparison, the cost of data collection and analysis are small. If they can serve to improve the decision even a small amount, they are worthwhile.

Identification of Possible Health Hazards

There are roughly 60,000 commonly used chemicals; as many as 1,000 are currently being introduced each year.[12] The labor force of just over 100 million workers is exposed to a vast range of conditions with implications for accident hazard as well as myriad substances that could lead to acute or chronic disorders such as cancer, genetic change, and birth defects. The U.S. industrial economy produces literally millions of types of raw materials, materials in process, and final goods and services, many of which offer potential risks to health.

Methods of Identification

Five methods are commonly used to identify hazardous substances: (1) case clusters, (2) structural toxicology, (3) laboratory study of simple test systems such as bacteria or cultured mammalian cells, (4) long-term animal bioassays, and (5) epidemiology. These methods differ in terms of the quality of information yielded, cost, and length of study.[13] Some of the methods, such as animal bioassays and epidemiology, can also be used to test causation and estimate potency.

CASE CLUSTERS. Case clusters, the oldest and most widely used method, are based on the identification of an abnormal pattern of disease. Typically a health professional, such as a physician, notices one or more cases of a rare disease or an unusual concentration of a common one and attempts to find the cause. This method has the lowest level of analytic sophistication. Intuition is used to infer the possible cause amid countless possibilities. Unfortunately, the incidence of disease is often sufficiently high that even casual observation correctly identifies a significant in-

11. Lester B. Lave, "Conflicting Objectives in Regulating the Automobile."

12. Thomas H. Maugh II, "Chemicals: How Many are There?"

13. For discussions, see Milton C. Weinstein, "Decision Making for Toxic Substances Control: Cost-Effective Information Development for the Control of Environmental Carcinogens"; Office of Technology Assessment, *Assessment of Technologies for Determining Cancer Risks from the Environment;* and Food Safety Council, "Proposed System for Food Safety Assessment."

crease. Finding the cause is more difficult, but often this too is obvious.

For example, Percival Pott inferred the cause of scrotal cancer among chimney sweeps;[14] four cases of angiosarcoma of the liver, an extremely rare condition, were sufficient to identify occupational exposure to vinyl chloride as hazardous;[15] and the prevalence of a few dozen cases of clear cell adenocarcinoma in young women, another extremely rare condition, was sufficient to identify diethylstilbestrol (DES) as a carcinogen for the fetus when given to pregnant women.[16] These examples show the power of case clusters in identifying hazards, at least when the resulting condition is extremely rare. When the health condition is more common in the general population, the method is not powerful. This method did not identify the hazardous nature of exposure to coke oven gases because there was no unique disease nor was lung cancer so much more prevalent as to compel attention.[17]

An obvious difficulty with this method is in determining whether the number of cases represents an event so unusual that it was unlikely to arise by chance. If the population at risk is unknown, this determination is extremely difficult. For example, if the exposed population is greater than believed, actual prevalence will be lower than inferred; if the age, sex, and genetic characteristics of the population are unknown, a seemingly high prevalence could rise from an unusual demographic mix. Similarly, an unusual set of personal habits might be the source of the disease, rather than some occupational or environmental exposure. Since the population at risk is rarely known in detail, the case cluster method necessarily yields no conclusive evidence, only rather vague suspicions.

While this sort of informal examination of human experience could provide evidence identifying possible hazards to be regulated, it can never provide conclusive evidence of a causal relationship because it cannot control confounding factors. This method is best used as a tool with which to raise hypotheses to be tested by more formal epidemiology or laboratory experimentation.

14. S. M. Wolfe, "Standards for Carcinogens: Science Affronted by Politics."

15. David D. Doniger, *The Law and Policy of Toxic Substances Control: A Case Study of Vinyl Chloride*.

16. A. L. Herbst and others, "Clear-Cell Adenocarcinoma of the Vagina and Cervix in Girls: Analysis of 1970 Registry Cases."

17. Carol K. Redmond and others found a high risk of lung cancer among coke oven workers, something not expected at the start of the study, in "Long-Term Mortality Study of Steelworkers: VI. Mortality from Malignant Neoplasms among Coke Oven Workers."

A less direct form of this method is the generalization from observed effects on animals and plants. Perhaps the most celebrated recent instance is the public concern for human health aroused by Rachel Carson's dramatic presentation of evidence that birds are killed or sterilized by insecticides.[18] While the danger to birds was clear, the danger to humans, if any, could not be determined without an appropriate investigation.

STRUCTURAL TOXICOLOGY. The second method for identifying hazards is structural toxicology, searching for similarities in chemical structure that might identify carcinogens.[19] For example, many of the coal tars are known to be human carcinogens, so one might presume that an untested coal tar is likely to be a carcinogen and thus tag it as a potential hazard. This method has exhibited little power in identifying carcinogens.

SIMPLE SYSTEMS. A method designed explicitly to identify possible hazards is in vitro testing using either simple systems such as bacteria or cultured mammalian cells.[20] The former tests can identify mutagenic effects and the latter tests can identify cell transformation as well as mutagenesis. The close association between mutagens and carcinogens leads to a general presumption that mutagenic substances are also carcinogenic. These tests are relatively inexpensive and quick; they can be used to screen hundreds or even thousands of chemicals. Since these tests have found more than 200 chemicals to be mutagenic,[21] there is no real possibility in the short term of subjecting all these possible carcinogens to epidemiological study or even to long-term animal bioassays. The issue is how to utilize the results of these tests to enhance scientific knowledge and the regulatory process rather than to paralyze them.

ANIMAL BIOASSAYS. Animal bioassays are laboratory experimentations, generally with rodents. Like epidemiology, long-term animal bioassays are time consuming and expensive; they are designed to test hypotheses rather than to explore possible associations between agents and disease. Unexpected results occasionally arise, however, and should be classified as suggestive associations. Short-term bioassays can also turn up suggestive results that need further exploration.

EPIDEMIOLOGY. Epidemiology is a more scientific, systematic form of

18. Rachel Carson, *Silent Spring*.

19. See I. M. Asher and C. Zervos, eds., *Structural Correlates of Carcinogenesis and Mutagenesis: A Guide to Testing Priorities?*

20. Frederick J. de Serres and John Ashby, eds., *Evaluation of Short-Term Tests for Carcinogens*.

21. 45 Fed. Reg. 5028 (1980).

case cluster analysis with an attempt to control for confounding factors in the experimental design or statistical analysis. On the borderline between the extremely informal case cluster analysis and the formal epidemiology to be discussed below are a series of exploratory studies designed to turn up hypotheses. For example, maps showing the incidence of cancer by area reveal thousands of "hot spots" that may reflect random variation, better diagnoses and recording procedures, genetic factors, general environmental factors, personal habits, or some combination of these factors. A few minutes of studying such a map can reveal many more hypotheses than could be tested in a lifetime.

These five methods would appear to offer a choice between data that are irrelevant (for example, short-term tests and bioassays) or inconclusive (for example, case clusters and epidemiology). At the current state of knowledge, refining the analysis enough to control for confounding factors requires animal test systems; the data are irrelevant in the sense that their implications for humans at much lower doses can only be guessed at. Since studies of humans are contaminated by confounding factors, the data are necessarily inconclusive. Actually, the two sets of methods, as well as the methods for identifying hazards, are complementary. Each has different costs and time requirements and generates different information. Each has a place within an integrated strategy for hazard identification and quantitative risk assessment.

Statistical models are used to extrapolate from animal bioassays to humans. Where the physiological mechanisms are understood, the statistical models can be designed to reflect this knowledge. With rare exceptions, however, the statistical models reflect a set of somewhat arbitrary assumptions. Unfortunately, equally plausible models give rise to vastly different estimates of risk. Uncertainty, from ignorance of physiological mechanisms to incomplete information about potency of a substance, dominates the decision. There is no good alternative to a model that treats ignorance and uncertainty explicitly; in addition to presenting the best estimate, the model must also provide a range of likely estimates. For example, differences in susceptibility among people due to genetic difference and individual habits must be accounted for in estimating risk.

There are conceptual difficulties in defining what constitutes an adverse health effect and practical difficulties in estimating the population at risk and their levels of exposure. The practical difficulties can be mitigated by focusing attention on data collection and modeling. The conceptual difficulties may be of overwhelming importance if imperceptible physical changes are perceived to be important health effects, even when there is no direct reason to regard the effects as important.

When a substance is suspected of being toxic, it is necessary to show that a substantial number of people are exposed to that substance at levels that present a hazard. Even though a substance is a potent carcinogen, no regulatory attention is required if the substance is not widely used or if the nature of the process guarantees that exposure is negligible.

Interpreting Data

None of these screening tests gives proof of carcinogenicity for humans, but each provides data that should play a greater or lesser role in the decision process, depending on the quality of the data. In particular, it is necessary to know the rate at which the tests tend to identify substances that are not hazardous (they identify false positives in order to avoid false negatives). Advancing toward both efficient regulation and scientific knowledge requires study of the implications of positive and negative results and of attempts to get more definitive answers. While science can wait for yet more data and a clearer understanding of physiological mechanisms, society must balance costly, perhaps unnecessary regulation against increased human risk.

If one of the techniques were so powerful that the vast majority of substances it identified were in fact carcinogens, one might be tempted to take regulatory action on the basis of this test alone. None of the current screening tests has that attribute, however. Indeed, testing and replication have been insufficient to establish thoroughly the power of any of these techniques to date.

If nothing is known about the health effects likely to result from a substance, none of the methods can be powerful in identifying a specific effect and estimating its magnitude. In contrast, when a good deal is known about the nature of the health effect and of mitigating and aggravating factors, any of the methods can be powerful in identifying effects. The most compelling conclusions can be drawn when there is coherence among the results of several methods and when these results are consistent with what is known from the fields of chemistry, biology, and pharmacology.[22]

These five tests tend to provide vast amounts of data, identifying

22. Mary O. Amdur, "Toxicological Guidelines for Research on Sulfur Oxides and Particulates."

more possible hazards than could be checked within a reasonable time period. Establishing whether suspect substances are hazardous is time consuming and expensive. For example, an imaginative scientist could hypothesize tens of thousands of suspect carcinogens from an inspection of the maps showing cancer incidence. If the use of these hypotheses is not considered carefully, the result can be paralysis of the regulatory process, because of the mountain of data, or paralysis of the economy, if all suspect chemicals are regulated.

For these exploratory methods to help rather than hinder the regulatory process, a systematic framework must be constructed for utilizing the information. A chemical found to be positive under one method could be tested by other screening methods in a protocol based on their cost and value of information. When the quality of information warrants, a suspect chemical could be subjected to the more costly and time-consuming methods of long-term animal bioassay or formal epidemiology. The result would be a hierarchy of tests or even a formal decision tree.[23] For example, when a possible hazard is identified by one procedure, such as a cancer map, further information might be derived from the in vitro tests. A positive result in a short-term test might warrant the expense of toxicological or epidemiological research to estimate the potency or dose-response relationship of the substance.

The types of regulatory actions that might be taken in response to information from the various tests range from using the data to set priorities for further tests to taking emergency action to abate exposure. The choice should depend on the costs of taking immediate action and the possible harm that might occur from delay, as well as legal and political pressures.

Current State of the Art

The most complete attempt by an agency to investigate the quality of information in each method and the proper regulatory response is the "Identification, Classification and Regulation of Potential Occupational Carcinogens" prepared by the Occupational Safety and Health Administration.[24] It describes alternative tests, expert opinion of their value, and how each should be used. It raises the relevant scientific issues,

23. See Weinstein, "Decision Making for Toxic Substances Control"; Lester B. Lave and others, "A Model for Selecting Short-Term Tests of Carcinogenicity"; and B. A. Bridges, "Evaluation of Mutagenicity and Carcinogenicity Using a Three-Tier System."

24. Published in 45 Fed. Reg. 5002–5296 (1980).

cites much of the pertinent literature, and quotes the testimony of experts. Unfortunately the document is marred by the attempt to interpret testimony to support the agency's proposal. Furthermore, OSHA assumes that evidence of carcinogenicity should never, or rarely, be rejected, while the failure to find carcinogenicity should rarely, if ever, be accepted. Only if the study could be shown to be grossly deficient would positive evidence be rejected; negative evidence would be rejected unless the study could disprove all criticism of its methods. Although there should be some bias toward giving more credence to positive than to negative studies, OSHA has gone too far. Furthermore, OSHA does not come to grips with the fact that workers are exposed to thousands of chemicals, and thus a qualitatively different solution for screening all potential carcinogens is needed.

The Consumer Product Safety Commission[25] and the EPA have attempted to deal with these issues. The commission's carcinogen document is much less ambitious than OSHA's. The EPA's policy has evolved over time and is set out in a series of documents, rather than a single comprehensive one.

Quantifying Risk Estimates: Epidemiology

Once a substance has been identified as a hazard with sufficient assurance to warrant committing years and hundreds of thousands of dollars to further exploration, epidemiology can be used to estimate the potency of the substance, the dose-response relationship. Human beings are subjected to health challenges through a combination of their choice of life-style (for example, cigarette smoking), occupational and other environmental exposure, and accidents. Much valuable information on the effects of exposures to various substances is contained in these nonexperimental situations.[26]

Methods Used to Isolate Causes

The characteristics of epidemiology stem from the fact that it is not an experimental science. The epidemiologist is confined to observing

25. Consumer Product Safety Commission, "Interim Policy and Procedure for Classifying, Evaluating and Regulating Carcinogens in Consumer Products," published in 43 Fed. Reg. 25657 (1978).

26. B. MacMahon, T. Pugh and J. Ipsen, *Epidemiologic Methods*.

and interpreting natural situations. Many possible causes are present simultaneously, and the general existence of a latency period means that it is extremely difficult to find a single or even central cause of a chronic disease. Indeed, it may not be useful to think in terms of a causal connection when many challenges are present in varying intensities and individuals differ in susceptibility.[27]

The classic epidemiological method is to examine persons to identify a disease and its cause; then the problem is to find the pathway for the agent. For example, typhus might be found to be the cause of death, and it is generally waterborne; the difficult tasks would be finding the source of the contaminated water and the easiest way to stop exposure. This approach works well with an acute infectious disease whose agent is evident.

More vexing are attempts to find causes and aggravating factors of chronic disease. The more subtle the effect and the longer the latency period, the more difficult it is to estimate a relationship. For a disease such as asbestosis, the cause of the disease (exposure to asbestos) is clear and the source of exposure is not hard to find. Even here, the current state of the disease is affected by other challenges, particularly cigarette smoking; Selikoff and associates found no excess lung cancer in nonsmoking asbestos workers.[28] The precise cause of illness is unknown for other diseases, such as lung cancer, in which case it could be any one or combination of agents. What is the cause of lung cancer in a cigarette-smoking asbestos worker living in a house with an unventilated gas heater in a polluted city? Surely each of the environmental challenges contributed to the disease in the sense that its occurrence might have been delayed if any of the insults were mitigated.

The most common epidemiological method is the case-controlled study in which people with a specified condition are matched with healthy people of the same age, race, sex, and other relevant characteristics; the latter become the control group.[29] These retrospective studies must assume that all relevant characteristics are identified and are matched, controlled statistically, or unrelated to the variables of interest. For example, workers, especially blue-collar workers, are known to be healthier than the population generally; thus a study contrasting workers

27. Gilbert S. Omenn and Robert D. Friedman, "Individual Differences in Susceptibility and Regulation of Environmental Hazards."

28. Irving J. Selikoff, E. Cuyler Hammond, and Jacob Churq, "Asbestos Exposure, Smoking, and Neoplasia."

29. Norman Breslow, "Design and Analysis of Case-Control Studies."

with the general population systematically neglects this difference in health status.

Retrospective case control studies can be done relatively quickly and cheaply. More expensive and time consuming are prospective cohort analyses in which study and control groups are selected and examined before the relevant exposure. Deterioration in some health index or physiological capacity is measured in the two groups during the study with the null hypothesis that the deterioration will be identical across groups. The assumption is that differences between the two groups are due only to random variation and the substance under study.

Among the advantages of a prospective study is the ability to get detailed measures of health status and exposure to substances over time. Often elaborate physical examinations and environmental monitoring are part of the protocol and subjects are followed for years. Unfortunately failure to observe a characteristic later found to be important can negate the value of a study; thus protocols specify observing myriad characteristics.

In prospective and retrospective studies of equal sample size and design quality, one would tend to have more confidence in the former type, since they offer greater ability to observe confounding characteristics and get better measures of the relevant characteristics. Carrying out the retrospective study would be both quicker and cheaper, however. If the same resources were devoted to the two studies, the retrospective one would have a larger sample size and might be worthy of equal or even greater confidence.

A final method for tracing out the causes of disease is statistical analysis to control for relevant physiological characteristics and environmental challenges in a study of general populations, often defined geographically. This method offers the advantages of large sample size and relatively low cost but has less complete controls for relevant factors. The inherent difficulties with epidemiology include the inability to control for all relevant factors and the need for inordinately large samples in order to deal with conditions of low incidence. Like each of the other methods, epidemiology alone is rarely sufficient to answer all the important questions.

Problems in Interpreting Results

Causality is a theoretical construct; it cannot be proved empirically. When scientists speak of proving causality, they are referring to a consensus among scientists.[30] Thus when someone says that cigarette smoking has been proved to cause lung cancer, he is referring to the belief held by the overwhelming number of scientists and supported by many studies in toxicology and epidemiology.[31]

It is important to understand the subjective nature of the conclusion that an observed association is causal. Neither laboratory experiments nor epidemiology can "prove" causality, but either or both can serve to convince scientists that the relationship is a causal one. The key is not the approach used, but the amount of confidence one can have in the individual studies. Laboratory experimental results are worthy of confidence because scientists can manipulate factors so as to control or randomize the principal confounding effects. But as the cost of an experiment rises, along with the time required for completion, fewer manipulations are done, and one can be less confident that an observed association is causal. Furthermore, a fundamental difficulty of these experiments is that they require generalization from effects observed in small mammals at high doses to expected effects in humans at low doses. Often epidemiology observes the relevant population at relevant dose levels and under relevant conditions, but this rich social-environmental context makes interpretation difficult.

The primary question in any epidemiological study is whether the significant associations are indicative of causal relationships or are simply random or spurious associations. A number of statistical and other tests have been proposed as guidelines for determining whether a significant association should be accepted as causal.[32] All these guidelines are only that; none can offer proof of causality.

Quantifying Risk Estimates: Long-Term Bioassays

The problems most difficult for epidemiology are the easiest ones for long-term bioassays, the other method for investigating exploratory hypotheses in depth. Since bioassays are laboratory experiments, they

30. Thomas S. Kuhn, *Structure of Scientific Revolutions*.

31. For recent comments, see Theodor D. Sterling, "A Critical Reassessment of the Evidence Bearing on Smoking as the Cause of Lung Cancer"; and Sterling, "Additional Comments on the Critical Assessment of the Evidence Bearing on Smoking as the Cause of Lung Cancer."

32. For example, see the discussion of Sir Austin B. Hill's criteria for statistical interpretation in Lester B. Lave and Eugene P. Seskin, *Air Pollution and Human Health*.

offer the ability to manipulate and control factors hypothesized to cause disease and also to observe physiological changes in more detail.

Methods Used in Animal Bioassays

Among the issues to be addressed in designing an animal bioassay are (1) the species and sex to be used, including whether to use crossbred or inbred animals and, if the latter, whether to select a strain with a high spontaneous tumor rate; (2) the exposure path, such as through feed, water, skin painting, inhalation, or implantation; (3) the length of test and sacrifice intervals for animals; (4) elements of experimental design such as the number of animals per group, levels of exposure, number of groups, and the use of a positive control; and (5) methods used in analyzing results, such as whether to examine all organs, whether to examine tumor type, and whether to test only hypotheses specified before the bioassay. In addition, the usual questions concerning animal husbandry, such as the choice of food, number of animals per cage, and type of cage must be addressed.[33]

The species can be selected on the basis of similarity to humans in the way the substance is metabolized, on the basis of the most sensitive species, or on the basis of convenience. While the first is the best criterion, the last seems to be most commonly used. The exposure path preferably should be the same as for humans, but almost invariably exposure is through food or water. Inbred animals provide a more homogeneous response and thus greater coherence in testing, but they may be deficient in a crucial immune response.

The other elements are grouped under the notion of experimental design questions. Generally there are three groups: control, high-dose, and low-dose.[34] The high group is exposed to as high a level as possible short of the toxic effects killing the animals during the experiment.[35] The low dose is generally at half that level.

Conducting an animal bioassay is a painstaking process. Animals must be kept free of disease and other health-endangering risks for two

33. National Cancer Institute, *Guidelines for Carcinogen Bioassay in Small Rodents*.

34. The high-dose group is designed to reveal an effect, given the small number of animals and the general ignorance about physiological mechanisms. The control group is necessary to isolate the effect of the substance. Finally, the low-dose group provides one data point on effect at a lower dose.

35. An adjustment is required as to the maximum dose the animals can tolerate over a prolonged period without acute toxicity.

to three years (or more for dogs and primates). Their food must not interfere with the experiment, and its composition must be known with confidence. Slips in management or animal husbandry will have the effect of increasing randomness and decreasing the power of the experiment. For example, a food containing an unrecognized carcinogen as a contaminant may increase the incidence of cancer in all groups and tend to obscure the effects of the test substance. There is also the possibility that the test substance may be a promoter in the presence of the unrecognized carcinogen or that they may interact positively or negatively.[36] A mistake in routine such as a dosage mix-up may result in the death of some animals or may exert some special effect on one of the groups. Many important bioassays have been marred by observed errors in feeding and record-keeping or by fires or disease epidemics.

Problems in Design and Interpretation

The animal bioassay is a rich structure with many possible variations. The selection of a design or the drawing of a conclusion inevitably leads to questions concerning why an alternative was not chosen and whether the conclusion is supportable. The fundamental difficulty is that often little is known about the underlying physiological processes in either humans or the experiment animal. The more that is known, the fewer arbitrary choices need be made. For example, knowing the metabolic pathways for a substance in humans and the resultant products allows selection of a test species and experimental design that mimic human exposure. Knowledge of the functional form for the dose-response relationship allows estimation of the parameters of the function with greater power and confidence.

Some scientists contend that no general conclusion about the effect on humans can be drawn from an animal bioassay.[37] The difficulties are that (1) large doses overwhelm defense mechanisms or produce peculiar metabolic processes (such as hormone imbalance); (2) species react differently (quantitatively and even qualitatively) to the same substance; (3) the absence of other environmental challenges excludes all interactions among challenges, may decrease resistance to the test substance, and precludes making quantitative estimates for humans; and (4) there

36. For example, vitamin C inhibits the formation of nitrosamines, which are potent carcinogens. See Weinstein, "Decision Making for Toxic Substances Control."

37. For example, Gio Batta Gori, "The Regulation of Carcinogenic Hazards."

are many conceptual difficulties in extrapolating from large doses in rodents to small doses in humans. These objections are formidable and are likely to be resolved only when the underlying physiological processes are better understood. However, scientists and regulators often act as if information that is less than completely certain is worthless. Information can be much less than certain and still prove valuable in making both scientific and regulatory decisions.

Some of these difficulties are inherent. For example, high doses are required to produce statistically significant effects in small test groups. The only alternative to such high doses is to increase the number of animals, and the costs of this are exorbitant.[38] Most of the experiments are not designed to facilitate estimation of a dose-response relationship. Rather, they are designed to elicit maximal response under tightly controlled conditions, even if that response cannot be related to human risks.[39]

Indeed, the choice of the number of animals per group is a crucial decision. Using too few animals precludes getting statistically significant results.[40] Adding more animals increases the power of the test, but at a diminishing rate since the power of the test rises with the square root of the number of animals in a group.[41] Shown in table 2-1 is the number of animals per group required to detect the presence of a carcinogen of the indicated potency 80 out of 100 times, using the usual 0.05 testing level. As the background incidence of the condition rises, the number of animals required per group to obtain statistically significant results increases rapidly. The chance of getting a significant result is alarmingly low for any economically manageable number of animals.

Another crucial parameter is the number of dose levels tested. If only three groups are used, the dose-response curve fitted to the data cannot be more complicated than a quadratic (or other three-parameter function). More important, having additional groups provides information with which to judge the inherent variability of the test animals (how

38. The largest bioassay run is the "megamouse" or ED_{01} experiment. For a description of the difficulties and cost, see Jeffrey A. Staffa and Myron A. Mehlman, eds., *Innovations in Cancer Risk Assessment (ED_{01} Study)*.

39. See Thomas Louis and Milton Weinstein, "Redesigning Bioassays to Enhance their Contribution to Regulation."

40. To simplify, a substance can be a carcinogen or not and the statistical test can conclude that it is a carcinogen or not. Since a carcinogen does not produce neoplasms in all test animals and since some neoplasms arise spontaneously, there is a danger of misclassifying a substance on the results of an experiment. David S. Salsburg, "Use of Statistics When Examining Lifetime Studies in Rodents to Detect Carcinogenicity."

41. The ability of a statistical test to classify substances correctly is called its power.

Table 2-1. Number of Animals Required to Show Statistical Significance at Varying Tumor Rates[a]

Background tumor rate (percent)	*Number of animals required*	
	At 5 percent above background rate	*At 10 percent above background rate*
1	143	55
5	330	105
10	540	155

Source: David W. Gaylor and Raymond E. Shapiro, "Extrapolation and Risk Estimation for Carcinogenesis," in Myron A. Mehlman, Raymond E. Shapiro, and Herbert Blumenthal, eds., *Advances in Modern Toxicology*, vol. 1, pt. 2: *New Concepts in Safety Evaluation* (Halsted Press, 1979), p. 79.

a. An 80 percent chance of detecting an increase at the 5 percent significance level.

much consistency in the dose-response relationship is observed across groups) and the quality of the experiment. As always, however, information gain and cost must be balanced.

Not only is variability introduced by differences among the animals and slight variations in the experiment, there is also variability in the preparation and histology. Failure to choose the right tissues for slides, careless preparation of the slides, or careless interpretation can waste years of work and hundreds of thousands of dollars. Worse still, it can lead to concluding that a carcinogenic substance is harmless or to the banning of an economically important substance that causes no harm.

Interpreting the slides is difficult and subject to differing expert judgments.[42] There is also controversy concerning whether benign neoplasms should be aggregated with malignant ones. A more general problem concerns the interpretation of exploratory data. Statistical tests are developed under the assumption that a specific hypothesis is to be tested, for example, that aflatoxin leads to an increase in the incidence of liver cancer in a particular set of test animals. In contrast, animal bioassays collect large amounts of data on many organs with no specific hypothesis of effect. If the usual statistical tests are applied to these data, it is erroneous to conclude effects to be statistically significant. For example, if ten organs are being inspected for evidence of carcinogenicity, it is incorrect to apply the usual test that assumes that a single organ is being tested. In such a case, what appeared to be a significant elevation in the cancer incidence for one organ could be due simply to

42. Independent review of the slides can reverse the conclusions of a study; for example, see the Newberne study and its interpretation. Paul M. Newberne, "Dietary Nitrite in the Rat"; Food and Drug Administration, *Re-evaluation of the Pathology Findings on Nitrite and Cancer: Histologic Lesions in Sprague-Dawley Rats;* and Food and Drug Administration, *Report of the Interagency Working Group on Nitrite Research.*

random variation. To test multiple hypotheses with an overall alpha equal to 0.05, the alpha for each test must be much smaller.

Failure to understand the underlying physiological processes can lead to procedures that are arbitrary and inappropriate. For example, extrapolation to humans is generally done in terms of dose per unit of body weight, body area, or concentration in inhaled or ingested substances. However, mammals differ by size, the ratios of food intake per unit of body weight or body areas, rates of respiration and of metabolism, and blood circulation. An extrapolation may have little predictive power. The methods used for extrapolating from mouse to man can have significantly different results, as seen in the following example. Since a human weighs about 2,500 times as much as a mouse, a dose of 1 milligram per day to a mouse would be equivalent to a dose of 2,500 milligrams per day to a human, if extrapolation were done by weight. If extrapolation were by surface area (which is proportional to weight to the two-thirds power), the mouse dose would be equivalent to a dose of 184 milligrams per day to a human. Thus if 1 milligram per day were the highest safe dose in a mouse, the highest safe dose in a human might vary from 184 to 2,500 milligrams per day.[43]

Current State of the Art

Standard protocols for conducting animal bioassays and interpreting the resulting data have been developed by institutions such as the National Cancer Institute.[44] Standard procedures and assumptions cover virtually all aspects of the bioassays, from the number of groups and animals per group chosen to the number of tissue slides taken and the nature of the statistical tests used.

Since the physiological mechanisms are not known in detail and since animal husbandry is an art, a manual on conducting animal bioassays will reflect current experience and a vast number of conjectures. Furthermore, questions such as the number of animals per group and the number of groups depend on the cost of testing and the cost to society of being wrong or imprecise. Without impugning the current guidelines, it is important to recognize that they contain many assumptions about fact and involve many trade-offs that must be reviewed periodically and

43. See Weinstein, "Decision Making for Toxic Substances Control," pp. 349–50.
44. National Cancer Institute, *Guidelines for Carcinogen Bioassay in Small Rodents*.

adjusted as knowledge, costs, and values change. Even when the general principles are seen to be correct, the application to any specific case must be governed by a rule of reason rather than unquestioning adherence.

Epidemiology and long-term bioassays are complementary, not competing methods. The strength of each is the weakness of the other. The most compelling results occur when both methods lead to similar conclusions.

Estimating the Dose-Response Relationship

Toxicology and epidemiology can provide quantitative data on the relationship between dose and response. Several formal and informal methods may be used to estimate a quantitative relationship between the dose and response that would allow estimation of health effects at different levels of exposure and thus different levels of control.

Statistical Models for Animal Bioassays

Since good epidemiological data are rarely available for chemicals suspected of being carcinogens, extrapolations from animal bioassays are the most frequent basis for inferring human risk. Problems abound with this method. The inherent problems with bioassays are compounded by arbitrary estimation and extrapolation techniques to produce large amounts of uncertainty concerning the estimated risk.

Two steps are required to estimate human risk from animal bioassay results.[45] The first is to extrapolate effects from lower animals to humans; the second is to extrapolate from high to low doses. This section is focused on the latter.[46] A functional form for the dose-response relationship must be assumed; if there are sufficient data, alternative functional forms can be tested.[47] In the simplest terms, one might conceive of a

45. Office of Technology Assessment, *Assessment of Technologies for Determining Cancer Risks from the Environment*.

46. A large literature examines statistical extrapolation of risks to humans. See the reviews in Office of Technology Assessment, *Assessment of Technologies for Determining Cancer Risks;* Food Safety Council, "Proposed System for Food Safety Assessment"; and also the references to extrapolation in the section on risk assessment in the subject-listing bibliography.

47. The shape of the dose-response relationship has been investigated most extensively

Figure 2-1. A Simple Dose-Response Curve

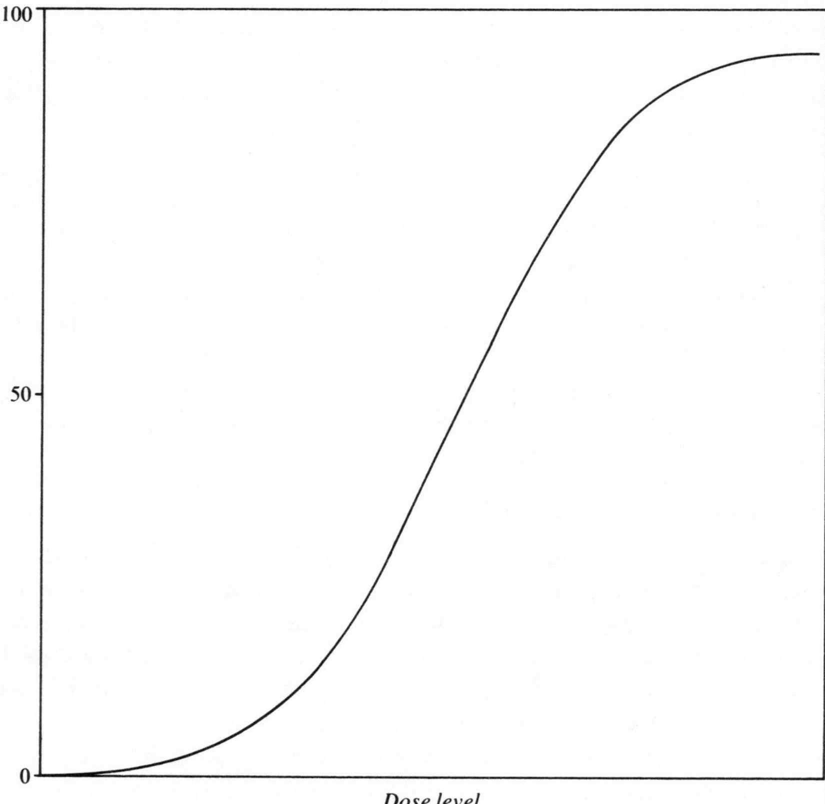

dose-response curve as shown in figure 2-1, where the proportion of the population manifesting a particular response increases with the dose. A few people might be extraordinarily sensitive to the substance because of genetic factors and previous environmental factors. More will be less sensitive because of either genetic and environmental factors, and some will display little reaction.

---

for ionizing radiation; see J. Martin Brown, "Linearity vs. Non-Linearity of Dose Response for Radiation Carcinogenesis"; Edward E. Pochin, "Assumption of Linearity in Dose-Effect Relationships"; and National Academy of Sciences, *The Effects on Populations of Exposure to Low Levels of Ionizing Radiation*. See also the analysis of ED_{01} in Staffa and Mehlman, eds., *Innovations in Cancer Risk Assessment*.

Conceiving of the dose-response relationship as deterministic is too simple a model to be useful in estimation. A stochastic element might be introduced into the dose-response relationship in either of two ways. Statistical models rely on the susceptibility of the population with an assumption that there is a tolerance distribution for the chemical being tested.[48] Stochastic biological models assume that the response is triggered by biological events that occur randomly.

Estimation requires assuming a particular functional form. In many cases the statistical model is developed directly from a simple biological model. For example, one biological model assumes each chemical molecule has an equal probability (compared with other molecules of the same substance) of causing change in a cell and that any change that makes a single cell carcinogenic has equal probability of producing a tumor. This "one-hit" theory is an extremely simple one, ignoring possible effects from a massive dose, the effectiveness of the defense mechanisms of the body at different levels of challenge, and the time required to produce the tumor. The resulting statistical model is a simple exponential in which any dose has a positive probability of producing cancer (no threshold) and response is directly proportional to dose at low levels of exposure (linear).

More complicated multistage biological models require that events take place in a sequence.[49] If the events occur out of order, no tumor is produced. The resulting statistical models are "multi-hit" and are more complicated to fit, requiring more data at different dose levels. The multi-hit model can be generalized to a much wider class of statistical models.[50] However, the biological analogue of these models is unclear.

A common observation from bioassays is that the time between exposure and tumor is inversely related to the rate of exposure, total dose and acute effects held constant.[51] This relationship between latency period and dose rate is particularly important for low-level exposure. In particular, if the dose rate is sufficiently low, the latency period can be longer than a human lifetime, which means there is a practical threshold

48. Kamta Rai and John Van Ryzin, "Risk Assessment of Toxic Environmental Substances Using a Generalized Multi-Hit Dose Response Model."

49. P. Armitage and R. Doll, "Stochastic Models for Carcinogenesis."

50. K. S. Crump and others, "Fundamental Carcinogenic Processes and Their Implications for Low Dose Risk Assessment," and Rai and Van Ryzin, "Risk Assessment of Toxic Environmental Substances."

51. The length of the latency period as a function of dose has been investigated by H. Druckrey, "Quantitative Aspects in Chemical Carcinogenesis"; H. B. Jones and A. Grendon, "Environmental Factors in the Origin of Cancer and Estimation of the Possible

for exposure to a carcinogen, even if the biological-mathematical models assume there is no threshold. The importance of this "time-to-tumor" concept has been demonstrated for ionizing radiation.[52] Recent work shows that such models fit the "megamouse" study data better than the class of models without a latency term.[53]

Having estimated the dose-response function, the standard method in regulation has been to define a virtually safe dose (VSD) as one having a small risk of producing the response. The choice of the quantitative level for which the risk is negligible is arbitrary; values such as 10^{-6} and 10^{-8} have been suggested. A more important objection is that the VSD depends on the estimates of the dose-response function but not on the precision with which the parameters are estimated. For example, the parameter estimates might be identical for bioassays with 40 animals and 4,000 animals, but confidence in the latter estimates would be much greater than in the former, other factors being constant. Accounting for the precision with which the parameters are estimated would have the effect of expanding the confidence interval. Thus if one insisted that the probability of the response occurring had to be less than 10^{-6}, the effect would be to lower the VSD even further. However, the current estimation and decision apparatus builds in arbitrary conservative factors at many stages; the cumulative effect of these is unknown and impossible to interpret, but it is large. A more thorough, careful estimation procedure should serve to eliminate many of the arbitrary assumptions and lead to decisions in which there is greater confidence. Scientists must estimate the most likely effect as well as the range of uncertainty. Unless this is done explicitly, risk estimates embodying arbitrary conservative factors are almost useless.

Dose-Response Curves in Epidemiology

The initial hypothesis to be tested in epidemiology is whether the estimated association is statistically significant. This test does not require

---

Hazard to Man"; Roy E. Albert and Bernard Altshuler, "Considerations Relating to the Formulation of Limits for Unavoidable Population Exposures to Environmental Carcinogens"; Alice S. Whittemore, "The Age Distribution of Human Cancer for Carcinogenic Exposures of Varying Intensity"; and Otto G. Raab, Steven A. Book, and Norris G. Parks, "Bone Cancer from Radium: Canine Dose Response Explains Data for Mice and Humans."

52. Raab, Book, and Parks, "Bone Cancer from Radium."

53. Society of Toxicology ED_{01} Task Force, "Reexamination of the ED_{01} Study—Risk Assessment Using Time."

an estimate of the gradient. Indeed, the vast majority of epidemiological studies do not attempt to estimate the quantitative relationship between dose and response.

A quantitative estimate is required to estimate risk at various doses, however. Regression analysis in one form or another is the usual technique for estimating a quantitative relationship.[54] As with toxicology, one must begin with some functional form. Often the data are not sufficient to distinguish among alternative functional forms or to estimate numerous parameters. Thus a simple relationship, such as a linear form, is usually fit.

The data can be adjusted for confounding factors—for example, calculating an age-sex-race adjusted mortality rate—or the confounding factors can be used as explanatory variables. The former has the advantage of decreasing the number of variables and making interpretation easier; the latter has the advantage of fewer assumptions (for example, about the nature of the way each confounding variable affects the relationship).

Statistical testing requires knowledge or hypotheses about the distribution of the stochastic element. When no assumptions can be justified, nonparametric tests can be used, although they are generally of much lower power.

To achieve results in which one can have confidence, all prior information must be built into the estimation; arbitrary assumptions required for statistical convenience must be avoided. For example, the longer life expectancy of women must be reflected in the model. Similarly, important simultaneous relationships must be modeled; for example, low income and disease are related in that low income leads to disease, but disease also leads to low income because the sick person cannot work.

There is never sufficient variation in the data and accuracy in the observations to allow unique functional forms to be discerned. Thus one should choose a functional form that is likely to be robust and simple to estimate. A large body of literature in statistics and econometrics has grown up concerning estimation.

Subjective Estimates

Many regulatory proceedings require that an expert or committee of experts arrive at a judgment concerning the effects on human health at

54. See for example, Frederick Mosteller and John W. Tukey, *Data Analysis and Regression: A Second Course in Statistics*.

alternate control levels. If there were a single quantitative study, this would be simple. But often a number of studies using methods as diverse as toxicology and epidemiology are analyzed; it is difficult to decide how to combine the information into a single dose-response relationship.

While blue-ribbon committees arrive at such judgments when asked, one cannot always have confidence in the resulting estimates. Unfortunately such informal methods produce different outcomes when the participants, procedures, or questions change. A more systematic procedure is needed that is credible to the public and less subject to change when participants or questions change. The EPA used a subjective decision analysis framework in its background analysis for the photochemical oxidant standard and is studying subjective frameworks more formally.[55]

There is no doubt that experts are making subjective judgments about the quantitative effects. However, the notion of making the process explicit causes intense controversy. Some people appear to prefer burying the assumptions and accommodations rather than to make the subjective judgments explicit. Much is to be gained from more systematic procedures.

Estimating the Population and Dose

After an estimated dose-response relationship is arrived at for a substance, the next step is a detailed estimation of the populations at risk and the dose they receive. A preliminary assessment is required at the hazard identification stage, but more detail is required here.

Methods Used

Information must be developed on the pathways by which toxic substances reach people. Then the concentration of the substance in each pathway and the dose received by humans must be measured. The measurement problem is linked to each pathway. Seemingly innocuous pathways can assume extraordinary importance because there is a concentration in the food chain. Rarely is the substance uniformly distributed across pathways or even over time within a pathway. Thus

55. See chapter 3.

it is important to estimate both the average exposure and the actual exposure to individuals, including the possibility of a superconcentrated dose.

The population at risk can be inferred from knowing the pathways and learning who works or lives at various sites or breathes air, drinks water, or eats food coming from a particular place. The problem can be complicated by particular habits, such as a taste for swordfish or chicken necks. Some people receive exposure during one period of their job or life and none thereafter. This inference is painstaking but relatively straightforward work.

Problems in Estimation

Exposure often takes place through a wide variety of pathways, with changes in concentration and chemical form. Some of these changes diffuse toxicity while others increase it. Determining all pathways is essentially impossible and is not required by statute.

Concentrations vary widely, depending on the time of day, day of year, weather, and so on. If the effect of the substance is nonlinear, the peak concentrations may be of greatest interest and action should be taken to lower peak exposure. Even within an industrial plant, large variations in exposure occur depending on the level of production, interval since maintenance, and whether control devices are working. Estimating an integrated dose is nearly impossible.

Worker selection may serve to remove sensitive persons (at least those with acute sensitivity) from areas of high exposure. Thus an exposed occupational population will not represent the general population and should not be used as a direct guide to the effects on the general population. One can expect that much larger effects will be displayed by those who are sensitive.

By devoting large amounts of resources to assessments, estimates of the exposed population and the dose levels can be improved. In practice, however, these estimates will contain major uncertainties because of variation over time and across locations.

Measuring Health Effects

So far in the discussion it has been assumed that health effects can be measured straightforwardly and without controversy, save possibly for problems with estimation. This is a crucial simplification that should be explored.

The first issue is what constitutes a health effect. At one extreme is mortality; at the other extreme are minute, unperceived changes in physiology (for example, increases in airway resistance) or perceived changes in well-being. If exposure to a chemical causes death, there is no doubt that the health effect is real and important. If it causes a minute and reversible but measurable change in physiology, the effect is real, but need be neither a health effect nor important. Similarly, if a person consistently perceives a change in physical well-being, even though this is not measurable, the effect is real but may not be related to health or be important. The underlying question is when a perceived or measured physiological change is important and when it can be considered disease.

The problem arises principally from laboratory studies with human subjects where exposure to a substance causes a small physiological change such as an increase in airway resistance. Such a change generally puts an additional strain on the subject, but it is unclear whether the change has long-term implications for health, even for someone who might be in poor health. This is particularly true when the change is imperceptible to the subject. A perceptible change that cannot be measured physiologically, such as slight eye irritation or an unpleasant odor, similarly has unclear implications for long-term health, although the immediate irritation is evident.

The measured or perceived effect may be a precursor of disease or may aggravate existing disease by an unmeasurable amount. In general it is impossible to relate the subtle effect observed in the laboratory to disease observed in the population. Thus one must often be content to specify the nature of the observed effect, whether physiological or perceived, and to elaborate some of the consequences. These effects can be arranged, at least roughly, along a scale from unmeasurable effects to death.

In generalizing from laboratory studies to the general population, it is important to recognize the heterogeneity of the population in terms of the distributions of age, sex, race, genetic inheritance, health state, current habits, access to medical care, education, and relevant history. For example, a slight increase in airway resistance could have markedly different implications for a healthy eighteen-year-old from those for an eighty-year-old with severe emphysema. While the vast majority of the population would be expected to display no reaction (or an unrecognizably small one), a sensitive minority might experience severe reactions, including premature death. This sensitive minority would be defined not only by current health state but by personal habits. For example, an increase in asbestos fibers in the air would be expected to have little or no effect on most people, but might have severe effects on cigarette smokers.[56]

Laboratory experiments with human volunteers (approved by human subjects committees) and animal bioassays could provide an extensive set of dose-response relationships that characterize the expected incidence of effects, from just perceived or just measured ones to severe disease or death. These curves might be combined with detailed information on the population at risk to generate estimates of the incidence of each condition in a particular population; each estimate would be subject to uncertainty. The output of such estimation might be thought of as a matrix, with effects of various magnitudes estimated for each subgroup in the population.

Such a matrix would be large, cumbersome and so difficult to interpret in many cases that it could be misleading. Each individual effect in each subgroup would be subject to large errors of estimation. The sum of effects across subgroups or across conditions within a subgroup would be estimated more reliably. However, aggregating either across subgroups or across conditions is difficult both conceptually and practically. Should a day of pain be assumed to have the same "social cost" regardless of whether it occurs to a child, an eighty-year-old, or a young adult? For the subgroup of octogenarians, how could one aggregate days of pain or minor discomfort with premature death?

A large literature on health status attempts to examine these issues, including people's subjective evaluations.[57] Not surprisingly, people do not like to think about such questions, but they can be induced to make judgments about what effects are commensurate and how all effects can be ranked.[58] Economists tend to assume that a common metric—dollars—exists and can be used to aggregate all the effects across all groups into a scalar measure of social cost.[59]

56. Selikoff, Hammond, and Churq, "Asbestos Exposure, Smoking, and Neoplasia."

57. Robert L. Berg, ed., *Health Status Indexes;* D. L. Patrick, J. W. Bush, and M. M. Chen, "Toward an Operational Definition of Health"; and Robert H. Brook and others, *Conceptualization and Measurement of Health for Adults in the Health Insurance Study.*

58. Berg, *Health Status Indexes.*

59. Lester B. Lave and Warren E. Weber, "A Benefit-Cost Analysis of Auto Safety Features."

Not everyone will agree about whether effects can be aggregated at all, or if so, by how much. While more information is displayed in the full matrix of effects, so many numbers make interpretation impossible. Wisdom seems to lie in displaying the full matrix and a range of aggregations so that a regulatory agency can find a comfortable generalization.

This matrix of physiological and perceived effects across subgroups in the population is subject to vast estimation difficulties. Data on human volunteers, on groups exposed to high concentrations, and on animals exposed to high concentrations are typically spotty. It is difficult to make the results comparable, and there is never a full range of estimated effects. In addition the data contain errors of observation and a host of difficulties previously described. Preparing the matrix of estimated effects requires heroic assumptions.

These formidable difficulties will cause some to throw up their hands and decide the task is impossible. An alternative to attempting estimation of the full matrix of effects is to concentrate on those cells for which there are better data and not to attempt to generalize to the other cells. Any estimation of effects involves generalization from lower mammals, healthy human volunteers, or groups subject to high exposure. No generalization is totally legitimate, and thus it is extremely difficult to estimate any effect for any subgroup.

As discussed above, one should not conclude that if the estimates have difficulties they are worthless to either science or regulatory decisions. Instead, the issue is modeling the uncertainty explicitly and using the information to take account of the uncertainties.

Coping with Uncertainty

Uncertainty is ubiquitous: few regulatory decisions are based on firm scientific evidence.[60] Instead, regulators are confronted with scientific literature that reduces the range of uncertainty but does not produce a single numerical estimate. Costs of complying with regulation are inherently uncertain. But even if all of these were known with confidence, uncertainty about the future state of the economy, about weather and other natural factors, and about technological innovation would become important.

60. Crandall and Lave, *The Scientific Basis of Health and Safety Regulation.*

The standard assumption in regulation has been that uncertainty is not important or that recognizing it is not important. Thus blue-ribbon panels have been asked to identify dose-response relationships or threshold values and consultants have been asked to estimate costs. The resulting estimates have been treated as facts. When opposed with estimates from adversaries, the approach has been to accept one or a compromise, but then to treat that estimate as a fact.

This approach is inherently unsatisfactory in that it neglects one of the most important aspects of the case. The magnitude and nature of uncertainties are important and should help shape the regulatory decision. Unfortunately the regulatory process does not encourage candor since congressional intervention or litigation is likely.

Uncertainty stemming from ignorance of the correct model or of crucial parameters must be distinguished from uncertainty due to ignorance of the outcome of a random process whose features are known. For example, the decision to ban cyclamate as a food additive in 1969 had vast uncertainty because the effect of consuming cyclamate was largely unknown, as were the health effects of substituting either saccharin or sugar for the banned chemical. In contrast, while it is impossible to know if a particular construction worker will be killed during a large construction job, the number of serious accidents can be predicted with confidence. When uncertainty is due to ignorance about structure or parameter values, a wide range of outcomes is possible. When uncertainty is due to not knowing the outcome of a random process that is understood, much more can be done to explore alternatives and to design a strategy to cope with the ignorance. Even when elements of the structure are unknown, however, careful modeling can explore the range of outcomes and design strategies to minimize loss.

Modeling Uncertainty

A common practice in estimating health effects or regulation costs when there is uncertainty is to pick a conservative figure in each instance where uncertainty is important and then to term the combination of these figures a "conservative estimate." While qualitatively correct, this approach makes no sense quantitatively. If a formal rule were adopted every time there was uncertainty to pick a figure that had one chance in twenty of occurring, the resulting estimate would have a minute chance of occurring; it could occur only if the unlikely event occurred at each stage. For example, if there were two places of uncertainty, the probability of the joint conservative event occurring would be only 1 in 400. If there were four stages in which uncertainty occurred, the probability of the joint conservative event occurring would be only 1 in 160,000. Thus, quantitatively, the probability of the joint conservative event occurring is so small that it rapidly becomes a remote event of no real interest.

Far better than choosing a conservative figure is picking a most likely estimate, along with upper and lower bounds (defined by probabilities of 0.05 or some similar number). One could then calculate the most probable overall estimate, along with upper- and lower-bound estimates occurring at each stage, guaranteeing that each had a minute probability of occurrence. Indeed, it would be preferable to sketch in the entire probability distribution that resulted from uncertainty at various stages.

The suggestion above is a rather simple illustration of how to model uncertainty. Generally, uncertainty occurs because some key parameter is unknown or because of an inherent stochastic factor. The nature of the uncertainty can focus attention on two key issues. The first is the uncertainty surrounding the final estimates of costs and effects. If values of zero and infinity are equally likely, and not much less probable than the most probable estimate, then it is obvious that science has done little to enlighten the decision. This means that the regulatory decision should attempt to promote flexibility and additional data collection and analysis so that a better decision can be made in the future. The second is that the analysis can isolate a particular parameter that is crucial to the decision. Often the agency can gain better information about this crucial parameter before making a decision or can phrase the regulation so that it is not entirely dependent on the parameter.

The lesson is that uncertainty must be modeled explicitly rather than regarded as nonexistent or as not being crucial for the regulatory decision. There is a need to increase understanding of the effects of each aspect of uncertainty in order to find the crucial questions to be investigated and to design regulatory decisions that will reflect the current state of uncertainty and help resolve it.

CHAPTER THREE

Revising the Ozone Standard

CHRISTOPHER H. MARRARO

THE Clean Air Amendments of 1970 required the Environmental Protection Agency to establish primary national ambient air quality standards (NAAQS).[1] The amendments require the administrator of the EPA to review the criteria published under the NAAQS at least every five years and permit him to revise standards and promulgate new ones as may be appropriate.[2] The EPA has established primary standards for seven pollutants: carbon monoxide, sulfur oxides, hydrocarbons, total suspended particulate matter, nitrogen dioxide, airborne lead, and photochemical oxidants.

Oxidants are an important constituent of photochemical smog. Ozone is the most prevalent in this class, and virtually all measurements of photochemical oxidants are actually of ozone.[3] The highest ozone concentrations typically occur during the summer months and are principally caused by hydrocarbon emissions from automobile exhausts, petroleum refinery emissions, chemical plants, and other industrial

1. These standards (42 U.S.C.7409) are to be achieved throughout the United States. They are enforced through the state implementation plans, which require reduction in pollutant emissions.

2. 42 U.S.C.7409(d)(1).

3. The chemical designation of the standard was changed from photochemical oxidant to ozone. The EPA states that "one reason for changing the chemical designation of the standard from photochemical oxidants to ozone is to correct an inconsistency between the title of the standard (photochemical oxidants) and the chemical species (ozone) that has always been measured by the reference method used to estimate ambient oxidant levels and determine compliance" [44 Fed. Reg. 8210 (1979)]. The standard applies only to ozone and does not establish permissible levels for other photochemical oxidants. *American Petroleum Institute* v. *Douglas M. Costle, Administrator, Environmental Protection Agency*, 661 F.2d 340 (D.C. Cir. 1981), cert. denied.

operations. But natural emissions, such as those from vegetation, also account for a significant portion of ambient ozone.

The ozone standard was the first national air quality standard to complete the revision process.[4] The EPA relaxed the primary one-hour standard from 0.08 part per million to 0.12 ppm; this decision was based on its interpretation of the medical evidence and on the use of a qualitative risk assessment technique.[5]

The EPA is required to review scientific evidence; it used two procedures for ozone. The lack of coordination between its two evaluation methods, haphazard procedures for reviewing the work that was done, and unclear direction and decisionmaking inside the EPA have contributed to the doubts about the newly promulgated ozone standard.

The procedural history is particularly important to this study since the new standard has been challenged in the courts and criticized extensively on the grounds that the EPA's evaluative procedures were inadequate. This report therefore is a review of the evidence and the proceedings on which the EPA based its decision to change the ozone standard. It is based on primary source materials, including the scientific literature, EPA reports, industry critiques, and interviews with health scientists and EPA policy experts who were involved in the revision process. Because this report concentrates on the review process, not all scientific studies available to the EPA are discussed or given equal treatment. Emphasis is placed on studies critical to the rule making and on important studies published after the revision. Finally, an attempt is made to determine whether risk assessment analysis, like that used in this case, can improve the decisionmaking process in other similar cases.

Background of the Revised Standard

The process by which the EPA revised the NAAQS for ozone in February 1979 from 0.08 ppm to 0.12 ppm took more than two years. The final decision, however, appears to be an arbitrary compromise stemming from the failure of the EPA's scientific method and bureaucratic procedures to yield a consensus.

4. The first attempt to revise an air quality standard was that of sulfur oxides [39 Fed. Reg. 25678 (1973)]; the revision was dropped.

5. 44 Fed. Reg. 8209 (1979). A primary one-hour standard is one deemed necessary to protect the public health. A secondary standard is one deemed necessary to protect the public welfare. Both are defined in section 109(b) of the Clean Air Act.

Examination of the ozone standard was reopened in September 1976,[6] when the EPA organized an international conference of scientists to review the original criteria document on which the current standard was based.[7] The initiative for revision came in part from a December 1976 petition to the EPA from the American Petroleum Institute, followed by a petition from the city of Houston.

After January 1977, when the report of the international conference was made public, the EPA began to move in earnest toward reevaluating the standard. In April 1977, the agency issued notice that it intended to revise the standard, and it assembled an ad hoc committee of its Science Advisory Board, whose task would be to review any new criteria the agency might develop.[8]

Inside the agency two evaluative procedures were being pursued. One, representing the EPA's conventional approach, was undertaken by the Advisory Panel on Health Effects, a group of outside experts often referred to as the Shy Advisory Panel because the chairman was Carl M. Shy. This panel was assembled by the EPA's Office of Air Quality Planning and Standards to review the scientific evidence to be contained in the criteria document. The ad hoc advisory panel, unlike the Science Advisory Board, was not mandated by statute.

The other procedure, a more novel undertaking, was done by Thomas Feagans, a staff member of the EPA's Office of Air Quality Planning and Standards, and William F. Biller, a consultant. They responded to a division director's desire to find an appropriate way to assess and identify what the Clean Air Act refers to as the "margin of safety" that would be appropriate for the new standard. Convinced of the usefulness of sophisticated judgmental evaluation, Feagans and Biller constructed a subjective probability analysis model for risk assessment. This model and its role in the final decision are at the center of the controversy over the new standard. The specific issue is whether the EPA intended to use the model as a tool for providing the answers that would shape the decision and whether it actually did.

6. An outline of the events leading to the revision is reported in Catherine Miller, "Case Study of the Revision of the National Ambient Air Quality Standard for Ozone."

7. The criteria document is a report of the scientific evidence on the causes, extent, and health and welfare health effects, and is required by the Clean Air Amendments of 1970, 42 U.S.C.4365(e)(1).

8. 42 Fed. Reg. 20493 (1977). The independent Science Advisory Board was established by Congress in the Environmental Research Development Demonstration Authorization Act of 1976 (90 Stat. 2069). The EPA is required to submit to the board for review and comment all proposed criteria documents and standards along with supporting scientific information.

The first time the two evaluative processes crossed paths was in June 1977, when the Feagans-Biller approach was presented to the Shy Advisory Panel. According to participants in the meeting, the panel was unenthusiastic; it did not reject the model entirely but chose not to adopt the method for its own investigation. Although a second discussion of the Feagans-Biller approach took place, the panel proceeded with its own plan of action; by July it was reviewing scientific studies on ozone exposure and was prepared to issue its final report.

In September the Advisory Panel issued the first draft of its criteria document, which was reviewed by the independent Science Advisory Board in November. Simultaneously Feagans and Biller were conducting interviews with nine experts, some of whom believed they were participating in an experimental procedure that would not be considered in designing a new standard for ozone.

By January 1978 the Advisory Panel's second draft of the criteria document was released. In the following month the Science Advisory Board received both the criteria document and the results of the Feagans-Biller assessment procedure. By this time the American Petroleum Institute had already submitted a critique of the Feagans-Biller approach to the EPA. In March, after this critical assessment and other dissatisfactions with the procedure had surfaced, the EPA belatedly asked the Science Advisory Board to review the Feagans-Biller model in a more formal context.

The EPA requested the review in the same month the Science Advisory Board voted to accept the Advisory Panel's criteria document, which was printed in April.[9] The document was released in June, when the EPA published a proposed ozone standard of 0.10 ppm.[10] The documentation in the *Federal Register* referred to the contribution of the Feagans-Biller model, although the method had not been officially sanctioned by the EPA or assessed by the Science Advisory Board.

Indeed, the EPA never accorded official status to the Feagans-Biller method. In interviews EPA personnel indicated that some officials regarded the method as a good idea, while others considered it "quan-

9. The approval of the Science Advisory Board was contingent on the EPA making several substantive revisions in the criteria document. These revisions were not made (Robert Van Vorhees, personal communication, fall 1980). The court in *API* v. *Costle* held that the act only requires that the EPA submit the criteria document to the board for advice and comment; it does not require the administrator to obtain approval of the board or to incorporate all suggested changes.

10. The proposal also included a secondary standard of 0.08 ppm for the one-hour average. 43 Fed. Reg. 26926 (1978).

titative nonsense." The Advisory Panel on Health Effects may have believed that Feagans was trespassing on its territory. At any rate, the panel proceeded with its own work and issued its conclusions without waiting for Feagans and Biller to present their results. But information and judgments produced by Feagans and Biller were mentioned in the rationale published for the proposed standard and even in that for the final standard. Feagans and Biller's information was at hand and seems to have been used before it was assessed, resulting in problems as soon as the proposed standard was published.

In July and August 1978, the months following the publication of the proposed standard, the EPA held public hearings in four cities. Soon afterward, critical evaluations of the Feagans-Biller method began to be received. The Regulatory Analysis Review Group of the Council on Wage and Price Stability submitted a critique, and the American Petroleum Institute again objected to the Feagans-Biller approach. The Council of Economic Advisers and officials in the Executive Office of the President expressed concern. At some time between the publication of the proposed 0.10 ppm standard in June 1978 and the publication of the final 0.12 ppm standard in February 1979, the EPA decided to disavow the Feagans-Biller risk assessment procedure and its results. The agency now claims that the information produced by the encoding sessions and subsequent analysis did not influence the final decision.

After the 0.12 ppm revised one-hour primary and secondary standard was promulgated, the American Petroleum Institute, the Natural Resources Defense Council, and several other groups petitioned the U.S. Court of Appeals for the District of Columbia Circuit to review the standard. Among the issues litigated were whether the standard for ozone was supported by the scientific evidence, whether the EPA violated the Clean Air Act by issuing standards more stringent than were required to protect the public health, and whether the decisionmaking process was adequate.[11]

Finally, the Feagans-Biller risk assessment technique was reviewed in April 1979 by an ad hoc subcommittee of the Science Advisory Board. Formal critiques were published by the subcommittee between September 1979 and December 1980.[12] The EPA is giving further study to this and related subjective techniques in response to a Science Advisory Board recommendation.

11. The court decided these issues in favor of the EPA; an analysis of the decision appears later in this chapter.

12. See footnote 30.

Analysis of Health Studies

A group of scientific studies (both epidemiological and laboratory) on the health effects of photochemical oxidants and ozone on humans was used by the Advisory Panel on Health Effects as the basis for reviewing the ozone standard. Many of these studies and two that were conducted after the review process are reported in detail in the appendix to this chapter.

Making judgments about health effects is difficult because of the increasing ability of scientists to detect subtle physiological changes resulting from exposure to a substance. Some detectable effects are so small as to be insignificant; others may be somewhat significant; still others may show clearly certain adverse health effects. For this reason it makes no sense to define all measurable physiological changes as adverse health effects. Therefore, although the studies examined in this report are analyzed in terms of statistically significant decrements of biological measurements, a distinction must be made between nonrandom changes in physiological effects and actual diseases or adverse health effects.

Unfortunately there is confusion about defining the terms *statistical significance* and *health effect* with respect to policy or regulatory decisions. Statistical significance is more dependent on sample size and the care with which the experiment was done than with the magnitude of an effect. It indicates whether one should have confidence that an observed effect is not due to random variation. When a study fails to find statistical significance, one cannot be confident that the observed association is valid. Even when the effect is statistically significant, however, it may be so small as to be irrelevant for regulatory purposes. Still, an exploratory study may find an association so important that it is prudent to take regulatory action, even though the association is statistically insignificant.

After reviewing the results of the health effect studies available to the agency, the EPA concluded that "the probable level of adverse effects in sensitive persons is in the range of 0.15 ppm to 0.25 ppm."[13] However, on the basis of studies relied upon in promulgating the revised standard

13. 44 Fed. Reg. 8126 (1979).

and studies reported after the revised standard was published, the lowest level at which there is evidence of statistically significant effects is 0.22 ppm.

However, many of the studies were sharply criticized by the president's Office of Science and Technology Policy as being inconclusive and flawed. It has been widely observed that they contain procedural inadequacies and contradictory results. Among the defects were failure to include data on smoking habits and respiratory illness; failure to account for factors such as temperature, humidity, and precipitation; failure to control for effects of other pollutants such as sulfur dioxide and nitrogen oxides; use of the unreliable potassium iodide method to measure oxidants; use of a nonrandom, small sample of healthy persons or of a sample biased toward more sensitive groups; failure to control the air in the environmental chamber being used, thus raising the possibility of extraneous pollutants having interfered with the results; and use of nonstandard methods to measure airway resistance.

Several areas of uncertainty exist with respect to short-term exposure and adverse health effects from photochemical oxidants. One of those is synergism—a positive interaction among pollutants. It is difficult to isolate the effect of a single pollutant in the epidemiological studies unless all other pollutants are controlled or at least measured.[14] Future investigations should monitor a large set of potentially relevant pollutants and investigate the possibility of interaction among them.

Another source of uncertainty is adaptation; it is not known what the effects are of repeated exposure to ozone, and it is likely that because of possible effects of adaptation, a dose-response curve for photochemical oxidants must take into account the frequency or length of exposure.[15] Temperature is also likely to be an important variable in assessing health effects of ozone.[16]

The Advisory Panel on Health Effects

All six members of the Advisory Panel on Health Effects were asked to estimate a dose-response curve after reviewing the literature reported

14. See the report of the study by Hazucha and Bates in the appendix, p. 87.

15. See the report of the study by Hackney and others in the appendix, pp. 83–86.

16. See the report of the studies by Hammer and others and Kagawa and Toyoma in the appendix, pp. 77–81.

in the criteria document.[17] At the time this panel met, the Office of Air Quality Planning and Standards had not yet decided if the Feagans-Biller risk assessment would be used in the decisionmaking to support the standard.[18] The Advisory Panel issued a summary statement that analyzed the health effects data and supported the existing 0.08 ppm standard.[19] The panel used a safety factor to move from the higher levels observed to produce physiological changes (0.15–0.25 ppm) down to an ambient standard that would protect the most sensitive groups. This method is termed the "qualitative" approach to risk assessment. No formal or structured technique was employed to obtain the effects level from the Advisory Panel; the 0.08 ppm standard resulted from panel discussions. A panel report issued June 10, 1977, was the result of a two-day meeting held on June 7–8, 1977. The report stated the panel's conclusion that an ozone level of 0.15–0.25 ppm aggravated asthma, emphysema, and chronic bronchitis, reduced pulmonary function, and caused chest discomfort and irritation of the respiratory tract.[20]

According to the report, "there is a convergence of toxicology, experimental human, and epidemiological studies demonstrating a small margin of difference between concentrations causing increased health risks and background levels." The Advisory Panel recommended against relaxing the 0.08 ppm standard, stating that "this standard provides very little margin of safety."[21]

The standard is essentially based on the short-term acute effects of ozone. It is important to realize, however, that a major, if not paramount, concern of the Advisory Panel in recommending the 0.08 ppm standard was the potential chronic effects of ozone.[22] Although no human health data are available in this area, at least two members of the panel were concerned specifically with the chronic effects of ozone on the developing lung and possible cytogenic effects. Further evidence of this concern was expressed in a letter to EPA Administrator Douglas Costle from five members of the panel.[23]

The Advisory Panel did not have the benefit of reviewing the Science

17. 43 Fed. Reg. 26966 (1978).

18. Miller, "Case Study of the Revision of the National Ambient Air Quality Standard for Ozone."

19. Environmental Protection Agency, *A Summary Statement from the Advisory Panel on Health Effects of Photochemical Oxidants*.

20. 44 Fed. Reg. 8126 (1979).

21. EPA, *Summary Statement from the Advisory Panel*.

22. Bernard D. Goldstein and David V. Bates, personal communication (August 1980).

23. Letter dated January 19, 1979.

Advisory Board's comments on the health effect studies contained in the first draft of the criteria document. Its report was presented at the board's review meeting (November 10–11, 1977) in the form of the first chapter of the criteria document. Resolution of various internal conflicts resulted in a final criteria document that excluded most of the conclusions voiced in the Shy Advisory Panel report.

Risk Assessment by Decision Analysis

In order to deal with the uncertainties described above, a quantitative approach to assessing risk was developed in the EPA's Office of Air Quality Planning and Standards. The method developed by Feagans and Biller is not a quantitative risk assessment, because it does not attempt to estimate the number of persons (or the percentage of the population) affected by specific doses. Quantitative risk assessment is not required by the Clean Air Act; instead, the act requires identification of a level of air quality that would protect the most sensitive groups in the population with an adequate margin of safety. The present method was developed in response to the EPA's need to identify the margin of safety required by the act.[24] The Feagans-Biller method is a decision analysis technique. It is used to estimate the probability that a given ambient concentration of ozone will constitute a health effects threshold. The threshold level was pragmatically defined by Feagans as that amount of effect the Clean Air Act seeks to prevent. The EPA has interpreted the act as requiring that the most sensitive group in the population be protected under conditions of normal daily activity. It defines a threshold as being "that concentration which is the health effect threshold concentration for the least sensitive member of the most sensitive one percent of the most sensitive group."[25]

The decision analysis technique established an interview process known as subjective probability encoding,[26] in which selected medical

24. Feagans stated in an interview (July 1980) that the risk assessment method was initiated in response to the search by Joseph Padgett, director of EPA's Strategies and Air Standards Division, for a method to deal with the margin of safety concept articulated by the Clean Air Act.

25. EPA, Office of Air Quality Planning and Standards, *A Method for Assessing the Health Risks Associated with Alternate Air Quality Standards for Ozone*, p. 25.

26. *Probability encoding* is a term used in the decision analysis literature to refer to the elicitation of subjective probability judgments and was pioneered by the Stanford Research Institute.

experts were asked to estimate a probable threshold subjectively. For the ozone application, nine experts were interviewed separately. The nine curves estimated were equally weighted and combined to get a "best" estimate curve. The results are presented in terms of the probability of suffering an adverse health effect at a specific concentration and are illustrated by ribbon graphs that seek to describe secondary uncertainty (a measure of uncertainty inherent in judgmental assessments).[27]

Experts' Judgments about Ozone

Judgments were elicited for each of the following four categories: (1) reduction in pulmonary function, (2) cough and chest discomfort, (3) reduced resistance to bacterial infection, and (4) aggravation of asthma and chronic bronchitis. Experts were asked to employ their own definitions of adverse health effects for each of these categories, to define for themselves which group of the population was most sensitive to ozone, and to focus on the most sensitive 1 percent of this group. The conditions of exposure were ambiguously defined. The experts were asked to base their judgments on the ambient air quality of "an average United States city." The level of exercise was specified to be light exercise such as jogging or tennis. This level, like the sensitive target population, was chosen because of the EPA's interpretation of the Clean Air Act. Each expert was also asked to describe the seriousness of the estimated health effects. Feagans stated in an interview that he defined encoding variables in consultation with the EPA's Office of General Counsel and "persons up the line."[28]

The experts were further told to take interaction effects among pollutants into account, but not to double-count for other NAAQS pollutants. The effect of adaptation was left to the discretion of each expert. For reduction in pulmonary function, the experts characterized

27. Feagans explains that the two primary uncertainties that give rise to the threshold risk are those about the health effects of threshold concentration and about what the maximum pollutant concentration in any area will be if a given standard is attained. In addition, there is a secondary uncertainty about how to best represent the primary uncertainties. The Feagans-Biller risk assessment method also contained a pollution concentration model for describing uncertainty concerning maximum pollutant concentrations that might occur under alternative air quality standards. The authors used a Weibull distribution to represent the one-hour average ozone concentrations that would be observed at a given location over a period of time. A subjective probability distribution was used to formulate the expected values critical to the air pollution sector of the model.

28. July 1980.

the sensitive population as asthmatics who were exercising and who were infrequently exposed. Adverse health effects were defined in terms of reduction in forced expiratory volume. For subjective symptoms of discomfort, including cough and chest symptoms, a health effect was defined to be a coughing spell or sore throat (sufficient to cause discomfort). The most susceptible group was determined to be children. Experts also considered these effects to be reversible. For reduced resistance to bacterial infections, the most susceptible group was thought to be young children. Increased severity of bacterial infections and possible risk to third parties were considered important health effects. For the fourth category, a health effect was defined to be an aggravation of asthma, emphysema, or chronic bronchitis. The effect was described as serious and the experts were divided about whether the sensitive group consisted of asthmatics or persons with emphysema.[29]

Evaluation of the Feagans-Biller Technique

As noted earlier, formal evaluations of the widely criticized Feagans-Biller technique have been submitted by the ad hoc subcommittee of the Science Advisory Board, the Regulatory Analysis Review Group, the American Petroleum Institute and member companies, and others.[30] They criticized the assumptions underlying the study, the way in which it was conducted, and the presentation of results.

The initial assumptions of the Feagans-Biller technique were challenged in several ways. First, critics complained that parameters of the study were poorly or even incorrectly defined. They noted that the selection of the most sensitive 1 percent of the population was an arbitrary choice based on, but not justified by, the Clean Air Act. This limitation, they felt, ignored the full range of sensitivities among individuals. Moreover, some believed that the selection of the population at risk should not have been made by Feagans and Biller and their subjects

29. For the results of the analysis, see 43 Fed. Reg. 26966–67 (1978); 44 Fed. Reg. 8216 (1979).

30. Information in this section was obtained from interviews with Granger Morgan, member of the ad hoc subcommittee of the Science Advisory Board (June and July 1980); Kay Jones, staff member of the Council on Environmental Quality (July 1980); Gordon Everett, consultant (September 1980); and Thomas Feagans (July 1980). See also EPA, "Review of a Method of Assessing the Health Risks Associated with Alternative Air Quality Standards for Ozone"; EPA, *Proposed Revisions to the National Ambient Air Quality Standard for Photochemical Oxidants: Report of the Regulatory Analysis Review Group;* and American Petroleum Institute, *An Evaluation of the Environmental Protection Agency's Risk Assessment Methodology Applied to Photochemical Oxidant (Ozone).*

but by EPA officials; the choice of this population, they argued, is a policy choice and should remain in the hands of decisionmakers who are responsible to the public.

Critics also complained that the term *adverse health effects* was poorly defined. Since this definition influences the results of the risk analysis, they contended, it must be carefully reached before interviews take place and must be uniformly expressed in all sessions. It was also noted that the EPA, in defining adverse health effects, should have taken into account the issues of adaptation to pollutants and the seriousness and reversibility of health effects.

Similarly, critics noted that the criterion of "ambient air of an average U.S. city" was inadequate, because experts could be basing judgments on widely varying ambient pollutant levels. Critics recommended that experts instead identify the fraction of the sensitive population that would suffer health effects at specific ambient ozone levels. (In the original study they were asked to identify the amount of ozone needed to affect 1, 5, and 10 percent of the most sensitive segment of the population.) Such an approach is more analogous to quantitative risk assessment. They suggested that head count models should be used in conjunction with subjective risk assessment techniques in order to estimate the number of persons who would be affected.

Another component of the model that was challenged, particularly by industry critics, was the test for pollution concentration and atmospheric meteorology conditions. Critics alleged that the Weibull distribution used by Feagans-Biller overestimates the risk of ozone exposure.

Doubt also was expressed about the model being adequately designed to elicit useful responses from interviewees, and the interview process was described as having been poorly organized and conducted in a haphazard fashion. Because this subjective analysis method is relatively cheap and produces results that appear quantitative, critics feared that subjective judgments might become a substitute for needed research.

The selection of experts was alleged to be arbitrary and unbalanced, resulting in a panel whose members were preponderantly affiliated with the EPA. Two panelists were chosen by Feagans alone, and five were chosen by him in consultation with the EPA Office of Research and Development. After concern was expressed about bias and the affiliations of the first two, Feagans chose two others.[31]

31. There was considerable overlap in the membership of the Advisory Panel and the Feagans-Biller panel. Four of the six members of the Advisory Panel were also among the nine men interviewed by Feagans and Biller. In addition, two authors of the scientific

Critics complained that the interview process was too haphazardly organized to "give the best professional judgment" of the health experts. For example, the first two encoding sessions ostensibly were held to demonstrate to EPA management that the procedure was feasible. But the results of these sessions were subsequently used in the analysis. This happened even though some experts agreed to participate only on the condition that this approach was experimental and that responses would not be used in the standard-setting process. Moreover, no member of the Stanford Research Institute (consultants for the technique) was present at these two sessions, and these consultants attended only three subsequent sessions. Finally, of the nine experts consulted, only two had the benefit of the Scientific Advisory Board's comments on the criteria document before they made their projections.

Another serious criticism of the interview method is that the experts were inadequately prepared to make the best projections possible under a subjective probability analysis regime. Critics noted the problems that result when subjects are required to make estimates in areas filled with uncertainty. Estimators are systematically overconfident under these circumstances (the distributions they project are narrower than they should be). Moreover, overconfidence *increases* with uncertainty about scientific fact, and the initial value chosen by the experts becomes an anchor point for their conclusions, thus biasing their results.[32]

The critics suggested that results could be improved in at least two ways. First, the experts could participate in preliminary interviews carefully designed to acclimate them to the subjective probability analysis technique and its attendant problems. Second, at least one critic suggested the use of Delphi techniques, which employ iterative encoding sessions after the experts have been exposed to each others' opinions;[33] such procedures might produce a firmer consensus.

Many complaints arose from the method used to weight the projections made by the experts during the encoding sessions. Critics believed it was inappropriate to give equal weight to each expert's projection and

---

studies used by the Advisory Panel were members of either the Advisory Panel or the group of nine experts.

32. See M. G. Morgan, M. Hendrion, and S. Morris, "Expert Judgments for Policy Analysis."

33. Three themes are common to most Delphi techniques: (1) consistency, (2) sharing of information and perspective among experts, and (3) convergence of judgments among experts. For an example of a Delphi technique applied to air pollution, see: Corvalis Environmental Research Laboratory, *Human Health Damages from Mobile Source Air Pollution: A Delphi Study* (EPA, 1978).

to combine the individual judgments into a single summary finding. The primary complaint about this method is that, although this choice of weighting affects the results, the authors made no attempt to justify their choice scientifically.[34]

Critics pointed out that the criteria document issued as a product of the interviews was so technical and so poorly presented that it could be useful only to other experts in the field. They strongly recommended that the results should be expressed in language accessible to a wider audience. They noted further that the standard was presented in misleading language. In the *Federal Register* the EPA reported that the encoded concentrations of ozone on which they relied are "probable or median effect levels as estimated from interviews with health experts."[35] As reported, these levels are neither median nor probable. They are simply the averages of concentrations at which experts estimated that the designated sensitive population would experience adverse health effects.

Finally, it was noted that the Science Advisory Board never reviewed the technique before it was used in the EPA's decisionmaking. Critics suggested that the board should be called on more consistently to perform oversight and review functions.

Feagans, Biller, and the EPA have responded to these criticisms by admitting that many are justified but arguing that this first application was preliminary. More resources are being put into improving the method for the future.

Risk Assessment in Decisionmaking

The promulgation notice in the *Federal Register* suggests that the EPA used the Feagans-Biller risk assessment technique to assess the margin of safety included in the standard and to justify the 0.12 ppm revision. The notice states:

> The risk assessment method is not being used to set the ozone standard. In determining what ozone standard has an adequate margin of safety, however,

34. One critic noted that sensitivity analysis shows that the method skewed data so that the lowermost, "left-hand" tail of the most conservative estimate drove the calculations, thus resulting in a hidden weighting in the program, which may not even have been recognized by those who manipulated the model. Everett suggested that a good test of the subjectivity analysis approach would have been to run each expert's curve of probabilities separately and then to compare the range of risk calculations that resulted.

35. 44 Fed. Reg. 8216 (1979).

the findings of the initial application of the risk assessment method to ozone have been considered.

While this (risk assessment) method cannot be used at this time as the sole tool for making that decision, the Agency does believe that the findings resulting from this initial application of the method do not permit any relaxation of the standard above 0.12 ppm.[36]

The EPA maintains that the risk assessment method was not used in the decision process and that inclusion of the statements in the *Federal Register* was unfortunate, the result of confusion in writing the promulgation notice.[37] Whether the Feagans-Biller technique was used to justify the 0.12 ppm standard is a controversial issue.[38]

The most extreme position taken by persons involved with the revision process is that the EPA had attempted to choose a reasonable number that was politically viable. The process was then worked backward, and the risk assessment was used as one mechanism to support the number. The 0.12 ppm proposed standard was considered early in the process in an internal action memorandum that outlines the health effects evidence, discusses the economic impacts, and determines the margin of safety for three alternatives: 0.08 ppm, 0.10 ppm, and 0.12 ppm.[39] The Feagans-Biller technique is mentioned in the memorandum as giving support for the probable effects level at 0.15 ppm. The EPA appears to have used the results of the risk assessment technique in the promulgation to lend support to the "probable effects" level of 0.15–0.25 ppm.[40] Further

36. 44 Fed. Reg. 8210, 8217 (1979).

37. This position was conveyed through a telephone interview with Joseph Padgett (August 1980). It has been corroborated by Feagans, who maintains that he had never been asked to interpret the risk numbers or risk ribbons for the administrator and notes that if a decision had been based on the risk assessment, he would have been asked to explain the significance of the numbers to either the administrator or other EPA management staff.

38. The use of the technique was at issue in *API* v. *Costle*.

39. Memorandum from David Hawkins, assistant administrator for air and waste management, to Douglas Costle, March 30, 1978.

40. The proposed rule stated that the "EPA concludes that the *demonstrated* human effects levels as cited in the criteria document vary from 0.15 ppm to 0.30 ppm" [43 Fed. Reg. 26966 (1978)]. However, the terminology the EPA used in the promulgation notice changed from "demonstrated" to "probable" effects levels at 0.15–0.25 ppm. To support this probable effects level, the EPA relied on health studies and on the judgments of the Advisory Panel on Health Effects *and* on the encoded average estimate of the judgments of health experts. This is substantiated by (1) the appearance in the promulgation notice of the table entitled "Probable Effect Level Estimates" [44 Fed. Reg. 8216 (1979)]; (2) the memorandum from Hawkins to Costle stating the "best estimate for effect level of 0.15 ppm is supported by 'the expert interview process' "; and (3) telephone interviews with EPA personnel who were closely involved with the revision process.

support for the hypothesis that the Feagans-Biller technique was considered in the decision process is the fact that the risk assessment document was included in the papers accompanying the action memorandum on which the final decision was based and presented to Costle.[41]

There is evidence that the EPA intended to use the technique to support the decision but then repudiated its use when sharp criticism was received after publication of the proposed rule. Feagans alleged that a decision not to use the technique was made between the time of the proposed rule and the time of the promulgation. Extensive criticism had been expressed by industry, the Regulatory Analysis Review Group, and, most important, by the health experts who were interviewed. Even Jack Hackney, a member of the encoding panel and a supporter of the concept of risk assessment, wrote a strong response to the EPA criticizing the use of the technique in the standard-setting process because he felt the process was inadequately developed and in an experimental stage.[42] The EPA would have had a difficult time justifying the use of a technique criticized by the very same health experts whose judgment the agency relied on in the elicitation process.

The Role of Executive Advisory Groups

The Council of Economic Advisers pressured the EPA to revise the standard upward from 0.10 ppm. The CEA criticism was contained in a report by the Regulatory Analysis Review Group, which was submitted to the EPA on October 16, 1978.[43] The report, written by Lawrence White, a former CEA senior staff member, criticized the EPA risk assessment technique, assessed the health evidence, and pointed out the marginal costs of meeting alternate standards of 0.08 ppm to 0.20 ppm (see table 3-1). White states that he did not propose alternative levels for the primary standard, but did point out that the marginal control costs were appreciably lower at 0.16 ppm than at 0.10 or 0.12 ppm. He suggested an alternative risk assessment strategy based on the concept that thresholds for health effects do not exist.[44] In November

41. Although the risk assessment draft document was submitted with the supporting papers, it was not mentioned in the three-page action memorandum.

42. Hackney submitted a written statement opposing the use of the technique in the revision process. Other experts were openly cautious about such use.

43. EPA, *Proposed Revisions to the National Ambient Air Quality Standard for Photochemical Oxidants: Report of the Regulatory Analysis Review Group.*

44. White felt that the proper position with respect to health effects is that there is a

Table 3-1. Estimates of the Annual Costs of Meeting Alternative Ozone Standards[a]
Billions of dollars

	Environmental Protection Agency estimates				*Regulatory Analysis Review Group estimates*			
Ozone standard (parts per million)	*Linear roll-back model*	*Mar-ginal costs*	*EKMA model*[b]	*Mar-ginal costs*	*Linear roll-back model*	*Mar-ginal costs*	*EKMA model*[b]	*Mar-ginal costs*
0.08	8.5		12.1		17.4		23.2	
		1.6		2.6		3.1		4.4
0.10	6.9		9.5		14.3		18.8	
		1.0		2.0		1.9		3.8
0.12	5.9		7.5		12.4		15.0	
		0.7		0.8		1.4		1.6
0.14	5.2		6.7		11.0		13.4	
		0.4		0.7		0.8		1.4
0.16	4.8		6.0		10.2		12.0	
		0.2		0.4		0.5		1.0
0.18	4.6		5.6		9.7		11.0	
		0.2		0.3		0.5		0.9
0.20	4.4		5.3		9.2		10.1	

Source: Adapted from Lawrence White, *Reforming Regulation: Processes and Problems* (Prentice-Hall, 1981), p. 62.
a. All costs are for calendar year 1987, in 1978 dollars.
b. EKMA: Environmental kinetic modeling approach.

1978 the EPA produced an internal memorandum that was a rebuttal to the Regulatory Analysis Review Group report, stating that the report had overestimated the costs of hydrocarbon control and that costs were irrelevant. A further rebuttal was drafted by White in December.[45] In the same month, concern was rising in the Executive Office of the President. Alfred Kahn, the chairman of the Council on Wage and Price Stability, became concerned about the ozone standard, and as a result, the Office of Science and Technology Policy began a review of the health studies. OSTP memorandums were prepared sharply criticizing the EPA's continued reliance on several of the studies used by the Advisory Panel. The memorandums evaluated these studies critically and found them to be inconclusive and flawed.

White reports that the staffs of the EPA and CEA held a number of meetings. The CEA argued that the costs were substantial, compared

no-threshold relationship. He notes that EPA health scientists agree with this position but that EPA policymakers, buttressed by the Clean Air Act, are promoting a threshold relationship for health effects. He suggests that a risk assessment, which is based on a no-threshold approach (such as the CAG risk assessment group), would not receive approval from EPA management for dealing with NAAQS standards because EPA policymakers are not likely to approve a no-threshold concept for air quality standards.

45. Lawrence White, *Reforming Regulation: Processes and Problems*, p. 66.

the ozone proposal to the proposed OSHA lead standard, and suggested that the ozone proposal would cost between ten and thirty times as much as the OSHA standard. Moreover, top CEA and OSTP members continually pointed out to senior EPA officials at other meetings that the health effects evidence would not support the probable effects level or the 0.10 ppm standard.

Throughout these December meetings, the EPA stressed that although the medical evidence was not solid, the uncertainties required extreme caution in selecting a standard.[46] The CEA, however, strongly emphasized the marginal costs of meeting alternative standards and also sharply criticized the application of the Feagans-Biller technique at these meetings. In fact, the CEA criticized the technique so relentlessly that the EPA senior officials stopped referring to risk assessment.

In January 1979 Costle informed the Executive Office of the President that a primary and secondary standard of 0.12 ppm was to be established. White reported that a last-minute series of meetings were held in which the Executive Office of the President suggested that a "0.12 ppm standard be kept but that four or five exceedances per year be allowed, which would have been statistically the equivalent of a 0.14 ppm standard with one exceedance."[47] When this proposal was rejected by the EPA, the CEA briefly considered appealing to the president. Although it is not certain that CEA efforts were responsible for moving the 0.10 ppm proposed standard to 0.12 ppm in the final rule, the CEA did exert strong pressure on the EPA. The EPA, although insisting that cost was irrelevant in setting the standard, continually objected to the cost estimates of the Regulatory Analysis Review Group. White argued that moving the standard to 0.12 ppm saved the country "between $1.0 and $3.8 billion per year, in perpetuity, starting in the mid-1980s."[48]

46. Kay Jones, who attended these meetings, noted (in an interview, July 1980) that David Hawkins was steadfast in desiring to maintain the 0.10 ppm proposed standard. Jones noted that during a final meeting in December 1978, Hawkins became infuriated with CEA persons and stated, "There are a hell of a lot of people getting sick from air pollution and we're going to do something about it." Others insist that Hawkins was instrumental in setting a tight standard, and he had a profound impact on the standard-setting process. He pressed hard for a 0.08 ppm standard, was reluctant to accept the 0.10 ppm standard, and grudgingly agreed to the 0.12 ppm standard.

47. White, *Reforming Regulation,* pp. 67–68. The EPA standard allows the 0.12 ppm level to be exceeded only once a year.

48. Ibid., p. 69.

Judicial Construction

The U.S. Court of Appeals for the District of Columbia Circuit was asked to review the 0.12 ppm standard by the American Petroleum Institute and several other groups. The court's ruling was issued on September 3, 1981.[49] The petition for review presented both substantive and procedural challenges. The industry and the state and local government intervenors essentially argued that the revised 0.12 ppm primary standard was arbitrary and irrational because adverse health effects have not been shown to exist below 0.25 ppm. They contended further that the 0.12 ppm standard was irrational because it was technologically impossible to attain that level in a number of geographic areas.[50] The American Petroleum Institute also argued that the administrator had erred in not considering attainability and cost justifications. The Natural Resources Defense Council argued that the 0.12 ppm primary standard was not sufficient to protect public health and that the administrator had failed to establish the adequate margin of safety mandated by the Clean Air Act.

The American Petroleum Institute also contended that the procedures followed by the EPA were seriously deficient. It was argued that the EPA had rejected the requirement of section 8 of the Environmental Research Development Demonstration Authorization Act that proposed standards be submitted to the Science Advisory Board for independent scientific review.[51] The Natural Resources Defense Council asserted that a series of illegal ex parte contacts (off the record comments) between the Executive Office of the President and EPA officials constituted a violation of the Clean Air Act.[52]

Judge Roger Robb, speaking for the court, upheld the standard in every respect. Although the court stated that "where the Administrator bases his conclusion as to an adequate margin of safety on a reasoned analysis and evidence of risk, the court will not reverse,"[53] it did not

49. *API* v. *Costle*.

50. The city of Houston contended that the 0.12 ppm limit could not be achieved in that jurisdiction because the background levels of ozone from natural sources (vegetation) already exceeded that level.

51. 42 U.S.C.4365.

52. 42 U.S.C.7607(d)(4)(B)(ii).

53. Slip opinion at 14.

attempt to scrutinize the evidence of risk or to examine the reasonableness of the analysis. The court noted that its duty was "to undertake a searching and careful inquiry into the facts" and reviewed the EPA decision under the "arbitrary and capricious" judicial standard of review that permits the court to give extreme deference to the judgment of the agency.[54] The court rejected the argument of the American Petroleum Institute that the standard was irrational and not supported by the health effects data, stating that "the record is replete with support for the final standards."[55] The court supported this statement by citing the findings of several of the health effects research experimenters. This is an important statement in view of the court's findings that the administrator is required to take into account in making his decision all the "relevant studies" revealed in the record.[56] The issue of what constitutes a scientifically relevant study is a key one if air quality standards are to be based on scientific merit. The EPA's assertion that the Clean Air Act permits only an assessment of health effects in promulgating health standards is an irrational interpretation if decisions are based on studies that are procedurally deficient, inconclusive, and generally irrelevant to the scientific issue at hand. The lesson here is that some attempt must be made by the scientific community and by regulators to outline the basic framework for what constitutes a relevant scientific study for decisionmaking purposes.

The court also found in favor of the agency on the procedural claims,[57] although it ruled that the EPA did violate section 8(e) of the Environmental Research Development Demonstration Authorization Act by failing to submit the proposed standard to the Science Advisory Board.[58] It excused this violation as harmless error under section 307(d)(8) of the Clean Air Act. The court held that "Section 8(e) makes the submission of any proposed standard to the SAB [Science Advisory Board] mandatory," but it could not find that "this error was so serious and related to matters of such central relevance to the rule that there is a substantial likelihood that the rule would have been significantly changed had the proposed standards been submitted to the SAB."[59] The court's interpretation of the Clean Air Act's "harmless error" provision undermines

54. This standard of review is mandated by the Clean Air Act, section 307.
55. Slip opinion at 15.
56. Slip opinion at 19.
57. *API* v. *Costle,* pp. 22–23.
58. Ibid., p. 22.
59. Ibid., p. 23.

the concept of independent scientific review embodied in section 8 of the Environmental Research Development Demonstration Authorization Act.[60] Indeed, what could be of more "central relevance" to an air quality standard than whether it is supported by relevant and credible scientific evidence? The independent scientific review process prescribed by the act ensures that the agency's technical assumptions and its interpretation of the scientific evidence will be open to scientific scrutiny. Because the Science Advisory Board has been highly critical of the EPA's interpretation of the scientific evidence for ozone, it is possible that further review by the board of the proposed standard could have significantly altered the 0.12 ppm revised standard. Independent review of the merits of the science used to justify an air quality standard is imperative in light of the great judicial deference accorded to agency decisionmaking. The courts must either take a hard look at the scientific assumptions and the EPA's conclusions, or require strict compliance with the procedural safeguards such as the independent scientific review provisions of the authorization act. Without these requirements, judicial review under the Clean Air Act is essentially a nullity.

Conclusions

Several conclusions concerning the health evidence and the use of risk assessment in setting the national ambient air quality standards under the Clean Air Act can be drawn from this case study.

First, EPA procedures were inadequately planned and were carried out clumsily. The power to make policy was vested everywhere and nowhere. Resources were dissipated on internal conflicts, while important questions remain unanswered.

Second, the scientific literature relied on by the EPA and the Advisory Panel on Health Effects was of uneven quality. Neither the EPA nor the panel seems to have assessed the scientific quality of each study and conclusions to discover which results were supported.

60. The act was enacted pursuant to a finding by a congressional subcommittee citing serious deficiencies in the EPA's interpretation of studies on the health effects of air pollution, including a tendency to find adverse effects when in fact no such effects existed. Section 8 directed the SAB to "review conflicting claims and advise the Administrator on the adequacy and reliability of the technical basis for rules and regulations." H.Rept. 722, 95 Cong. 1 sess. (Government Printing Office, 1977).

Third, the Advisory Panel on Health Effects made its final recommendation (a standard of 0.08 ppm) in part on the basis of concerns not addressed by the scientific studies. The panel was concerned about the potential chronic adverse health effects of ozone exposure. Review of the literature on animal experiments suggests that this concern may have been legitimate, particularly with respect to developing lung tissue. The work of the panel highlights the need for more sophisticated studies of the long-term effects of exposure to low levels of ambient ozone.

Fourth, the interviews revealed serious inadequacies in the subjective probability analysis conceived as an alternative risk assessment method. Such judgmental analysis can and should be an adjunct tool in regulatory decisionmaking. But the history of the approach used here is largely an object lesson demonstrating the potential weaknesses of such methods.

Finally, major attempts were made by various offices in the executive branch to influence the EPA at the end of the decisionmaking process. The extent of internal conflict, suspect data, and unanswered questions meant that decisions within the range at issue were necessarily arbitrary.

My recommendations are all variations on a single theme: the need for more careful, coherent planning.

1. The Clean Air Act's mandate for five-year reviews of all standards should be incorporated into the EPA's programmatic planning schedule. The ad hoc character of this review process should give way to more orderly procedures.

2. The agency should vest the evaluation authority in a body capable of carrying out its job relatively free from the interference of internal agency politics or outside pressures.

3. The agency should have a continuing program to support and solicit well-designed experimental studies in order to improve the quality and breadth of the body of evidence available to environmental decisionmakers.

4. Subjective probability analysis should be viewed as an aid in assessing areas of uncertainty rather than as a substitute for experimentation and hard evidence. Any such analysis should be carefully designed to avoid the weaknesses inherent in such methods.

5. The responsibility for making final regulatory decisions should rest clearly with EPA officials charged with making policy. The political component of a regulatory decision should be acknowledged; it is a legitimate element in any decision affecting millions of citizens. Certainly it should never be allowed to hide behind shaky claims of scientific justification.

Appendix: Studies of Health Effects of Ozone

Most of the health effects studies used by the EPA Advisory Panel on Health Effects in reviewing the ozone standard are discussed in detail in this appendix and are also shown in table 3-2. Two studies discussed here were conducted after the EPA review process. The studies fall into two categories: epidemiological and laboratory.

Epidemiological Studies

HAMMER AND OTHERS. EPA scientists studied photochemical oxidant exposure at two Los Angeles nursing schools, using data from October 1961 through June 1964.[61] Student nurses—healthy, young, and predominantly white—completed daily symptom diaries, recording the incidence of headache, eye discomfort, cough, and chest discomfort. To minimize bias, neither faculty nor students were informed that the relation of these symptoms to air pollution was of major interest. One defect may have biased the results, however. Although available, data on smoking habits and respiratory illness were not used in the analysis.

Maximum hourly measurements of photochemical oxidants, carbon monoxide, nitrogen dioxide, and daily maximum temperatures were monitored simultaneously at stations located 1.5 to 3.0 kilometers from the nursing schools. No validation techniques were reported to show that ozone levels at the schools matched those at the monitoring stations. A daily percentage of students reporting each symptom was calculated and compared with the daily hourly measurements of pollutants. Threshold functions were calculated for both simple and "adjusted" symptom rates in relation to photochemical oxidant concentrations.[62]

Cough and chest discomfort both remained relatively constant until a photochemical oxidant range of 0.30–0.39 ppm was reached. Headache without fever occurred more often above oxidant levels of 0.30–0.39 ppm. Daily eye discomfort frequency, a secondary "welfare" effect, increased continuously as photochemical oxidant levels exceeded 0.15–0.19 ppm.

Dose-response curves were estimated using a "hockey stick" or

61. D. I. Hammer and others, "The Los Angeles Student Nurse Study."
62. "Adjusted" symptom rates excluded symptoms accompanied by fever or chills.

Table 3-2. Effects of Exposure to Ozone as Reported in Studies Used by the Environmental Protection Agency[a]

Effect	*Study*	*Concentration producing effect (parts per million)*	*Comments*
Aggravation of asthma	Schoettlin and Landau (1961)	0.25	Report incorrectly concludes observing effects at levels as low as 0.20 ppm
Reduction in pulmonary function	Hazucha and others (1973); Hazucha and Bates (1975)	0.37	No adequate air purification system
	Kagawa and Toyoma (1975, 1976)	0.01–0.30	Pulmonary function strongly correlates with temperature; sulfur dioxide and ozone correlate with same factors
	Von Nieding and others (1976)	0.10	Advisory Panel report used Von Nieding to support its conclusion that changes in lung function may occur below 0.25 ppm and some risk may occur in range of 0.15–0.25 ppm
Chest discomfort	Hammer and others (1974)	0.30	Hockey stick function in Hammer found invalid
	DeLucia and Adams (1977)	0.15	Study results must be interpreted in light of stressful exercise levels
No significant pulmonary changes	Linn and others (1978)	0.20–0.25	If adaptation was a factor, responses of subjects would be underestimated
No consistent physiological changes	Hackney and others (1975)	0.25	Population biased toward more sensitive groups

Source: Adapted from 44 Fed. Reg. 8214 (1979).

a. Additional studies were cited by the Environmental Protection Agency but are not discussed in this paper and not listed in this table. See the Bibliography for complete citations of the studies listed here.

linear, piecewise continuous function. For headache without fever, the computed threshold for the appearance of adverse effects was 0.05 ppm oxidant. For simple eye discomfort, the computed threshold was 0.15 ppm with an estimated 95 percent confidence limit of 0.14–0.17 ppm. Computed thresholds for cough and chest discomfort were 0.26 ppm and 0.30 ppm, respectively.

The major problem with the study is the invalidity of the hockey stick function used to estimate threshold values. This function presumes that the data belong to two linear regimes,[63] and at best it is an approximation to a more complicated form. The authors did not demonstrate that the data conformed to this assumption.

They acknowledged that nitrates and sulfates measured at the same site in April 1970 were at moderately high levels. Since these pollutants were not controlled in the analysis, they, rather than photochemical oxidants, may have been responsible for the observed effects. In epidemiological studies by Kagawa and others, investigators have shown that accounting statistically for temperatures greatly reduces the association between health effects and photochemical oxidants.[64] Although the authors acknowledge that the weak relationship between oxidants and eye discomfort is most likely due to their concomitant association with daily maximum temperature, they do not analyze the degree to which temperature may be causing the effect.

The significance of an increase in headache is also questionable. Not only is the curve shallow, indicating little association, but the biological plausibility of this finding is questionable. The general biological knowledge of ozone as a pulmonary irritant does not support the observed association between exposure and headache.

The findings of the study would also have been more convincing if other factors, such as the day of the week, had been specifically controlled and if symptom relationship with other meteorological variables such as humidity and precipitation had been examined. Finally, the potassium iodide technique used to measure oxidants has proved unreliable.[65]

The authors of the study conclude that photochemical oxidants at

63. Alan Gittelsohn, "Evaluation of Hockey Stick Functions Used to Establish Pollution Health Effect Thresholds."

64. J. Kagawa and T. Toyoma, "Photochemical Air Pollution: Its Effects on Respiratory Function of Elementary School Children"; and J. Kagawa, T. Toyoma, and M. Nakaza, "Pulmonary Function Tests in Children Exposed to Air Pollution."

65. C. S. Burton and others, "Oxidant/Ozone Ambient Measurement Method: Assessment and Evaluation."

ambient levels may produce the four symptoms examined. But the study determines neither at what levels effects occur nor that oxidants alone are responsible for effects in the subject population.

SCHOETTLIN AND LANDAU. One hundred and thirty-seven patients participated in the investigation of the relationship between asthma attacks and photochemical oxidants; the experimental protocol required the subjects to keep diaries on the prevalence and severity of their attacks.[66] A failure of the study was due in part to the lack of control for effects of other pollutants such as sulfur dioxide and nitrogen oxide. A further deficiency was that again the unreliable potassium iodide method was used to measure oxidants.

The coefficient of determination (R^2) between daily attacks and daily maximum hourly oxidant levels reached was only 0.14. Analysis of subpopulations according to sex, age, and length of residence within the Los Angeles area resulted in a range of R^2s, the largest being only 0.18. The mean number of patients having attacks on days when the oxidant level was above the median (0.13 ppm) was compared with the mean number of patients having attacks when the oxidant level was below the median. No significant difference was found in the average number of patients having attacks on days measuring above or below the median oxidant level. However, the authors did report that the comparison between the mean number of patients having attacks on days with oxidant levels above 0.25 ppm differed significantly from the number when the level was lower. Most attacks were characterized as mild. Schoettlin and Landau do not assert that the relationship between oxidant levels and asthma attacks is causal. They state that "all correlations led to the conclusion that there was relatively little association between oxidant levels and attacks of asthma."[67]

KAGAWA AND TOYOMA. The authors studied the effects of environmental pollutants, including ozone and total oxidants, on the pulmonary function of twenty children in an elementary school in Tokyo.[68] The results show that pulmonary function tests were significantly correlated with temperature far more often than with any other environmental factor. Oxidants and nitrogen dioxide frequently correlated with pul-

66. C. E. Schoettlin and E. Landau, "Air Pollution and Asthmatic Attacks in the Los Angeles Area."

67. Ibid., p. 547.

68. Kagawa and Toyoma, "Photochemical Air Pollution"; and Kagawa, Toyoma and Nakaza, "Pulmonary Function Tests in Children Exposed to Air Pollution."

monary function. In 25 percent of the subjects, ozone was significantly correlated with some pulmonary function. However, the analysis showed that sulfur dioxide and ozone tended to correlate significantly with the same factors, suggesting that both ozone and sulfur dioxide may exert effects on the upper airways. Since temperature was found to be highly correlated with the pulmonary test results, the authors calculated partial correlations correcting for the effects of temperature. Significant partial correlations with ozone occurred for three subjects. A constraint placed on the results of this study is that physiological measurements were taken indoors, while the aerometric measurements were outdoor ambient measurements. The relationship of indoor measurements to ambient level is not analyzed. A further constraint is that the authors do not describe the specific levels of ozone where significant associations with physiological measurements were observed. The reported range of ozone concentration was from 0.01 ppm–0.30 ppm.

Laboratory Studies

DELUCIA AND ADAMS. The effects of ozone on the pulmonary function and ventilatory patterns of six healthy nonsmoking male subjects were studied after exposure for one hour to zero ppm, 0.15 ppm, or 0.30 ppm of ozone, while at rest or steadily exercising at 25 percent, 45 percent, and 65 percent of maximum oxygen uptake (V max).[69] The ozone was administered through a mouthpiece, and subjects were not informed whether they were receiving ozone for any of the twelve conditions imposed.

The results show little discernible effect of ozone inhalation on respiratory indices during the 25 percent and 45 percent exercise protocols. However, a significant decrease in forced expiratory volume (FEV) was observed following the 65 percent, 0.30 ppm exposure protocol. A nonsignificant diminution was noted at 45 percent V max for this concentration. Significant changes in FEV were transitory, returning to near normal values following four hours of recovery.

A significant decrease in mid-maximum flow rate (MMFR) was also noted during the 65 percent, 0.30 ppm exposure protocol. Four hours

69. A. J. DeLucia and W. C. Adams, "Effects of Ozone Inhalation During Exercise on Pulmonary Function and Blood Biochemistry." David Hawkins stated in an interview that the EPA's conclusion that probable health effects occurred at 0.15 ppm exposure to ozone was the result of reliance by the EPA on the DeLucia and Adams report.

following this protocol, MMFR was still 9.4 percent lower than control values. Subjective symptoms of discomfort were reported during the most stressful exercise periods, including headache, wheezing, and congestion.

The results of the DeLucia and Adams study indicate that healthy subjects, when exposed to 0.30 ppm ozone during stressful exercise periods, may experience a temporary reduction in pulmonary function measurements. Further, they may also experience subjective symptoms of discomfort when exposed to 0.15 to 0.30 ppm ozone during strenuous exercise. The results of the DeLucia and Adams study, however, must be interpreted carefully.

Since the sample population consisted of only six healthy persons, including the authors themselves, who were not randomly selected, the results are open to question. Failure to find a significant association between exposure levels and reduction in pulmonary function at 0.15 ppm does not conclusively support the absence of association in a larger, more randomly selected population.

The results of the study are valid only for healthy persons, since the six subjects tested were above average in physical fitness.[70] One subject reported a previous history of compromised respiratory function, having received medication to suppress an asthmatic condition five years before the study. Although the authors reported that the sensitive subject could not complete a full hour of exercise at 65 percent, 0.30 ppm, they would not ascribe a causal relationship between exercise performance and exposure. In fact, they stated that reductions in work performance by this subject "may be related to altered exercise ventilatory patterns" rather than to changes in maximal or subnormal maximum oxygen uptake.[71]

Study results must be interpreted in light of the stressful exercise levels to which subjects were exposed. Significant decreases in pulmonary function were observed *only* during the 65 percent, 0.30 ppm exposure protocol. DeLucia noted that the 65 percent exercise level is what a physician would prescribe to "get into shape."[72] For the most fit persons, 65 percent V max would be like running six to seven miles in an hour or playing competitive handball for an hour.

70. DeLucia press conference, January 25, 1979, transcript by American Petroleum Institute.

71. DeLucia and Adams, "Effects of Ozone Inhalation," p. 79.

72. DeLucia press conference.

A Dasibi ozone analyzer was used to monitor the ozone exposure levels. DeLucia has acknowledged that there may have been errors in calibrating the Dasibi analyzer so that the 0.15 ppm and 0.30 ppm levels used in the experiment might actually have been 0.12 ppm and 0.24 ppm.

DeLucia and Adams reported that the nature of the effect on pulmonary function was temporary. DeLucia reported that "by and large the effects were already diminished by four hours and essentially gone by twenty-four hours."[73]

It is critical to note that three-fourths of the subjective discomfort symptoms were limited to the most vigorous exercise situations. Further, Everett indicated that the symptoms that occurred only with ozone exposure were chest tightness, pain on deep inhalation, and wheezing.[74] Only two subjects reported headache. Subject 1 experienced headache at the 65 percent "workload" (zero ppm) and subject 6 experienced headache at rest with 0.30 ppm ozone exposure. DeLucia stated that the other protocols resulted in few symptoms other than one reported by a subject who thought he was breathing ozone when he was actually breathing filtered air.

Strenuous levels of exercise exacerbated the effects of ozone toxicity in the six healthy males examined, and pulmonary function measurements significantly decreased during stressful exercise periods at 0.30 ppm exposure. The effects on pulmonary function from exposure to ozone were transient, however. Subjective symptoms of discomfort occurred during the most vigorous exercise protocols—at 65 percent V max, 0.15 ppm–0.30 ppm, and at 45 percent V max at 0.30 ppm. Because of possible errors in the calibration of the ozone monitor, these levels could have been 0.12 ppm–0.24 ppm at 65 percent V max and 0.24 ppm at 45 percent V max.

HACKNEY AND OTHERS. In a study by Hackney and associates, normal and sensitive persons were exposed to ozone for two hours at concentrations of 0.25, 0.37, or 0.50 ppm.[75] Secondary stresses of heat and intermittent light exercise, sufficient to double ventilation in one minute, were applied.

The subject population consisted of thirteen adult males. All were

73. Ibid.

74. Gordon Everett, consultant, personal communication (September 1980).

75. J. Hackney and others, "Experimental Studies on Human Health Effects of Air Pollutants: Two Hour Exposure to Ozone Alone and in Combination with Other Pollutant Gases."

residents of Los Angeles and, because of adaptation, may have been less reactive than persons from smog-free environments. Two persons who had a history of asthma and four who had histories of allergy were included in the study.

All subjects were exposed in a chamber where careful attention was given to environmental control and pollutant monitoring. Extreme care was taken in controlling the pollutants and in filtering particles. A battery of tests were performed while the subject was still under exposure. In addition, a venous blood sample was taken for biochemical analysis, and the subject was interviewed for symptoms according to a standard questionnaire. During each week of the study, the first two or three days were devoted to control (sham) exposures in order to establish baseline measurements of functions.

The first group of seven persons (including three with a history of allergies) who were exposed on two successive days to 0.50 ppm showed decreases in some respiratory functions.[76] Changes in the measurements in most cases did not become statistically significant until the second exposure day. Biochemical analyses revealed increased erythrocyte fragility. The four normal subjects showed few symptoms.

The group exhibited no consistent physiological changes when exposed to 0.25 ppm ozone. Closing capacity, however, did show a significant alteration. Increases in respiratory volume and decreases in diffusion capacity were observed in some exposures. Few biochemical changes were detected in this exposure group.

A second mixed group of three sensitive and two normal subjects showed few physiological changes when exposed to 0.37 ppm, but one reactive subject who had a history of smog sensitivity showed substantial decreases in some pulmonary functions. This subject reported symptoms similar to those of a reactive subject in the 0.50 ppm exposure group. Biochemical changes were detected but were less severe than changes seen in the 0.50 ppm exposure group.

Hackney, in a recent interview, reported that the subject population was biased toward the more sensitive groups and that therefore the results represented "worst-case" situations.[77] He believes that his experimental design allows extensive testing before and after exposure and is capable of identifying minute changes in pulmonary function tests.

76. The allergies were defined by symptoms of wheezing, dermatitis when in contact with special antigens, or a history of chronic hay fever.

77. June 1980.

Of greater importance than the issue of sample size and selection, however, is the issue of the most sensitive part of the population and whether studies demonstrate (rather than assume) a most sensitive part. With time, it is beginning to appear that asthmatics may be no more sensitive than a "normal" population that includes persons subject to respiratory allergic reactions.[78] Where data from repeated small samples of a large population begin to cluster (as in the ozone data), one can have increased confidence that the small population is "representative" even if not randomly selected.

The results reported from this investigation agree with worst-case studies conducted by the same authors.[79] Those studies, using the same experimental procedure, indicated that four normal subjects failed to show decreases in basic pulmonary measurements when exposed to 0.50 ppm for four hours. Slight but inconsistent decreases in other functions were reported.

The four sensitive subjects tested, however, developed marked respiratory symptoms and physiological changes. All four experienced strong subjective symptoms, including coughs, substernal pain, and wheezing. In addition, three out of four could not complete two successive days of testing. The symptoms generally moderated soon after exposure was terminated; sensitive subjects were not affected at 0.25 ppm, but mild physiological changes were detected at 0.37–0.50 ppm. The authors speculated that response at the 0.37 ppm exposure appeared only because this exposure was made in the third week of testing.

Increased erythrocyte fragility and a downward trend in red cell acetylcholinesterase acute activity were detected. These biochemical responses also occur in clean air under stresses from heat and exercise. Unlike the physiological responses, these biochemical responses may not reverse.[80] Hackney stated that the biochemical effects of ozone could not be separated from those of heat or exercise. Increased erythrocyte fragility occurred during the 0.50 ppm exposure protocol and to a lesser degree at 0.37 ppm and could not be detected at 0.25 ppm.

All subjects tested were from southern California, where ambient photochemical oxidant concentrations are generally high. Small but

78. Bates, personal communication (July 1980).

79. J. Hackney and others, "Experimental Studies on Human Health Effects of Air Pollutants, II: Four-Hour Exposure to Ozone Alone and in Combination with Other Pollutant Gases."

80. Goldstein, personal communication (September 1980).

significant differences in reactivity to ozone were found between southern Californians, regularly exposed to ozone, and Canadians, rarely exposed to high concentrations. In a highly controlled experiment both subjective symptoms and physiological reactivity were greater in the Canadians when exposed to 0.37 ppm ozone for two hours. These results may indicate that humans adapt to photochemical oxidants.

Exposed for two hours to 0.50 ppm ozone, sensitive subjects performing light exercise showed statistically significant decrements in basic pulmonary function measurements. After exposure for two hours to 0.25 ppm ozone, sensitive subjects did not show meaningful decrements in basic pulmonary function measurements. Sensitive subjects exposed for two hours to 0.37 ppm ozone may show decrements in basic pulmonary function measurements. Exposure for two hours at 0.25 ppm ozone produced few if any symptoms of discomfort in sensitive subjects. During exposure for two hours at 0.37 ppm and at 0.50 ppm, however, subjective symptoms were present.

In the worst-case study marked symptoms of discomfort occurred during the four-hour exposure to 0.50 ppm. At higher concentrations, the effects of exposure on pulmonary measurements were more pronounced in sensitive subjects after repeated exposures. Adverse health effects resulting from exposure to a level of 0.37 ppm cannot be determined from the present experiments, based on their biochemical measurements. It is probable that humans can adapt to repetitive, short exposures to photochemical smog (ozone) at concentrations up to 0.37 ppm or even 0.50 ppm.

HAZUCHA AND OTHERS. Two groups of normal subjects, smokers and nonsmokers, were exposed to either 0.37 ppm or 0.75 ppm ozone for two hours in an environmental chamber.[81] Exposure to both levels resulted in significant decreases in forced vital capacity at one and two hours, regardless of smoking habits. Statistically significant changes from control values occurred in both groups after a two-hour exposure to 0.37 ppm. Changes in MMFR and 50 percent V max were the most pronounced. The validity of the study is suspect, however, because the air entering the chamber was not carefully controlled. An extraneous pollutant might have affected the accuracy of the instruments monitoring the test pollutant or interacted with the test pollutant and modified the subject's biological response.

81. M. Hazucha and others, "Pulmonary Function in Man After Short-Term Exposure to Ozone."

HAZUCHA AND BATES. The authors investigated the synergistic effects of ozone and sulfur dioxide on pulmonary functions.[82] Eight subjects were exposed to 0.37 ppm ozone and 0.37 ppm sulfur dioxide for two hours in an environmental chamber. The authors found that a significant decrease in MMFR occurred for the group as a whole under exposure to 0.37 ppm ozone in combination with 0.37 ppm sulfur dioxide for thirty minutes. Forced expiratory volume decreased to 78 percent of its initial value after exposure to the combined pollutants. Recovery was apparent one-half hour after exposure. The most critical deficiency of the study is that there was no adequate air purification system. Quite probably undetected pollutants reacted with the test gases and interfered with the results. In a follow-up investigation by Bell and associates a series of highly controlled studies were initiated to attempt to reproduce the results of Hazucha and Bates.[83] The results of the Bell study suggest less severe effects than do those of Hazucha and Bates. The Bell group concludes that sulfur aerosols (sulfates) may have formed in the Hazucha and Bates study chamber due to the lack of an adequate air purification system.

LINN AND OTHERS. Linn and associates assessed pulmonary, biochemical, and symptom responses of twenty-two clinically diagnosed asthmatics exposed for two hours to 0.20–0.25 ppm ozone.[84] The authors report no significant difference in pulmonary function measurements. Symptoms increased slightly but not significantly with exposure to ozone. Small but significant group mean blood biochemical changes occurred with exposure to ozone. Hemoglobin concentration showed a significant decrease on ozone exposure days. Acetylcholinesterase activity showed the greatest overall change, decreasing with each successive day of ozone exposure. A possible confounding factor is the phenomenon of adaptation.[85] The authors acknowledge that if adaptation was a factor in their study, the responses of the subjects would tend to underestimate that of populations not commonly exposed to increased ambient oxidant concentrations.

82. M. Hazucha and D. V. Bates, "Combined Effects of Ozone and Sulfur Dioxide on Human Pulmonary Function."

83. K. Bell and others, "Respiratory Effects of Exposure to Ozone Plus Sulfur Dioxide in Southern Californians and Eastern Canadians."

84. W. Linn and others, "Health Effects of Ozone Exposure in Asthmatics."

85. J. Hackney and others, "Effects of Ozone Exposure in Canadians and Southern Californians."

VON NIEDING AND OTHERS. Von Nieding and associates exposed twelve healthy male volunteers for two hours to 0.1 ppm ozone and to ozone in combination with nitrogen dioxide and sulfur oxides.[86] Subjects were exposed in an environmental chamber where temperature and humidity were held constant. The results show that airway resistance was significantly higher at the end of a two-hour exposure to 0.1 ppm ozone. In addition, the alveolar-arterial gradient increased with decreasing oxygen tension. The general consensus of those who have evaluated the study is that its interpretation of observed physiological changes as adverse health effects "is unlikely to be correct and cannot be accepted unless confirmed by further work under highly controlled conditions."[87] The essential points of criticism are that the air purification system was primitive; hydrocarbon, carbon monoxide, or particles could have caused the observed results. Further, airway resistance was measured by a nonstandard method, and subsequent investigations by Linn and associates, using the same method employed by Von Nieding, could not detect the significant changes in oxygen tension found by the latter.[88] The EPA Science Advisory Board offered extensive criticisms of the Von Nieding study,[89] whose results make little biological sense when viewed in terms of the biological and chemical nature of the pollutant.

Studies Reported after the EPA Revised Standard

Although the studies reported in this section were not available to the EPA at the time of the revision, they are well designed and their results should be considered in any future revision of the ozone standard.

LINN AND OTHERS. Short-term effects from air pollution were investigated by Linn and associates in a single-blind experiment.[90] The authors

86. A. Von Nieding, "Studies of the Combined Effects of Nitrogen Dioxide, Sulfur Oxide, and Oxygen on Human Lung Function." Von Nieding indicated in 1978 at the Conference on Pollutants and High Risk Groups at the University of Massachusetts that his "normal population" was drawn from patients under an outpatient treatment program for chronic bronchitis resulting from occupational respiratory exposure problems.

87. R. Frank, J. Hackney, and P. Mueller, "Report on Visit to Von Nieding Laboratory," p. 165.

88. W. S. Linn and others, "Effect of Low-Level Exposure to Ozone on Arterial Oxygenation in Humans."

89. Transcript of the meeting of the Science Advisory Board, February 23, 1978, pp. 510–11. John Knelson, chief at EPA's Health Effects Research Laboratory, also felt that the study should be strongly qualified.

90. W. Linn and others, "Short-Term Respiratory Effects of Polluted Ambient Air: A Laboratory Study of Volunteers in a High-Oxidant Community."

attempted to combine the major advantages of a clinical study (maximum control) with one of the major advantages of an epidemiological approach (opportunity to study the long-term effects of ambient air pollution). Thirty asthmatics and thirty-four normal subjects were exposed to pollutants in a mobile laboratory that could be supplied with either polluted ambient air or purified air.

All subjects lived and worked near the test site in a Los Angeles suburb. The normal classification excluded asthma but did not exclude upper respiratory allergies. Asthmatics were diagnosed by a physician; clinically, they were quite heterogeneous. It is important to note that of the thirty-four "normal" subjects, twenty-five had a history of respiratory allergies. The authors concluded that the observed result that asthmatics did not react more severely than the normal subjects may be artificial and invalid because the normal group included an atypically large proportion of persons sensitive to upper respiratory insults.

Although the subjects were not randomly selected and therefore were not representative of the general population, the deliberate choice of a location expected to provide oxidant exposure conditions among the most severe in the United States, together with a population of highly sensitive subjects, allows confidence that the levels of response observed should be greater than those experienced by the general population.

The study involved a series of experiments. First, twenty-two ambient exposures and twenty purified-air control studies were performed between July and October 1978. Subjects were exposed for two hours and performed intermittent light exercise, sufficient to double ventilation per minute. As a control method, subjects were acclimated to the odor of ozone in the chamber. Lung function and symptoms were evaluated before and after exposure. Purified-air control studies then took place at least three weeks after exposure. Air conditioning controlled the chamber temperature and relative humidity. A validation study was performed next on a separate group of twelve healthy subjects to verify that responses to ambient air inside the chamber did not differ from those observed outside. Finally, an additional follow-up study was initiated after all exposures had been completed on those subjects who appeared to be most reactive to ambient pollution. The purpose was to determine whether ambient air produced toxic responses more severe than could be attributed to ozone alone.

Air monitoring results showed that mean ambient exposure concentrations were 0.22 ppm ozone and 200 micrograms per cubic meter for total suspended particulates, and that the levels of sulfur dioxide were quite low. The authors report that atmospheric conditions (high humidity) were conducive to interaction between ozone and sulfur dioxide to form sulfate aerosols. The results of the lung function covariance analyses showed that all forced expiratory measures and total lung capacity changed significantly during the ambient exposures as compared with purified air exposures.

In asthmatics the increase in reported symptoms was insignificant. In addition, a small significant increase in reported symptoms was seen in normal subjects with ambient exposures relative to control. The bulk of the increase in symptom scores was attributable to headache and fatigue. Multiple regression analyses indicated that increased levels of ozone had a detrimental effect on all pulmonary function variables.

In the validation experiments, the mean concentration of ozone in the chamber was 0.22 ppm (0.12–0.32 ppm), while the mean corresponding outdoor concentration was 0.24 ppm (0.16–0.33 ppm). Changes in $FEV_{1.0}$ between indoor and outdoor protocols were not significant ($p > 0.05$), suggesting no real difference between indoor and outdoor responses.

A very important result observed in the follow-up studies was that the ambient photochemical pollution had greater effects on the twelve highly reactive subjects than did the purified air with ozone. This result suggests that laboratory experiments with a limited number of pollutants may underestimate the effects of air pollution on human health in the real world environment.

The results of this investigation showed statistically significant changes in lung function and symptom responses when subjects were exposed to ambient air. The magnitude of these changes was small, however. The authors stated that "the physiological changes appeared too small to be perceived by the subjects or to affect their performance measurably." The authors intimated that these changes cannot be considered an adverse health effect. They further stated that "all the significant changes found were quite small; they were often no larger than the changes in pre-exposure measurements between study days, and could be considered close to or within the noise level of repeated measurements in an individual subject over a short time. Whether such small changes are of any health consequence remains a matter of conjecture."[91]

With respect to multiple regression analysis, significant associations may be spurious or due to chance because only a few significant

91. Ibid., p. 251.

associations were found in many groups. It must be recognized that the regression analysis as used here cannot confirm or deny a cause-effect relationship. Moreover, subjects termed highly reactive did contribute to the significant associations and these subjects received the highest doses. Thus the results may only indicate a statistically significant response to exposure at the highest doses.

The high prevalence of respiratory allergy in the "normal" group led the authors to state that other factors such as antigens could possibly have been responsible for the observed results. Previous studies by these authors under highly controlled experimental conditions have shown no function decrements at 0.20–0.25 ppm ozone in normal subjects and asthmatics. Those studies suggest that function changes observed in the present experiment were partially due to unmeasured substances such as pollen.

I conclude that significant but small physiological responses occurred in the generally sensitive population when exposed to ambient air pollution containing about 0.22 ppm of ozone. But it cannot be concluded from this investigation that asthmatics react more severely than normal subjects. The subjects tested and the environmental conditions imply that the investigation may have represented a worst case because normal subjects had a high prevalence of respiratory allergy. A small increase in symptoms resulted from exposure to ambient air as compared to control values, but the bulk of this increase was due to headache and fatigue and cannot be ascribed completely to elevated ozone levels since other pollutants were present.

WHITTEMORE AND KORN. The authors examined daily asthma attack diaries of sixteen panels (432 subjects) of asthmatics who resided in the Los Angeles area.[92] The subject population consisted of adult and juvenile persons (under sixteen years of age) who were determined from interviews to be asthmatics. A person was selected to participate in a panel if he had experienced at least one attack in the year before the study, had a history of wheezing and dyspnea with each attack, and lived within two miles of the community's air monitoring stations.

The data were collected by the EPA during 1972–75. Subjects were asked about demographic characteristics and smoking habits. They received a diary each week and were asked to record when and where asthma attacks occurred and to specify whether they took medication.

92. A. Whittemore and E. Korn, "Asthma and Air Pollution in the Los Angeles Area."

They received no details about the investigation and were told only that it concerned the role of environmental factors in asthma.

Daily attack rates were tested against daily levels of photochemical oxidants, total suspended particulate matter (TSP), minimum temperature, relative humidity, and wind speed. Measurements were taken by county air pollution control districts. Day of the week effects were also analyzed. A new statistical method that estimates each person's response separately was used to analyze the data. Days with missing pollutant or attack data were dropped from the analysis. The results show that the variable with the largest effect on the panelists' daily attack probability was the presence of an asthma attack on the preceding day. The results also show a small but significant association between oxidant, TSP, and asthma attack. The high interpanel variability of the coefficients for temperature and humidity suggests that these factors vary from person to person. Wind speed had no observable effect on the asthma attack rate.

A limitation of this study is the absence of data on important pollutants and other environmental and sociological factors. Measurements were taken for TSP, respirable suspended particulate matter, suspended nitrates, and suspended sulfates. Since these contaminants were highly correlated, TSP was used as a surrogate for these pollutants. This surrogate may be inadequate, however. Finally, no data on pollen and smoking were used, which may mask results.

The results of this study show a slight but statistically significant increase in asthma attacks associated with increases in levels of oxidants and TSP. The effects are so small they could be due to confounding factors and are of little significance.

Summary of the Findings

Most of the studies discussed in the last section were cited in the promulgation notice as support for EPA's "probable effects" level of 0.15–0.25 ppm. The major general findings are summarized below.

BIOCHEMICAL EFFECTS. Hackney reported increased erythrocyte fragility at 0.50 ppm ozone exposure. Linn reported small changes in actylcholinesterase activity and hemoglobin concentration for clinically diagnosed asthmatics exposed for two hours at 0.20–0.25 ppm. The importance of these changes is unknown. Hackney stated in an interview that these observed biochemical changes were not uniquely related to the pollutant.[93] Similar results occurred in control experiments under stresses of heat and light exercise. Hackney believes that biochemical changes are small at concentrations below 0.25 ppm. This conclusion is supported by the results of the DeLucia and Adams study, in which no differences in blood biochemical parameters were observed following a two-hour exposure to 0.15 ppm ozone at strenuous exercise levels.

PULMONARY DYSFUNCTION. Several experts stated in interviews that the most reliable measure for ozone-associated lung function changes is forced expiratory volume ($FEV_{1.0}$). The results of $FEV_{1.0}$ tests also correlate well with changes in reported symptoms. The results from clinical studies on humans show statistically significant reductions in $FEV_{1.0}$ at concentrations from 0.22–0.75 ppm for a two- to four-hour exposure. The results of the clinical investigations are based on data obtained from clinically diagnosed asthmatics as well as from normal subjects. However, Bates stated in an interview that asthmatics do not appear to show greater sensitivity to ozone than normal people do with respect to reductions of $FEV_{1.0}$.[94] Bates is supported by experimental results found by Linn and associates.[95] But great individual variation in sensitivity to ozone occurs within different groups tested.

Sensitivity to ozone is affected by the level of exercise. A key finding of the DeLucia and Adams study is that strenuous levels of exercise exacerbate the adverse effects of ozone. Both Hackney and Bates have stated that exercise is required to identify meaningful reductions in pulmonary function.

Hackney has reported that epidemiological studies of short-term clinical effects are generally in agreement with the controlled exposure studies in that they find significantly increased incidence of respiratory complaints at times of high ambient ozone levels.[96] Hackney referred to the results of the study by Hammer and associates, which showed significant increases in cough and chest discomfort at ambient concentrations of 0.30 ppm ozone (reported threshold at 0.26 ppm).[97] Further evidence of increased incidence of respiratory complaints when subjects (normal and asthmatic) are exposed to ambient ozone levels is presented

93. June 1980.

94. July 1980.

95. Linn and others, "Short-Term Respiratory Effects of Polluted Ambient Air."

96. J. Hackney and W. S. Linn, "Experimental Evaluation of Air Pollution in Humans as a Basis for Estimating Risk."

97. Hackney also was referring to the study done by Schoettlin and Landau, "Air Pollution and Asthmatic Attacks in the Los Angeles Area."

by Linn and associates.[98] In that study, reductions in $FEV_{1.0}$ approaches statistically significant levels at ambient exposures of 0.22 ppm (0.16 ppm–0.38 ppm).

SYMPTOMS. The results of clinical investigations have conclusively demonstrated that exposure to ozone at concentrations of 0.37–0.75 ppm can have debilitating effects on both normal and sensitive populations. Hackney and Bates have both shown that subjects exposed for short periods at these concentrations develop substernal pain, cough, and wheezing, and that some are unable to complete experimental protocols requiring subjects to perform intermittent light exercise for two hours.

Subjective symptoms of substernal soreness and wheezing have been recorded in both sensitive and normal subjects for exposure concentrations of 0.24–0.30 ppm ozone. These responses have been termed "slight" and have not resulted in termination of the experimental protocol. Epidemiological studies and clinical studies in which subjects are exposed to ambient air also show small but significant increases in subjective symptoms including chest discomfort and wheezing at concentrations of 0.22–0.39 ppm ozone.

Exercise level is a critical factor in producing subjective symptoms. Such symptoms, including coughing and wheezing, have been observed in normal subjects exposed to 0.15–0.30 ppm ozone. The exercise level at which these results were observed, however, was highly strenuous and would not be considered normal daily activity.[99] With respect to subjective symptoms of discomfort experienced by persons exposed to 0.15 ppm ozone (light exercise), Bates has commented that he would expect that out of 1,000 persons, only a few (less than 10) would experience subjective discomfort evidenced by soreness in the chest.

The importance of symptomatology has been stressed by Hackney, who believes that the results are surprisingly quantitative. He feels that the results are consistent and correlate well with changes in $FEV_{1.0}$.

ASTHMA ATTACKS. Two epidemiological studies have associated incidence of asthma attacks with levels of photochemical oxidant. Schoettlin and Landau reported that in their study the mean number of patients having attacks on days with oxidant levels above 0.25 ppm differed significantly from the number of patients having attacks when the level

98. Linn and others, "Short-Term Respiratory Effects of Polluted Ambient Air."
99. DeLucia press conference.

was lower.[100] Whittemore and Korn showed a small but significant association between asthma attack rates and oxidants at daily median ambient concentrations from about 0.12–0.15 ppm.[101] Attacks were characterized as mild. Unfortunately the lack of control for other environmental factors suggests that the effects cannot be ascribed solely or even predominantly to ozone.

EFFECT OF OZONE ON THE DEVELOPING LUNG. The potential effect of ozone on the developing lung was raised by Bates as an area of important concern.[102] Although he felt that this effect is not well understood, he believes that it is important and thus calls for a cautious attitude in considering an air quality standard.

Robert Frank, a respiratory physiologist who served on the Science Advisory Board overseeing the criteria document for ozone, also conjectured that this effect may be important.[103] Evidence of this effect in human populations is virtually nonexistent, but animal investigations have shown changes in the elasticity of the lung, damage to the small airways, and shifts in the type of mucous glycoprotein synthesized.[104] These investigations have also shown increased collagen synthesis rates. In general, the animal experiments demonstrate that the smallest alveolar airspaces are affected and that ozone may cause effects in the defense mechanisms of the lung similar to those in the macrophages. Frank hypothesized that ozone may interact biochemically with structural proteins of the lung to affect its elasticity. The effect is similar to an aging process, and the result may be a chronic adverse health effect for persons with long exposures. While information is too preliminary to carry weight in a decisionmaking process to promulgate a quality standard, Frank believes effects on the developing lung require further research.

Goldstein has reviewed the general toxicity of ozone and possible chronic effects.[105] The toxicity of ozone has generally been ascribed to its oxidizing properties, particularly lipid peroxidation, but toxicity is

100. Schoettlin and Landau, "Air Pollution and Asthmatic Attacks in the Los Angeles Area."

101. Whittemore and Korn, "Asthma and Air Pollution."

102. Interview (July 1980).

103. Interview (August 1980).

104. D. Bartlett, C. S. Faulkner, and K. Cook, "Effect of Chronic Ozone Exposure on Lung Elasticity in Young Rats"; and J. A. Last, "Collagen and Mucopolysaccharide Synthesis after Acute and Chronic Exposure to Oxidant Gases."

105. Bernard D. Goldstein, "Experimental and Clinical Problems of Effects of Photochemical Pollutants."

due as well to other biochemical reactions of ozone. DeLucia observed that exposure to 0.8 ppm ozone for one week results in an increase in nonprotein sulfhydryl groups in rats and monkey lungs.[106] Goldstein also reports that at higher levels ranging upward from 4 ppm for four hours, ozone produces fatal pulmonary edema in a number of species.[107]

Ozone may also be a possible mutagenic agent.[108] Chromosomal alterations in the circulating lymphocytes of hamsters exposed to 0.20 ppm ozone have been reported by Zelac and associates.[109] In addition, an increase in lung tumor incidence in animals chronically exposed to ozone has been reported by Werthamer and associates and by Stokinger.[110]

Ozone may be further implicated in the potentiation of respiratory tract infections.[111] Goldstein notes that extrapulmonary effects of ozone have been demonstrated in laboratory animals.[112] Studies by Menzel have shown that Heinz bodies formed in the circulatory red cells of mice exposed to ozone will also result from injected ozonides.[113] Changes in the circulating red cells of humans experimentally exposed to ozone have been reported by Buckley and associates, suggesting that extrapulmonary effects also may occur in humans.[114]

Ozone may have beneficial effects for man. A recent study by Sweet and associates shows that the growth of human cancer cells from lung, breast, and uterine tumors was selectively inhibited in a dose-dependent manner by ozone.[115]

EVIDENCE FOR HEALTH EFFECTS BELOW 0.22 PPM. The evidence for any health effects below 0.22 ppm ozone (two hours' exposure) is slight and inconclusive. The studies relied on by the EPA to show "probable

106. DeLucia and Adams, "Effects of Ozone Inhalation."

107. Goldstein, "Experimental and Clinical Problems."

108. Ibid.

109. R. E. Zelac and others, "Inhaled Ozone as a Mutagen."

110. S. Werthamer, L. H. Schwartz, and L. Soskind, "Bronchial Epithelial Alterations and Pulmonary Neoplasia Induced by Ozone"; and H. E. Stokinger, "Effects of Air Pollution on Animals."

111. D. L. Coffin and E. J. Bloomer, "Alterations of the Pathogenic Role of Streptococci Group C in Mice Conferred by Previous Exposure to Ozone"; and E. Goldstein and others, "Adverse Influence of Ozone on Pulmonary Bactericidal Activity of Lung."

112. Interview (September 1980).

113. Daniel B. Menzel and others, "Heinz Bodies Formed in Erythrocytes by Fatty Acid Ozonides and Ozone."

114. Ramon D. Buckley and others, "Ozone and Human Blood."

115. F. Sweet, K. Ming-Shian Kao, and S. D. Lee, "Ozone Selectively Inhibits Growth of Human Cancer Cells."

effects'' between 0.15 and 0.22 ppm contain procedural inadequacies and contradictory results. The Japanese epidemiological studies are inconclusive because they cannot distinguish between effects caused by ozone, sulfur dioxide, and other pollutants. Von Nieding's work has been discredited as being procedurally deficient by health experts including James Whittenberger, chairman of the EPA's ad hoc subcommittee of the Science Advisory Board. The DeLucia and Adams investigation does not support adverse health effects at 0.15 ppm. Results obtained in a follow-up study by Savin and Adams do not support adverse health effects at 0.15 ppm.[116] These authors report that exposure of healthy young men to either 0.15 ppm or 0.30 ppm ozone for no more than thirty minutes of progressively heavier exercise to volitional fatigue is insufficient to cause a significant decrease in work capacity.

Whittenberger, Hackney, and Knelson stated in personal interviews that there are no demonstrated short-term acute health effects below 0.25 ppm.[117]

116. W. Savin and W. Adams, ''Effects of Ozone Inhalation on Work Performance and VO_2 Max.''

117. Interviews with Whittenberger (August 1980); Hackney (June 1980); and Knelson (August 1980).

CHAPTER FOUR

Regulating Benzene

THOMAS R. BARTMAN

BENZENE is a clear, colorless liquid used extensively in the petrochemical and refining industries. An estimated 11 billion pounds of benzene were produced domestically in 1976. It is used as the raw material for other organic chemicals, some detergents, and pesticides and is a constituent of gasoline.

The Occupational Safety and Health Administration estimates that over 190,000 workers are occupationally exposed to benzene.[1] The Environmental Protection Agency estimates that 110 million people are exposed to atmospheric benzene at concentrations of a few parts per billion to 0.5 part per million.[2]

Benzene evaporates rapidly and enters the body primarily through inhalation.[3] It diffuses quickly through the lungs and is readily absorbed. Epidemiological studies, animal bioassays, and other reports have implicated benzene in increased incidences of leukemia, nonmalignant blood disorders, and effects on chromosomes and animal embryonic development. Exposure to high concentrations (more than 100 ppm) has been accepted as leukemia-producing (leukemogenic) in humans on the basis of numerous individual medical reports, observed coincidences between the introduction of benzene and increased leukemia rates in

1. U.S. Department of Labor, Occupational Safety and Health Administration, *Economic Impact Statement: Benzene*, vol. 1, p. 5-2.

2. In contrast to occupational exposures (eight hours a day for a limited number of days) in low parts per million, ambient air concentrations in the low parts per billion involve both constant exposure and a population including children and old people more sensitive than worker cohorts. Environmental Protection Agency, *Assessment of Human Exposures to Atmospheric Benzene*, p. 5.

3. For a general review of benzene's health effects, see Sidney Laskin and Bernard D. Goldstein, eds., "Benzene Toxicity, A Critical Evaluation"; Environmental Protection Agency, *Assessment of Health Effects of Benzene Germane to Low-Level Exposure*; and R. Snyder and J. J. Kocsis, "Current Concepts of Benzene Toxicity."

occupational settings, and epidemiological studies. A small number of controversial studies link leukemias to benzene at lower exposures.

The typical symptom of benzene exposure is a reduction in platelets and red and white blood cells (pancytopenia). While mild effects caused by low exposures are apparently reversible, exposure can also lead to aplastic anemia and leukemia. Occupational studies have offered some evidence of effects at 40 ppm and perhaps lower.

Research into fetal development in rodents has indicated that benzene is probably not teratogenic, but exposure has produced such fetotoxic effects in rodents as reduced litters, retarded embryonic development, and fetal resorptions. Dose-response correlations for these effects are inconsistent, especially at low doses. The relevance of animal studies to benzene effects on humans is clouded by the differences in fetal development.

Occupational and animal studies show that benzene, like other known carcinogens, causes chromosomal alterations. Benzene exposure reduces DNA synthesis, an effect that evidently persists for considerable periods. Chromosomal effects following occupational inhalation exposure of around 2 ppm have been reported. While the significance of effects on chromosome number and structure is quite uncertain, such effects may participate in the transition from a nonmalignant blood disorder to leukemia.

All the studies linking human exposure to benzene with adverse health effects are plagued by the lack of direct measurement of exposure and often by small samples and inexact diagnoses. Only a few observations in widely scattered time periods are available. While animals have been exposed to specific concentrations, extrapolation of these exposures to humans is difficult because of the lack of a developed animal model.

The overall picture of benzene's effects on human health is both unpleasant and unclear. At high levels, benzene is plainly toxic to humans in numerous ways. The levels at which the various pernicious effects take place is in doubt, however. First, it is hard to prove that benzene is a cause of leukemia. Long latency between exposure and onset of disease and the small absolute increase in the incidence of leukemia are confounding factors. Unlike polyvinyl chloride monomer, which is associated with a rare form of liver cancer, benzene is not related to a unique or specific cancer. Second, benzene appears to affect animals differently from human subjects, thus making the relevancy of animal bioassays suspect. Third, the chronic health consequences of mild nonmalignant blood disorders and chromosomal damage observed in subjects who have been exposed to benzene are largely unknown. In short, regulators can conclude that benzene is a powerful poison, but they are faced with great uncertainty concerning what doses of benzene produce what incidence of pancytopenia, aplastic anemia, and leukemia.

OSHA's Role in Regulating Benzene

The Occupational Safety and Health Act requires that in regulating toxic materials the agency "set the standard which most adequately assures, to the extent feasible, on the basis of the best available evidence, that no employee will suffer material impairment of health or functional capacity."[4]

The present Occupational Safety and Health Administration standard for benzene was adopted from the American National Standards Institute in 1971. Based on benzene's general toxic effects on the blood, the standard prescribes an eight-hour time-weighted average of 10 ppm and a ceiling concentration of 25 ppm and permits excursions to a peak of 50 ppm for no more than ten minutes per eight-hour period.

In 1974 the National Institute for Occupational Safety and Health (NIOSH), the research complement of OSHA, compiled a criteria document on occupational exposure to benzene that acknowledged benzene's suspected leukemogenicity but nevertheless recommended retaining the 10 ppm time-weighted average and 25 ppm ceiling standard due to insufficiently conclusive data.[5]

Setting a New Standard

In the middle and late 1970s pressures began to build for a reexamination of the benzene standard. Benzene had long been of concern to the rubberworkers' union; a number of studies had found excess leukemia deaths associated with solvent use in that industry. But for three years after the chemical was designated a suspected leukemogen in the 1974 NIOSH criteria document, OSHA continued to reject pressures for a benzene standard because it viewed the data as insufficient to justify a new standard.

4. Sec. 6(b)5.
5. National Institute for Occupational Safety and Health, *Occupational Exposure to Benzene*.

In a letter dated April 23, 1976, the United Rubber, Cork, Linoleum, and Plastic Workers of America urged the secretary of labor to issue an emergency standard regulating benzene.[6] Secretary William J. Usery denied the request on May 18, 1976, noting the lack of sufficient scientific evidence to warrant a change and indicating that other measures to control benzene exposure were being taken.[7]

Later in 1976 a panel of scientists at the National Academy of Sciences reviewed for the EPA the information on health effects of benzene and concluded that benzene should be considered a suspect leukemogen.[8] In August 1976 NIOSH submitted a revised criteria document that found benzene to be a leukemogen. NIOSH recommended that since no safe level for benzene exposure could be established, no worker should be exposed to more than 1 ppm. A 1 ppm emergency standard was recommended to the assistant secretary of labor by letter on October 27, 1976.[9]

Based on the recommendations of NIOSH, OSHA issued voluntary "Guidelines for Control of Occupational Exposure to Benzene" on January 14, 1977. The guidelines, based on benzene's leukemogenicity, urged that benzene concentrations in air not exceed an eight-hour time-weighted average of 1 ppm per eight-hour shift. On April 15, 1977, NIOSH conveyed preliminary findings of its epidemiological study of two Ohio rubber manufacturing plants to OSHA and again urged the setting of a 1 ppm emergency standard.[10]

In 1977 Eula Bingham, the newly designated assistant secretary of labor for OSHA, began to prepare an emergency standard for benzene even before she was confirmed. Bingham, a toxicologist, was familiar with the scientific data on benzene and believed that it should be regulated to the lowest feasible level. She was also interested in the advocacy function of OSHA. In some quarters OSHA's past refusal to regulate benzene was seen as symbolic of a failure to regulate toxic chemicals,[11] and Bingham wanted benzene regulation to be a sign of OSHA's concern about toxic agents.

6. 43 Fed. Reg. 5919 (1978).

7. W. J. Usery, Jr., letter to Peter Bommarito (May 14, 1976).

8. National Academy of Sciences, Committee on Toxicology, *Health Effects of Benzene: A Review*.

9. 43 Fed. Reg. 5919 (1978).

10. Ibid.

11. Union pressure aside, OSHA was criticized in 1977 in a General Accounting Office report to a House oversight hearing for its slowness in promulgating health standards, as

Legal Challenges

On May 3, 1977, OSHA issued a 1 ppm emergency temporary standard (ETS) for occupational exposure to benzene to take effect on May 21.[12] The Fifth Circuit Court of Appeals, ruling on legal challenges,[13] issued a temporary restraining order on May 20, 1977, and the emergency standard never went into effect.

On May 27, 1977, OSHA published a proposed permanent standard incorporating the 1 ppm ceiling. The standard also prohibited any dermal contact with benzene. OSHA subsequently amended it to exempt dermal contact with liquids containing no more than 1 percent benzene (no more than 0.1 percent as of 1981). OSHA held hearings on the standard from July 19 to August 10 with testimony from agencies, affected industries, unions, and other members of the public. OSHA also published a draft environmental impact statement for its standard on May 27.[14]

The circuit court ruled on the challenges to OSHA's 1 ppm permanent standard on October 5, 1978, setting aside the standard.[15] The court cited the absence of substantial evidence showing a reasonable relationship between measurable benefits sought and the significant cost of the regulation to the affected industries. The court also set aside OSHA's prohibition of dermal contact, holding that the standard was based on dated and inconclusive data.

The Supreme Court heard oral argument October 10, 1979, in OSHA's appeal of the circuit court's decision. The government argued that the benzene standard was based on the best available scientific evidence. It further contended that both the lack of data on a safe level of exposure to benzene and the policy assumption that there is no safe exposure level

---

opposed to safety standards, as a result of new interest in OSHA health standards generated by Bingham's predecessor, Morton Corn. *Performance of the Occupational Safety and Health Administration,* Hearings before the House Committee on Governmental Operations.

12. 42 Fed. Reg. 22516 (1977). Before issuing an emergency temporary standard, OSHA must find "that employees are exposed to grave danger from exposure to substances or agents determined to be toxic or physically harmful or from new hazards, and . . . that such emergency standard is necessary to protect employees from such danger." 29 USC 655(c).

13. Petitioners, including the American Petroleum Institute and other industry groups, attacked the reduction of the exposure standard to 1 ppm, the prohibition of dermal contact, and engineering and work practice prescriptions.

14. 42 Fed. Reg. 27452, 27455 (1977).

15. *American Petroleum Institute* v. *OSHA*, 581 F. 2d 493 (5th Cir. 1978).

for a carcinogen required that the standard be set at the lowest feasible level, namely 1 ppm. The government also argued that the Occupational Safety and Health Act did not require that a standard be based on a cost-benefit analysis.

The American Petroleum Institute and associated groups argued that studies did not show an excess risk of leukemia at low concentrations of benzene and that OSHA had failed to show that the standard would produce material or appreciable benefits.

The Supreme Court affirmed the circuit court's decision on July 2, 1980.[16] Justice John Paul Stevens, joined by two others, wrote a plurality opinion holding that OSHA had not shown that a significant health risk was associated with the existing 10 ppm standard. Rather, OSHA had lowered the benzene standard based on a series of inadequately tested assumptions about the risk at 10 ppm and about a reduction in risk that might result from a 1 ppm standard. OSHA lacked statutory authority to regulate to a completely risk-free level; the agency had to demonstrate that appreciable benefits would result from reducing exposure and had made no attempt to show that chronic exposure to 10 ppm of benzene would result in a significant risk of material health impairment.

Justice Lewis F. Powell, Jr., stated in a separate opinion that while OSHA had tried to demonstrate a hazard at 10 ppm, the agency failed to demonstrate that the economic effects of the standard bore a reasonable relationship to its expected benefits. Justice William H. Rehnquist argued to vacate the standard because Congress had unlawfully delegated authority to OSHA without providing ascertainable standards for exercising that authority. Justice Thurgood Marshall's dissent, in which he was joined by three others, asserted that the plurality's requirement of a threshold showing of significant risk at 10 ppm had no statutory basis.

OSHA's Case

OSHA had argued before the Supreme Court that in making judgments about specific hazards the agency has the duty to set a standard at the level that assures the greatest protection.[17] Since OSHA's policy is that there is no safe exposure level for a carcinogen, it claimed that feasibility was the only proper limit to its standard.

16. *Industrial Union Department, AFL-CIO* v. *American Petroleum Institute and others,* 448 U.S. 607 (1980).

17. Ibid., Brief for Federal Parties, 1979.

The primary basis of OSHA's standard was evidence of benzene leukemogenicity.[18] Review of the scientific literature revealed adverse effects at low exposure levels. OSHA conceded there were unanswered questions about benzene's carcinogenicity, but argued that the Occupational Safety and Health Act did not permit the agency to wait for answers while workers were being exposed to a life-threatening substance. The only acceptable criterion was feasibility.

OSHA engaged a consulting firm to study the feasibility of the agency's 1 ppm standard. OSHA had selected this level because it is technically difficult to measure lower concentrations, and 1 ppm approaches background levels (an assertion contradicted by the EPA); an even lower standard, OSHA argued, would require cleaning the ambient air.[19] Finally, OSHA felt that a level of 1 ppm was readily achievable and that if 1 ppm had been found infeasible, it would have explored other standards.

An emergency temporary standard is an extraordinary measure. In promulgating such a standard in May 1977, after having refused for three years to revise the standard, OSHA had to find a new scientific basis for increased regulation of benzene. Bingham, who was aware of Peter Infante's study of Ohio rubberworkers in progress, sought the results as a new basis for an emergency standard. The study was rushed into print in *The Lancet* when the follow-up was only 75 percent complete.[20] OSHA relied heavily on the Infante study in its emergency standard promulgation and apparently attributed to it quantitative significance concerning the effects of low benzene dosage, not recognizing its lack of quantitative significance. (See appendix A for details of the study.)

The economic impact statement concluded that a 1 ppm standard was feasible. Compliance was estimated to impose investment costs of

18. This and subsequent sections of this chapter were based in part on interviews with Peter F. Infante, OSHA; Jim Vail, former project director for benzene at OSHA; Grover Wrenn, former health standards director at OSHA; Robert E. McGaughy, deputy director, Carcinogen Assessment Group; Diane Berkley, Solicitor's Office, OSHA; Ed Klein, Solicitor's Office, OSHA; Morton Corn, former administrator of OSHA; Richard Johnson, formerly EPA project manager for benzene; Bernard Goldstein, Rutgers University; Dante Picciano, former research scientist, Dow Chemical Company; Barbara Bankoff, special assistant to the administrator for air quality, EPA; Robert Kelham, EPA; Michael Dusetzina, EPA.

19. Occupational Safety and Health Administration, *Transcript of Proceedings, Informal Hearing on Proposed Standard for Exposure to Benzene*.

20. P. F. Infante and others, "Leukemia in Benzene Workers."

around \$267 million, first-year operating costs of about \$124 million and annual costs of \$74 million.[21]

OSHA's case rested on two grounds: benzene is a proven leukemogen, and no more restrictive controls were feasible. The standard was promulgated with little attention given to the opinions of OSHA's scientific staff, who knew and informed Bingham of the problems with the proposed standard, primarily the lack of new data.

In promulgating this standard, the agency relied on the history of judicial deference to administrative discretion.[22] The courts had agreed that the Occupational Safety and Health Act did not require a quantitative risk assessment. While the act may mandate quantitative methods for setting priorities, the act's basic requirement is for "feasibility," the meaning of which is loose and ambiguous.

Before the benzene case, courts had upheld OSHA's definition of feasibility as a measure of both economic cost and technological capability of the regulated industry.[23] Courts reviewing emergency temporary standards have become concerned with the probability that an asserted hazard poses an actual hazard and with the gravity or severity of the harm threatened. The Court of Appeals for the Third Circuit has held that OSHA must show more than "some probability" that a substance is carcinogenic; OSHA need not show actual harm, however, but simply that harm would result.[24]

OSHA and Risk Assessment

In answer to these challenges OSHA argued repeatedly that the data were insufficient for a risk assessment. OSHA stated that it was not opposed in principle to quantitative risk assessment, particularly in setting priorities and estimating benefits once a standard was set, but it

21. OSHA, *Economic Impact Statement,* vol. 1, pp. 1–8.

22. Courts have at most required that OSHA be explicit in its rationale for a particular standard. See *Dry Color Manufacturers Association* v. *Department of Labor,* 486 F.2d 98 (3d Cir. 1973). See also *Industrial Union Department, AFL-CIO* v. *Hodgson,* 499 F.2d 467 (D.C. Cir. 1974): where "choice [of a regulatory course] purports to be based on existence of certain determinable facts, the Secretary must . . . find those facts from evidence in the record. . . . When the Secretary is obliged to make policy judgments where no factual certainties exist . . . he should so state and go on to identify the considerations he found persuasive."

23. For example, D.C. Circuit in *Industrial Union Dept.* v. *Hodgson.*

24. *Dry Color Manufacturers Association* v. *Department of Labor* (reviewing emergency temporary standards for fourteen carcinogens).

would not use it in setting exposure levels.[25] Another element in its rejection of risk analysis included the policy concern that the secretary of labor not be associated with any quantitative method that appeared to set a dollar value on human life. Indeed, OSHA interpreted the Occupational Safety and Health Act as precluding a balancing of benefits and costs.[26] OSHA understood its duty was to set a standard assuring "to the extent feasible" that "no employee will suffer material impairment of health."[27] Assuming no safe level exists for a carcinogen, the standard could not be less restrictive than the constraints of technical and economic feasibility would allow.[28]

OSHA did offer quantitative risk assessment in its Supreme Court brief after the Fifth Circuit Court of Appeals had criticized its failure to engage in a balancing of costs and benefits. This effort seemed intended primarily to show the crude nature of risk assessment and how different assumptions could produce a significantly different result based on the same data.

OSHA's most recent position on risk assessment is enunciated in its policy for the general regulation of carcinogens.[29] After reviewing the uncertainties of risk assessment and proposing models for interpreting animal studies, OSHA concluded that the uncertainties of extrapolating from high doses in animals to low doses in humans are too great to be useful to risk-benefit balancing and setting exposure limits. Quantitative risk analysis can help set priorities by comparing relative risks, and it can be used to assess how much risk reduction has resulted from regulatory action. OSHA further suggests that risk assessment should state the range of risk based on cautious assumptions about the uncertainty.

OSHA's review of the research on benzene's health effects, with the exception of its initial reliance on the problematic Infante study, was thorough and accurate.[30] OSHA issued the new exposure standard based

25. *Industrial Union Department* v. *American Petroleum Institute*, Brief for Federal Parties.

26. Ibid.

27. 29 U.S.C.655(b)(5).

28. Under the prior rule of judicial deference, OSHA may have had adequate evidence to justify its standard. A change in judicial atmosphere, however, and a hastily prepared promulgation conspired against the standard's chances for success.

29. 45 Fed. Reg. 5001 (1980).

30. OSHA's assessment that the results were significant is a matter of policy-based judgment.

primarily on benzene leukemogenicity.[31] While OSHA may have made a less substantial showing of the standard's basis than it had in past regulations, no legal precedent led it to expect it would have to do more than detail safety concerns.

In sum, OSHA did not use risk assessment even to set priorities before deciding to regulate benzene. To add quantitative substantiation to its case, OSHA could have pointed to evidence of benzene leukemogenicity at exposure levels around 100 ppm and established a safety factor based on recognized scientific uncertainties about benzene's effects and about extrapolation. Since the 1 ppm standard, ostensibly based on feasibility, must itself have been based on some sort of balancing, it could have explicitly considered other levels of feasibility or cost, including 5 and 0.5 ppm. Finally, it could have adapted to its own showing of health effects a quantitative risk assessment like that produced by the EPA, which finds health effects at levels in the low parts per billion. In the wake of the Supreme Court's ruling on benzene, OSHA will certainly have to employ quantitative means of substantiating health effects for other toxic substances in the future.

The EPA Role in Regulating Benzene

In 1975 benzene was listed among ten high-volume industrial chemicals for which limited-budget, fast assessments were undertaken by the EPA in setting priorities by regulating airborne pollutants. These assessments considered the sources of emissions, the populations exposed, and potential technological controls. Subsequently the EPA collated the priority lists of various agencies and bodies based on the biological hazards and environmental impacts of pollutants and identified benzene as a high priority. In 1976 the recommendation of NIOSH that an emergency standard should be issued for benzene added momentum to the EPA's effort. And finally, on April 4, 1977, the Environmental Defense Fund petitioned the EPA to list benzene as a hazardous air pollutant under section 112 of the Clean Air Act. Following consultations with OSHA and NIOSH and in response to the petition, the EPA listed

31. OSHA, however, issued its emergency temporary standard under the impression that the Infante study offered data about low benzene concentrations, and the association of benzene and leukemia was reasonably well established before the Infante study.

benzene as a hazardous air pollutant on June 8, 1977.[32] During 1978 the EPA issued an "Assessment of Health Effects of Benzene Germane to Low-Level Exposure," its Carcinogen Assessment Group's (CAG) evaluation of benzene's leukemogenic risk, and an "Assessment of Human Exposure to Atmospheric Benzene." These documents formed the basis of the EPA's plan to regulate benzene emissions from various sources.

As a first step, the EPA proposed a "National Emission Standard for Hazardous Air Pollutants; Benzene Emissions from Maleic Anhydride Plants" on April 18, 1980.[33] The proposed standard would require 97 percent control (100 percent for new plants) of benzene emissions from maleic anhydride plants.[34] Hearings on the proposed standard were held in August 1980. Comments by interested parties included the claim that using the same data and modified assumptions, the EPA's risk assessment model shows that the risk of benzene exposure at ambient levels was not significant. The EPA has subsequently not made its maleic anhydride standard final but has proposed standards for other emission sources.[35]

The scientific staff dealing with benzene at the EPA did not feel political pressure for the listing of benzene, though policymakers might have. The EPA's constituency is not as focused as OSHA's, and it most likely had less influence over specific programs. The EPA has authority under section 112 of the Clean Air Act to regulate "hazardous air pollutants," which "in the judgment of the Administrator may cause, or contribute to, an increase in mortality or an increase in serious irreversible, or incapacitating reversible, illness."[36]

The scientific basis for the EPA's regulation, exhaustively reviewed in its health effects document, comprised the same studies on which the OSHA benzene standard was based. The EPA recognized that this evidence primarily involved research into occupational exposure at levels higher than those found in the ambient air, but noted the administrator's "generic determination that, in view of the existing state of

32. 42 Fed. Reg. 29332 (1977).

33. 45 Fed. Reg. 26660 (1980).

34. Regulation of maleic anhydride plant emissions constituting 35 percent of emissions from chemical manufacturing was undertaken under section 112 of the Clean Air Act, which covers only stationary sources. The largest portion of benzene in the ambient air results from mobile emissions.

35. "Benzene Emissions from Benzene Storage Vessels," 45 Fed. Reg. 83952 (1980).

36. 42 Fed. Reg. 29322 (1977).

scientific knowledge, prudent public health policy requires that carcinogens be considered for regulatory purposes to pose some finite risk of cancer at any exposure level above zero.''[37]

The EPA and Risk Assessment

The EPA used quantitative risk assessment in a general balancing of the risks and costs of options to arrive at its final standard.[38] The comparison of options took account of environmental impact (the degree of reduction in benzene emissions), the energy impact of particular methods of controls (such as carbon adsorption and thermal incineration), and aspects of economic impact. The option chosen, 97 percent control with best available technology (and 100 percent control in new plants), is expected to result in only 0.03 to 0.19 death a year.[39] It was estimated to cost $6.6 million in capital, $2.5 million in additional annual costs, possibly one plant closing, and a 1.2 percent price increase for maleic anhydride.

The EPA's compilation of a human exposure survey and quantitative risk assessment in addition to the usual health effects document was an innovation intended to establish the parameters of risk associated with benzene. The actual role of the risk assessment in regulating benzene emissions is unclear. The health effects and human exposure documents were evidently considered the substantial bases for action. The risk assessment, based on benzene leukemogenicity, does not cover the other effects to which the general population is exposed. Although the listing of benzene as a hazardous air pollutant in 1977 signifies only the identification of a potential hazard, no substance so listed has subsequently been removed from the list. Thus the qualitative evaluation of health effects of benzene largely determined its regulation. The quantitative risk assessment, developed after the listing of benzene in 1977, was used as supplementary evidence of a hazard. It evidently was a factor in assigning priorities to various sources of benzene emissions and thus in regulating maleic anhydride. It was an element in the risk-benefit balancing on which the choice of a regulatory option was based.

37. 44 Fed. Reg. 58646 (1979).

38. Ibid.

39. The CAG estimated 3.39 deaths would result from emissions from chemical manufacturing in general. See EPA, CAG, ''Final Report on Population Risk from Ambient Benzene Exposure,'' table 5.

The EPA has specified the general role of risk assessment in setting ambient air standards in "National Emission Standards for Identifying, Assessing and Regulating Airborne Substances Posing a Risk of Cancer."[40] Citing the uncertainties, the EPA limits the use of risk assessment to providing supplementary evidence in support of a finding of significant risk: the assessment cannot be ignored if it shows risk but is too crude to be the basis for not listing a substance. Thus the EPA will conduct a quantitative risk assessment for agents listed as carcinogens under section 112. The risk assessment will be used to set priorities for regulations of particular source categories and to determine the degree of control required in final emission standards for those source categories.

The Carcinogen Assessment Group

The Carcinogen Assessment Group's risk assessment model for benzene is plausible, and the CAG generally made reasonable assumptions in the face of limited evidence. A review of the risk assessment (given in detail in appendix B) indicates that the CAG might have been more explicit about the uncertainties of its assumptions. It would have been helpful for the group to have considered several values, for example in the estimation of dosage, to indicate a range for the calculated risk. In addition, its estimated confidence interval (there is a 95 percent chance the true number will be between 34 and 235 leukemias per year induced in the U.S. population by benzene) must be interpreted carefully; it refers only to the standard error in the estimate, calculated using standard assumptions. No account is taken of the uncertainties that arise from the unknown exposure levels in each case, misdiagnosed cases (false positives and negatives), exposure to other leukemogens, and latency periods.

The CAG quantitative risk assessment extrapolates down to low exposures on the basis of the linear nonthreshold model. As table 4-1 indicates, all the expected leukemias effectively occur at levels below 4 ppb. Less extreme functional forms for a dose-response relation would, by contrast, indicate almost zero deaths below 10 ppb.

The *Assessment of Human Exposures to Atmospheric Benzene*, commissioned by the EPA from the Stanford Research Institute, is subject

40. 44 Fed. Reg. 58642 (1979).

Table 4-1. Expected Number of Benzene-Caused Leukemia Deaths per Year

Annual average benzene concentrations (parts per billion)	*Number of people exposed (thousands)*	*Exposure index (millions of ppb-person-years)*	*Expected number of benzene-caused leukemia deaths per year*
10.0	80	0.80	0.27
4.1–10.0	200	1.40	0.48
1.1– 4.0	110,000	275.00	99.40
0.1– 1.0	7,000	3.85	1.31
Total	. . .	281.05	101.46

Source: Adapted from table 1-22 in Environmental Protection Agency, *Assessment of Human Exposures to Atmospheric Benzene* (EPA, 1978). The expected leukemias are calculated following the CAG quantitative risk assessment method.

to uncertainty due to the paucity of information on which it was based as well as to the exposure modeling technique employed.[41] The unsettled uncertainties, the cost and problems of providing large samples, and the possible lack of occupational settings in which benzene can be isolated as the only contaminant will hamper the production of more precise, quantifiable information in the future despite the substantial amount of research devoted to benzene. Epidemiological studies cannot provide the answer since it would be impossible to verify that thousands of workers were exposed to 5–15 ppm of benzene over several decades and be sure that exposure was never higher and that exposure to other leukemogens was controlled. For a quantitative supplement to findings of health effects, the regulatory agencies must turn to extrapolation from epidemiological and toxicological studies. Such extrapolations cannot be mathematical straitjackets, as the Supreme Court recognized. But used with explicit awareness of their limitations, they offer a significant basis for regulatory decision, as the EPA's use of risk assessment suggests.

The subsequent history of the EPA's quantitative risk assessment indicates the ultimate limit on the use of quantitative methods. Commenters at the EPA's maleic anhydride hearings, having criticized specific assumptions underlying the EPA's calculations, concluded that the same data, but under somewhat modified assumptions, would show that in fact no risk is associated with atmospheric exposure to benzene. Some of the EPA's assumptions, however, were necessarily influenced

41. A detailed critique of the exposure assessment was submitted by the API in its comments on the draft health assessment, December 9, 1977.

by its policy of conservative interpretation of risk. Once a quantitative showing of risk has been factored into the decisionmaking process, the judgment on whether the risk is significant is basically a matter of policy.

How Toxic Is Benzene?

The effects of benzene on the hematopoietic tissue have been recognized for one hundred years and have served as the basis for past benzene standards. An acute dose affects the central nervous system, quickly inducing a light anesthesia followed by depression and respiratory failure. The narcotic threshold is 1,000 ppm and acute toxic effects follow exposure to concentrations below 10,000 ppm. A subacute, chronic dose produces changes first in the bone marrow, slowing the maturation process of red blood cells, and next inhibits the production of white blood cells.[42]

Attempts to correlate concentration and effect in chronic inhalation studies have had inconsistent results.[43] Animal studies have given insight into the mechanism of benzene effects on the blood, but in view of their inconsistent results and their uncertainties, past animal studies have presented inconclusive dose-response data.

The results of human epidemiological studies are complicated by a worker's likely exposure to multiple agents in the workplace. Benzene has been isolated as the common denominator in various occupational settings where blood effects were found. Moreover, benzene has induced in animals blood effects that are not produced by other chemical agents.[44]

Chronic benzene exposure is associated with both the occurrence of pancytopenia and interference with cell production in the marrow. Some evidence suggests that exposure shortens the survival of the circulating cells and reduces the counts of particular cell types or combinations of cell types. Symptoms of mild anemia are lassitude, tiredness, dizziness, headaches, and shortness of breath. Recovery is likely in a mild case of pancytopenia if benzene exposure is halted, although there have been reports of leukemia developing after apparent full recovery.[45]

42. Basil K. J. Leong, "Experimental Benzene Intoxication."

43. Complete surveys are found in Bernard D. Goldstein, "Hematotoxicity in Humans"; and EPA, *Assessment of Health Effects of Benzene Germane to Low-Level Exposure*.

44. Goldstein, "Hematotoxicity in Humans."

45. EPA, *Assessment of Health Effects of Benzene Germane to Low-Level Exposure*.

Severe pancytopenia may be accompanied by hemorrhagic effects, with the possibility of fatal bleeding. Aplastic anemia, which has a 50 percent mortality rate, occurs at high exposure levels. Benzene's influence on blood-forming tissues may debilitate the human immunological system, with the potential result that immunological defenses may be overwhelmed by other disease. It has been speculated that leukemia is the terminal stage of pancytopenia.[46] Benzene may allow the development of acute leukemia by hampering the immune surveillance function that normally weeds out abnormal cells. However, there is evidence that a relatively small percentage of workers with pancytopenia will develop serious effects, particularly if occupational conditions improve.[47]

The true incidence of benzene-induced pancytopenia may be underreported because mild blood disorders will be overlooked unless they are the focus of search.[48] Similarly, benzene's role in a particular hematological case may be overlooked owing to its ubiquity.

A study of rotogravure workers exposed to benzene levels of 11–160 ppm for several years uncovered six cases of benzene poisoning (among 332 workers) severe enough to require hospitalization. There were also hematological abnormalities. A study of 217 apparently healthy shoeworkers (reported in detail in appendix A) exposed to a maximum of 210–650 ppm for uncertain periods found 51 with benzene-associated abnormalities, including 41 cases of leukopenia.[49] In one of the only studies of long-term effects, a few of the thirty-eight exposed workers showed persistent abnormal blood changes, and one case showed mild benzene poisoning long after exposure at levels averaging 40 ppm. There were, however, no significant effects thirteen years after the use of solvents containing benzene had been discontinued.[50] Finally, a Korean study found hematological effects after exposure at 20 ppm and attempted to extrapolate down to effects at 10 ppm.[51] But the study is very difficult to evaluate because of insufficient information on exposures and on the work force, aside from difficulties of comparing its Korean population

46. E. C. Vigliani, "Leukemia Associated with Benzene Exposure."

47. Goldstein, "Hematotoxicity in Humans."

48. Ibid.

49. M. Aksoy and others, "Hematological Effects of Chronic Benzene Poisoning in 217 Workers."

50. L. D. Pagnotto and others, "Industrial Benzene Exposure from Petroleum Naphtha. I: Rubber Coating Industry."

51. Im Won Chang, "Study on the Threshold Limit Value of Benzene and Early Diagnosis of Benzene Poisoning."

to an American occupational cohort. In sum, epidemiological studies generally have lacked data on dosage and have been based on small populations.

While the association of benzene and changes in the human hematopoietic system seems well established, with some evidence of effects at relatively low doses, the data are insufficient to allow a confident construction of a dose-response curve. The relationship of benzene-induced blood changes to leukemic developments is unclear, and there is little study of long-term effects of slight blood changes. The mild disorders that result from low doses appear reversible.

Effects on Fetal Development

Teratological studies have examined the effects of benzene on fetal development.[52] Generalization of the rodent data to humans is complicated by the differences in metabolism and embryonic development among species, particularly for rodents, which are used for reasons of cost and practicality. Rats and mice have respiratory rates five to ten times the rate of humans, which may mean that an ambient concentration gives the animals a higher dose.

The differences between the placentas of rodents and humans further complicate extrapolating findings in rats to human effects.[53] Finally, rats and mice show spontaneous abnormalities similar to effects caused by benzene. A sizable control population is required to determine the extent of these abnormalities, which may also result from factors such as fasting.

Results of these studies must be considered in light of the technical parameters of teratological study. Exposure is focused on the period of organogenesis for the purpose of studying abnormal growth.[54] This ten-day exposure during the period of gestation is unlikely to have any close correspondence to human occupational exposure, which would begin before conception. The duration of exposure is not long enough to

52. For a review of teratological studies, see Consumer Product Safety Commission Report, "Review and Analysis of the Literature Pertaining to the Reproductive Effects of Exposure to Benzene." This is a new area of research; little data was available to the EPA's assessment of health effects and OSHA did not cover it.

53. And there is evidently no human equivalent to the finding of fetal resorptions in rats.

54. Pregnant rats are not exposed before organogenesis because the fetus may be killed, vitiating the teratological study.

produce the hematological effects of benzene exposure that might well be dangerous to in utero development in cases of aplastic anemia.[55]

In sum, studies of benzene's effect on embryonic development indicate that benzene is apparently not a teratogen in rats at exposure levels under 500 ppm. Benzene's fetotoxic effects may occur at lower levels, but evidence is contradictory. The fact that this line of research must rely on animals complicates its significance for the study of benzene effects on humans.[56]

Chromosomal Effects

Research has turned to the examination of benzene's effects on cells and chromosomes.[57] Benzene depresses formation of human marrow cells in vitro.

The most common finding of benzene cytogenetic studies has involved chromosomal alterations, like those produced by ionizing radiation, which are linked to cancer.[58] The significance of an increased incidence of chromosomal alterations is not certain: breaks may be repaired, but a larger incidence may increase the possibility of mutation. The persistence of change after exposure at least suggests that damage has occurred.[59] Chromosome changes have also been associated with specific cancers. Finally, effects have so far been found only in somatic cells rather than in germinal cells, so a relation of benzene to hereditary damage is not known.

Human effects are best studied using cytogenetic studies; four studies involving a few workers receiving occupational exposure at subacute doses found an association between benzene exposure and chromosome irregularities.[60] One study found an increased rate of chromosomal alterations at the outer limit of normal rates associated with exposure

55. W. Deichman, W. E. MacDonald, and E. Bernal, "The Hemopoietic Tissue Toxicity of Benzene Vapors."

56. Two early studies suggested reproductive effects in humans, but they are crude and have not been replicated.

57. For a more complete survey, see Sandra R. Wolman, "Cytologic and Cytogenetic Effects of Benzene." This area of research is relatively new. OSHA's review of benzene health effects did not explore it in depth.

58. M. Kissling and B. Speck, "Chromosome Aberration in Experimental Benzene Intoxication."

59. A. M. Forni and others, "Chromosome Changes and Their Evolution in Subjects with Past Exposure to Benzene."

60. G. Hartwich and G. Schwanitz, "Chromosomenuntersuchungen Nachchronischer Benzol-Exposition"; A. M. Forni, D. Pacifico, and A. Limonta, "Chromosome Studies

levels well under 25 ppm. A second study found a significant increase in unstable chromosomal changes one to eighteen years after acute benzene poisoning. A third study found that exposures in the range of 25–160 ppm resulted in a significant increase in the number of aberrant cells. Finally, a controversial study of workers exposed to a wide range of benzene concentrations found the same number of abnormal cells as in the controls but twice the percentage of chromosome breaks (0.67 percent), three times the percentage of marker chromosomes (1.6 percent), and ten times the percentage of controls showing both aberrations.

The significance of cytogenetic studies of occupational exposure is limited by lack of data on dosage, the generally small size of populations, an inability to control for possible varied degrees of latency in the subjects, and by the often low number of aberrations in workers (around 1 percent). There is a spontaneous incidence of chromosomal aberrations in the general population of 2.6–3.0 percent, which might be an artifact of current laboratory techniques.

The association of benzene with cytogenetic damage is subject to further uncertainty due to the still early stage of research. Some noncarcinogens and nonmutagens (for example, caffeine) produce chromosomal damage. Conversely, carcinogens do not necessarily damage cultured chromosomes in vitro. Finally, the significance of such aberrations is uncertain: it is not clear whether chromosomal alterations are causative or whether they are perhaps accidental or exceptional occurrences such as accompany the attack of any disease.

Leukemogenicity

The association of benzene and adult acute, generally fatal, leukemias is based on numerous individual case reports.[61] One survey of leukemia patients found a significant number with histories of benzene exposure.[62]

---

in Workers Exposed to Benzene, Toluene, or Both"; I. M. Tough and W. Court-Brown, "Chromosome Aberrations and Exposure to Ambient Benzene"; Tough and others, "Chromosome Studies on Workers Exposed to Atmospheric Benzene"; and D. Picciano, "Cytogenetic Study of Workers Exposed to Benzene."

61. For a review of benzene leukemogenicity, see Goldstein, "Hematotoxicity in Humans"; Leong, "Experimental Benzene Intoxication"; and EPA, *Assessment of Health Effects of Benzene Germane to Low-Level Exposure.*

62. R. Girard, F. Tolot, and J. Bourret, "Hydrocarbures, benzeniques et hemopathies graves."

Most important, instances of increased leukemia rates have been found to follow chronologically outbreaks of industrial benzene poisoning.

The mechanism of benzene leukemogenicity is unknown. This uncertainty hampers research into dose-response relationships. Further, uncertainty surrounds benzene's association with the various types of leukemia. European studies of occupationally exposed populations have indicated a relationship between benzene and acute myelogenous and acute myelomonocytic leukemias. Other studies have found some correspondence with chronic lymphocytic leukemia.

Until recently research has been seriously complicated by the unavailability of an animal bioassay showing benzene's leukemogenicity. Recent preliminary results indicating leukemia induction in rodents should reassure scientists previously hesitant to acknowledge benzene's leukemogenicity.

There are few large-scale epidemiological studies on benzene leukemogenicity. Past epidemiological studies have lacked precise measures of benzene exposure. They have confirmed the qualitative association of benzene and leukemia. Since the ambient dose of benzene is so low and the normal incidence of leukemia is about eight deaths per 100,000 persons per year, large sample sizes would be required for significant results. The unavailability of large samples for which there are controls of environmental factors, accurate dosage data, and a sufficient time period to take latency effects into account contributes to the uncertainty of research into benzene leukemogenicity. Long latency periods (fifteen to twenty-seven years) complicate diagnosis. Ubiquity makes it difficult to isolate benzene as a contaminant.[63]

Quantitative Risk Assessment

While there are many case reports of leukemia linked to benzene exposure, any hope of linking the incidence of leukemia to the dose of benzene rests on several epidemiological studies. As reviewed in appen-

63. See, for example, E. C. Vigliani, "Occupational Animal Factors." By contrast, the latency period for leukemia from ionizing radiation is only two to four years. See National Academy of Sciences, Advisory Committee on the Biological Effects of Ionizing Radiation, *The Effects on Populations of Exposure to Low Levels of Ionizing Radiation.* If the latency period for benzene leukemia is this short, the dose-response curve would be different from that estimated by the EPA and other investigators.

dix A, each of the four case studies relied on by OSHA and the EPA in seeking to regulate benzene has difficulties in defining the level and period of benzene exposure in order to estimate dose. Generally, the population at risk is not well defined, there is some doubt about the number of leukemia cases that resulted, and there is general uncertainty in each study. For example, benzene concentrations in the air workers breathe is generally not measured at all, is measured only at peak concentrations, or is measured only once in several years.

Although each study has severe shortcomings, the four studies together can be used to provide at least crude estimates of the dose-response relationship by which benzene produces leukemia. In doing so it is important to look carefully at what is known about exposure levels and the population at risk. Rather than making conservative assumptions at each stage, it is more helpful to arrive at a best estimate and upper and lower bounds. In amalgamating the studies, it is important to weight each by the quality of its information, as represented by the size of the population studied and the quality of the data.

Appendix B describes the CAG's risk assessment, an important intellectual contribution to decisionmaking about carcinogens. It describes the details of the calculations by which the EPA derived quantitative risk estimates from the uncertain epidemiological studies. While the general method is admirable, there are specific assumptions that seem overly conservative or simply inexplicable. For example, the CAG includes leukemias that Infante did not find and for which there is little evidence of their being produced by occupational exposures. The CAG also assumes that benzene concentration levels in Infante's plant dropped in proportion to gradually tightening state occupational standards.

An alternative dose-response relationship is estimated, using what appear to be more reasonable assumptions. The new estimate also includes specific upper and lower bound estimates and attempts to take account of the amount of information in the various epidemiological studies. While the details of the calculation and of the differences in assumptions may seem esoteric, their implications for the number of leukemias that could be saved by tightening the standard are quite important. Furthermore, there is probably little disagreement over the most probable assumptions to be used in the estimation. The different estimates and different assumptions result more from disagreement over whether the risk assessment should represent a best estimate or be highly conservative.

Conclusion

OSHA's failure to do a quantitative risk analysis meant it had no real idea of the estimated cost per leukemia prevented. While the quantitative risk analyses of the EPA and this chapter are far from certain, they indicate that between eighteen and ninety leukemias a year result from current environmental exposure, using quite conservative assumptions about the nature of the dose-response relationship. The analysis does not indicate whether the OSHA and EPA standards are worthwhile, but it does serve to indicate the possible benefit of controlling benzene.

By assumption, any exposure to benzene carries with it an increased risk of leukemia. Since there is a natural exposure to benzene, even without petrochemicals, the risk of leukemia due to benzene cannot be eliminated. Thus society is faced with the painful decision of setting standards for occupational and public health exposure, knowing that some excess risk will remain, at least in theory. This analysis, however, along with estimates of the cost of meeting the standard, can provide society with some idea of the implications of setting one standard versus another.

Appendix A: Epidemiological Studies

The first three studies discussed below provided the basis for OSHA's findings of benzene's leukemogenicity and for the EPA's quantitative risk assessment. Along with the Thorpe study, they are the only substantial epidemiological studies. Each of these studies has major problems.

Infante Study

The epidemiological study by Peter F. Infante of NIOSH involved a cohort combining workers from two Ohio plants producing a natural rubber cast film known as Pliofilm by "essentially identical" processes.[64]

64. Infante and others, "Leukemia in Benzene Workers."

Benzene was established to be the only significant airborne contaminant.[65]

The study cohort comprised 748 workers employed and exposed to benzene at the two plants between January 1, 1940, and December 31, 1949. Follow-up covered the period from first employment to June 30, 1975. As controls, Infante chose a group of 1,447 white males from a fiberglass manufacturing factory situated in a geographically similar area and the U.S. white male population during the 1940s, adjusted for age.

Levels of exposure to benzene at the selected sites before 1946 are unknown.[66] In 1946 installation of an exhaust ventilation system significantly reduced exposure. After a survey of the Pliofilm process in 1946, the Industrial Commission of Ohio reported that "tests were made with benzol detectors and the results indicate that concentrations have been reduced to a safe level and in most instances range from zero to 10 or 15 parts per million."[67] A total of 112 surveys were conducted in one plant in the period between 1963 and 1974. Infante notes that these and earlier surveys indicate that employee exposure was generally within the recommended limits for the respective year.

Infante found 140 deaths from all causes; 187.6 were expected from his U.S. white male control group. He attributed the lower mortality rate of the rubber workers to incomplete follow-up, and it may also be due to the "healthy worker effect," the generally healthy character of workers in comparison with the general population. Infante found, however, a significant excess of hematopoietic malignancies, chiefly of leukemia deaths. Seven workers died from myelogenous or monocytic leukemias, as compared with an expected 1.38 deaths (based on all white males), and an expected 1.48 deaths (based on the fiberglass workers), a fivefold excess risk.

In a supplemental letter to *The Lancet,* Infante referred to reports of additional leukemias among Pliofilm workers.[68] Infante did not include these additional deaths in his findings since they were not located by his

65. As noted above, the Infante study was heavily relied on in OSHA's promulgation of an emergency temporary standard and was a focus of industry attacks on the permanent standard in the 1978 OSHA hearings.

66. OSHA, *Proposed Standard for Exposure to Benzene.*

67. Industrial Commission of Ohio, Report, 1946, cited in Infante and others, "Leukemia in Benzene Workers," p. 76.

68. P. F. Infante, "Reply," p. 868.

own study. He did correct his estimates of the number of expected deaths from 1.38 to 1.25 for white males.

Infante's report of a significant excess incidence of fatal leukemias in an industrial setting in which benzene was claimed to be the only contaminant supports the qualitative association of benzene and leukemia. The study's limited usefulness, however, arises from the paucity of its dosage data. Infante gives no information on the duration of worker exposure.[69] It is unclear why he did not use employment records to determine this. He also evidently lacked records of prior employment that might have been the source of workers' exposure to benzene or other contaminants.

Data on contamination at the site are limited and uncertain. Exposure levels before 1946 were not recorded. The Ohio Industrial Commission reported an exposure level of 10–15 ppm in most places and "safe" levels elsewhere. These safe levels were those recommended for the various years, a level of 100 ppm for 1941–46, a 50 ppm time-weighted average in 1947, and a level of 35 ppm in 1948. The fact that recommended exposure levels decreased over the period of study is no guarantee that the actual exposure declined. The total of 112 air surveys in one plant between 1963 and 1974 amount to less than one sampling a month. Further, though uniform exposure could be determined for most production areas, certain sites in the production process were subject to significantly higher exposures. The use of respirators was recommended for such sites, but there is no assurance that respirators were used at these times. Testimony revealed unrecorded temporary excursions significantly above the recommended safe level, 350 ppm and beyond, resulting from accidental drenching, for example. Finally, some doubt exists about whether sampling and measurement techniques in the 1940s were capable of accurately measuring levels as low as 10 ppm.

Infante's cohort of white men directly exposed to benzene was poorly defined. The use of populations from two separate plants with different amounts of available exposure data leaves some doubt on the comparability of environmental and occupational exposure data.[70] Infante plausibly justified the combining of two separate plants as a means of

69. Indeed, the OSHA hearings indicated that workers were included in the study on the basis of as little as one day of employment exposure.

70. I. Tabershaw and S. Lamm, "Letter," points out that one plant also manufactured products other than Pliofilm, and that turnover was greater at one plant than at the other.

significantly enlarging the study population with workers all involved in essentially identical processes.

Infante's estimate of the exposure levels of workers in his study was low, although there are data to the contrary. The Infante study documents the qualitative association of benzene and leukemia but provides little evidence on doses that may be associated with leukemia.

Aksoy Study

Muzaffer Aksoy has published a series of studies of health effects among Turkish shoeworkers.[71] Observing leukemic patients in Istanbul hospitals, his primary conclusion was that an increase in cases among shoeworkers coincided with the introduction of benzene as a solvent for adhesives. He has reported that about one-fourth of the 217 apparently healthy shoeworkers selected at random exhibited hematological abnormalities associated with acute benzene poisoning after exposure to between 30 and 210 ppm for from three months to seventeen years.[72]

In the study specifically relied on in the EPA's risk assessment, Aksoy reported twenty-six cases of leukemia among shoeworkers admitted to Istanbul hospitals during the period 1967–73.[73] The data may not include all cases. The concentration of benzene in poorly ventilated workshops was estimated to be as high as 210–650 ppm. The duration of exposure ranged from four months to fifteen years (average 9.7 years). Ages at the time of diagnosis ranged from sixteen to fifty-eight (average 34.2). Official records indicated that 28,500 workers were involved in shoe manufacturing, leading Aksoy to calculate an incidence of leukemia of 13 per 100,000, roughly twice the usual incidence for Western nations and about four times the estimated incidence of leukemia in Turkey.

71. Aksoy and others, "Hematological Effects of Chronic Benzene Poisoning in 217 Workers"; Aksoy and others, "Details of Blood Changes in Thirty-Two Patients with Pancytopenia Associated with Long-Term Exposure to Benzene"; Aksoy and others, "Acute Leukemia Due to Chronic Exposure to Benzene"; Aksoy and others, "Acute Leukemia in Two Generations Following Chronic Exposure to Benzene"; Aksoy, "Leukemia in Shoe-Workers Exposed Chronically to Benzene"; and Aksoy, S. Erdem, and G. Dincol, "Types of Leukemia in Chronic Benzene Poisoning." Aksoy's findings were relied on both by OSHA and the EPA in setting standards and Aksoy was presented as an OSHA witness at its 1978 administrative hearings.

72. Aksoy and others, "Hematological Effects of Chronic Benzene Poisoning in 217 Workers."

73. Aksoy, "Leukemia in Shoe-Workers Exposed Chronically to Benzene," pp. 837–38. Three cases were acute lymphoblastic leukemia, which are as yet inconclusively associated with benzene. See Goldstein, "Hematoxicity in Humans."

Aksoy can give only the roughest of indications of exposure level, since there were few measurements of benzene concentration in the workplace. The hot climate and poor ventilation made it likely that many workers experienced exposures that were frequently more than 500 ppm. Since shops were in or adjacent to living quarters, it is also likely that high benzene exposures continued outside working hours. The estimate of the population at risk and the number of leukemias was also problematic. While various assumptions can be employed to estimate dose-response relationships, one cannot have confidence in a particular estimate.

Aksoy's large cohort and significant number of cases support the qualitative association between benzene exposure and leukemia. His rough dosage figures, however, are difficult to quantify in establishing a dose-response relationship. Furthermore, comparison of these results to an American occupational setting is problematic.

Ott Study

M. Gerald Ott, in a 1978 epidemiological study of workers exposed in the petrochemical industry, examined 594 workers at a Dow Chemical plant.[74] The study covered employment between 1940 and 1973. Ott notes that sufficient allowance was made for the development of latent effects. On the basis of employment records, Ott located workers in particular departments and associated them with particular durations of exposure and ranges of benzene concentration (from 2 ppm to 25 ppm). Ott found no statistically significant excess rate of death generally or from any cause other than leukemia. He identified two deaths due to leukemia and a third in which leukemia was noted as a significant condition, the primary cause of death being bronchopneumonia. This result, compared with an expected incidence of 0.8, yielded a result of borderline statistical significance.[75]

74. This industry-sponsored study was published after the Infante results and the OSHA emergency temporary standard promulgation. It was cited by industry in the OSHA hearings as a negative study and was used by the EPA to broaden the data base in its calculation of the benzene risk assessment. M. G. Ott and others, "Mortality among Individuals Occupationally Exposed to Benzene."

75. Evaluation of two of the leukemia cases is, in fact, complicated by documented exposure of one to vinyl chloride and an exposure level up to 200 ppm of benzene, while the other had worked in veneer manufacturing, which is associated with increased risk of myelocytic leukemia. The cause of death in the third case was given on the certificate as bronchopneumonia with leukemia as a significant concurrent condition.

Because of Ott's access to work histories and industrial hygiene records, he has been able to give a better estimate of benzene dosage than those in the other studies, and he has tabulated his findings in detail. Ott points out the uncertainty due to the likelihood that long-term employees were exposed to a wide range of chemicals and exposure levels; two of the leukemia cases had had previous exposure to potentially carcinogenic chemicals.

Ott does not discuss air-sampling methods. His historic records of hygienic surveys are presumably subject to doubt based on the limited technical capability of measuring low concentration in the 1940s, the difficulty of accounting for temporary excursions, and the possibly inadequate number of air samples.

The major limit on the study's utility arises from its small sample size. While the resultant leukemia deaths are suggestive, their statistical inconclusiveness makes use of the study's figures difficult. This study has both the lowest concentrations of benzene and the smallest worker population of three major studies. It is important because it is the only one reporting documented exposures below 25 ppm.

Thorpe Study

Among the limited number of epidemiological studies are several sponsored by the petroleum industry.[76] J. J. Thorpe's study examined employment records for 1962–71 of eight Exxon affiliates in Europe with a combined population and duration of exposure of 38,000 man-years. He found eighteen cases (23.23 expected) of diagnosed leukemia occurring at four of the plants, an incidence judged equivalent to that in the general population of comparable age.

Thorpe acknowledged several limitations of his study; for example, exposure levels for job categories were known, if at all, only as "much less than the recommended level of 25 ppm." There is no record of the duration of a worker's exposure to various levels of benzene. The Thorpe study indicates, however, that there was no outstanding incidence in the refining industry. While it does not eliminate a risk of leukemia due to benzene, the study can be used to place an upper bound on the quantitative effect of benzene.

76. J. J. Thorpe, "Epidemiological Survey of Leukemia in Persons Potentially Exposed to Benzene"; R. A. Stallones, "Report on Mortality from Leukemia"; and I. Tabershaw, "Mortality Study among Refinery Workers."

It is apparent from this brief review that all the studies share a similar flaw. A link between benzene and leukemia exists in each study, but the dose required to produce this response is not certain. In the face of such inconclusive data, a method designed to estimate the possible effects of a range of doses would be immensely helpful.

Appendix B: Review of the EPA Risk Assessment

The Carcinogen Assessment Group of the EPA undertook a quantitative risk assessment, based on the first three studies discussed in appendix A.[77]

In the mathematical model employed, the CAG assumed that for low exposures, the lifetime probability of leukemia (P) may be represented by the linear equation

$$P = A + Bx,$$

where

A = the leukemia rate in the absence of benzene,
x = the average lifetime background benzene exposure in ppm,
B = the change in the leukemia rate per 1 ppm benzene.

Assuming that the relative leukemia risk, R, of benzene-exposed workers relative to that of the general population is independent of the length or age of exposure but depends only on the total exposure, it follows that

$$R = \frac{P_2}{P_1} = \frac{A + B(x_1 + x_2)}{A + Bx_1}$$

or

$$RP_1 = A + B(x_1 + x_2),$$

so that

$$B = \frac{P_1(R - 1)}{x_2}$$

77. See also the review and recalculations in Ralph H. Luken and Stephen G. Miller, "The Benefits and Costs of Regulating Benzene."

where

x_1 = the ambient air level of benzene,
x_2 = the industrial level of benzene,
P_1 = the lifetime probability of dying of leukemia with no industrial benzene exposure;
P_2 = the lifetime probability of dying of leukemia with industrial benzene exposure.[78]

Infante Risk Estimates

The CAG accepted Infante's recalculation, based on his more complete follow-up, of the expected incidence of leukemia from 1.38 to 1.25 per 100,000. The CAG also added to Infante's seven leukemia cases two additional ones reported by Marvin Sakol that were "probably" in Infante's cohort.[79] According to the CAG's calculation:

$$R = \frac{7 + 2}{1.25} = 7.20.$$

Since the original leukemias were not discovered in the framework of the original study (indeed Infante omitted them from his own calculation of the leukemia incidence in his letter to *The Lancet*), they are omitted from the calculation of relative risk to give the following:

$$R = \frac{7}{1.25} = 5.60.$$

The CAG assumed on the basis of Infante's information and other testimony that exposure before 1946 was at least 15 ppm and less than or equal to 100 ppm.

Based on the doubtful assumption that the recommended levels were the actual levels for the years of the study,[80] the CAG estimated a

78. Estimates of R and x_2 are obtained from the epidemiological studies. The exposure values for x_1 are obtained from EPA, CAG, *Assessment of Human Exposures to Atmospheric Benzene*. The estimation of the lifetime probability, P_1 and P_2, of death due to various forms of leukemia for a member of the general population is based on data from the "Vital Statistics of the United States," 1973, vol. II.

79. See Infante and others, "Letter." The CAG was persuaded by Sakol's conviction that leukemia deaths were consistently underreported for reasons associated with workmen's compensation, according to Bob McGaughy of the CAG (personal communication, summer 1980).

80. The CAG tabulates the *recommended* exposure limits for the particular years, for example, 1940–46, 100–15 ppm; 1947, 50 ppm; 1948–56, 35 ppm. The CAG arrives at a time-weighted average of 23.3–39.9 ppm.

continuous lifetime exposure level of 40.36 ppm for workers starting before 1946 and an exposure duration of thirty-five years. Exposure was assumed to be 23.7 ppm for newer workers, with an exposure duration of twenty-five years. It is doubtful that, as assumed, a worker starting in 1940 or in 1946 stayed in Pliofilm during his whole working life. The group included workers who may have been employed as little as one day. The CAG produced the following estimates of exposures:[81]

Employed before 1946 $$40.36 \times \frac{240}{365} \times \frac{1}{3} \times \frac{35}{70} = 4.4 \text{ ppm}$$

Employed after 1946 $$23.7 \times \frac{240}{365} \times \frac{1}{3} \times \frac{25}{70} = 1.8 \text{ ppm.}$$

CAG calculated the geometric mean of these continuous exposures as $4.4 \times 1.8 = 2.81$. Because of uncertainties about actual exposure levels and duration of employment, both high and low estimated lifetime averages will be used in subsequent calculations to indicate the range of exposures.

CAG estimated:

$$B = \frac{P_1(R - 1)}{x_2} = 0.006732 \times \frac{(7.20 - 1)}{2.81} = 0.014854.$$

Using the lower number of deaths (seven) found by Infante (resulting in the relative risk estimate of 5.6) and using both the high and low estimates of lifetime exposure arrived at above, I calculated the following estimates of the change in the leukemia rate per 1 ppm benzene:

Low: $$B = 0.006732 \times \frac{(5.6 - 1)}{4.4} = 0.007038$$

High: $$B = 0.006732 \times \frac{(5.6 - 1)}{1.8} = 0.0172.$$

Aksoy Risk Estimates

In using Aksoy's results to calculate the leukemia rate per unit of benzene exposure, the CAG first estimated the incidence of leukemia

81. The level of exposure is 40.36, 240 is the number of working days per year, one-third is the proportion of the day spent on the job, and 35 is the number of years spent on the job.

using the figure of twenty-six cases out of a population of 28,500 shoeworkers at risk during the 6⅔ years of observation. The CAG, eliminating the case of lymphoblastic leukemia "not thought to be associated with benzene exposure,"[82] estimated the incidence among shoeworkers to be 13.15 per 100,000. Modifying the available estimate of the incidence of all leukemias in the Turkish population (2.5 to 3.0 per 100,000), the CAG calculated an expected incidence of nonlymphoblastic leukemia of 0.66 per 100,000. The actual incidence of leukemia in the general Turkish population is uncertain; still, the cancer rate in less developed Turkey is presumably lower, and the CAG's estimated number of expected deaths is reasonably conservative.

The CAG arrived at the incidence of leukemia associated with occupational benzene exposure as follows:

$$R = \frac{13.15}{0.66} = 19.92.$$

The CAG used Aksoy's estimate that the benzene concentration in the shop outside of working hours was 15–30 ppm and the level during working hours was 150–210 ppm. It then took the geometric mean of these exposures, assuming they are of equal duration: 63.6 ppm.

Assuming a ten-hour working day, a 300-day working year, an average age at the end of observation of fifty, and an average period of exposure of 9.7 years, the CAG calculated lifetime average exposure as:

$$x_2 = 63.6 \times \frac{(10)}{24} \times \frac{(300)}{365} \times \frac{(9.7)}{50} = 4.22 \text{ ppm}.$$

In the calculations that follow, the CAG did not take into account this nonworking-hour concentration. But considering that the shoeworkers' shops are most likely attached to their abodes, this exposure level represents a background exposure that must be distinguished from the background ambient air exposure of American workers, which is on the order of a few parts per billion. Instead of taking the mean of these exposures and weighting them for ten hours of work a day, a ten-hour working exposure at the high level is assumed and a ten-hour nonworking-hour exposure is added to the background level. In addition, the figures used by the CAG are low. Aksoy has noted the poor ventilation of the shoeworkers' shops; the low boiling point of benzene would lead to

82. EPA, CAG, "Final Report," p. 15.

higher concentrations in a warm climate. In any case, Aksoy himself uses the range of 210–650 ppm.[83] I use these modified assumptions and figures in calculating lifetime average exposure:

$$\left[\left(\frac{(15 + 30)}{2}\right)\left(\frac{10}{24}\right) + \left(\frac{210 + 650}{2}\right)\left(\frac{10}{24}\right)\right] \times \left(\frac{300}{365}\right) \times \left(\frac{9.7}{50}\right) = 30.1 \text{ ppm.}$$

To indicate the range of possible exposure, I also calculate lifetime exposure on the basis of the CAG's more conservative figure for working-hour exposure:

$$\left[\left(\frac{(15 + 30)}{2}\right)\left(\frac{10}{24}\right) + \left(\frac{150 + 210}{2}\right)\left(\frac{10}{24}\right)\right] \times \left(\frac{300}{365}\right) \times \left(\frac{9.7}{50}\right) = 13.5 \text{ ppm.}$$

CAG applied its average exposure figure to the equation given earlier:

$$B = \frac{P_1(R - 1)}{x_2}$$

$$B = 0.004517 \times \frac{(19.92 - 1)}{4.22} = 0.020252.$$

I use the higher exposure figure and account for the relatively high background exposure:

$$B = 0.04517 \times \frac{(19.92 - 1)}{30.1} = 0.0284.$$

Observing three deaths with 0.8 expected ($p < 0.047$) gives a relative risk of:

$$R = \frac{3}{0.8} = 3.75.$$

Ott Risk Estimates

Ott estimated the ppm-months of exposure of each worker from records and plant benzene measurements and tabulated them in terms

83. Aksoy, "Leukemia in Shoe-Workers Chronically Exposed to Benzene."

of observed and expected deaths corresponding to duration of exposure.[84] Using Ott's results, the CAG took the average of each exposure level and weighted averages by expected deaths:

$$\frac{(250 \times 65.1 + 750 \times 16.2 + 1250 \times 32.8)}{65.1 + 16.2 + 32.8} = 608.46 \text{ ppm-months.}$$

The CAG then calculated the average lifetime exposure on the assumptions of an eight-hour day, a 240-day working year, and an average age at the end of the observation period of sixty-five years.

$$\frac{(608.46)}{(12)} \times \frac{(8)}{(24)} \times \frac{(240)}{(365)} \times \frac{(1)}{(65)} = 0.171 \text{ ppm.}$$

The object of weighting exposure by expected mortality values is to introduce an element of duration and proportionality (deaths correspond to level of exposure and time), but exposure can be correlated more directly with time by weighting the mean exposure level in a production area by duration of exposure in that area.

Ott gives the number of workers who spent a certain number of years in a particular production area:

Production area	*Less than 1 year*	*1–9 years*	*10–19 years*	*20+ years*
I	9	36	20	43
II	21	64	23	27
III	96	139	39	24

The average number of years spent in a particular production area is derived from the table by weighting the mean number of years in a range by the number of workers in that range:

I. $(9 \times 1 + 36 \times 5 + 20 \times 15 + 43 \times 30)/(9 + 36 + 20 + 43) = 16.47$

II. $(3 \times 1 + 12 \times 5 + 1 \times 15 + 5 \times 30)/(3 + 12 + 1 + 5) = 10.85$

III. $(1 \times 1 + 13 \times 5 + 13 \times 15 + 10 \times 3)/(1 + 13 + 13 + 10) = 7.86$

These figures for the average number of years spent in a production area are used to weight the mean exposure level for each production area, to

84. Ott and others, "Mortality among Individuals Occupationally Exposed to Benzene," table 7.

derive the average occupational exposure. Ott gives the ranges of exposure level for the production areas:

I. Low (2–9 ppm TWA), very low (<2 ppm TWA)
II. High (25+ ppm TWA), moderate (10–24 ppm TWA), low, very low
III. High

$$\frac{(3 \times 16.47 + 13 \times 10.85 + 30 \times 15.16)}{16.47 + 10.85 + 15.16}$$

$$= 15.19 \text{ ppm average occupational exposure.}$$

Using the CAG's assumption of an eight-hour day and 240-day working year and estimating the average duration of years on the job to be 15.5, the average lifetime exposure can be calculated thusly:

$$15.19 \times \frac{240}{365} \times \frac{1}{3} \times \frac{(15.50)}{70} = 0.737 \text{ ppm.}$$

Using the equation

$$B = \frac{P_1(R - 1)}{x_2},$$

the CAG calculates the lifetime probability of leukemia per unit exposure to be

$$B = 0.002884 \times \frac{(3.75 - 1)}{0.171} = 0.04638.$$

Substituting my value for the lifetime average exposure, I estimate that

$$B = 0.002884 \times \frac{(3.75 - 1)}{0.737} = 0.01076.$$

Combined Risk Estimate

Finally, the CAG took the geometric mean of its values for B to compute the total probability of deaths due to 1 ppm of benzene in the air breathed over a lifetime:

$$B = \frac{1}{3}(0.014854 \times 0.020252 \times 0.046380) = 0.02407.$$

However, because the studies vary considerably in population size and thus should not be accorded equal statistical weight, I weight my estimates of the lifetime probability of leukemia per unit of benzene (*B*) by the square root of the population on which the probability is calculated:

$$B = \frac{(0.007038 \times 748) + (0.00284 \times 28)}{500 + (0.01076 \times 594)} = 0.004236.$$

With *D* representing units in 10^6 parts per billion person-years, the expected number of leukemia deaths a year (*M*) may be estimated approximately by the relationship

$$M_D = \frac{(0.024074 \times D \times 10^3)}{70.96} = 0.339262D,$$

where 0.024074 is the geometric mean of the slope parameters of the three studies and 70.96 is the average life expectancy in the United States. By this equation and using my weighted average of the slope parameters, I calculate:

$$M_D = \frac{(0.004236 \times D \times 10^3)}{70.96} = 0.059696D.$$

Using exposure figures for sources from the "Assessment of Human Exposures" document, the CAG calculated expected deaths as shown in table 4-2.

Table 4-2. Expected Deaths by Source of Exposure

Sources of exposure	*Exposure index (millions of ppb-person-years)*	*CAG expected number of benzene-caused leukemia deaths per year*	*My recalculation of expected deaths*
Chemical manufacturing	8.5	2.88	0.57
Coke ovens	0.2	0.07	0.01
Petroleum refineries	2.5	0.85	0.17
Automobile emissions	150.0	50.89	9.98
Gasoline service stations	19.0	6.44	1.26
Self-service gasoline	1.6	0.54	0.11
Total	181.8	61.67	12.10

Source: EPA, Carcinogen Assessment Group, "Final Report on Population Risk from Ambient Benzene Exposure" (EPA, 1979), table 4.

Table 4-3. Expected Deaths by Vicinity of Residence

Vicinity of residence	*Exposure index (millions of ppb-person-years)*	*CAG expected number of benzene-caused leukemia deaths per year*	*My recalculation of expected deaths*
Chemical manufacturing	10.0	3.39	0.67
Coke ovens	0.2	0.07	0.01
Petroleum refineries	4.5	1.53	0.29
Urban areas	250.0	84.80	16.63
Total	264.7	89.80	17.60

Source: EPA, Carcinogen Assessment Group, "Final Report on Population Risk from Ambient Benzene Exposure," table 5.

The CAG also used exposure figures based on a second model that does not assume a static population but tries to follow a typical person through a typical day; a primary factor in this approach is the location of the person's residence. The CAG then calculates deaths as shown in table 4-3.

I find that about eighteen leukemia deaths a year can be expected from ambient benzene exposure; the CAG's calculations result in ninety expected deaths.

CHAPTER FIVE

Regulating Coke Oven Emissions

DWIGHT D. BRIGGS *and* LESTER B. LAVE

MAKING COAL into coke requires heating the coal to high temperatures in an oven with too little air to permit combustion. Heating drives off impurities, leaving a pure fuel that can be used for making steel. In the process, coke oven gases are emitted, consisting of carbon monoxide, coal tars, sulfur oxides, and other chemicals. Workers are exposed to these gases as they escape through cracks in oven doors or piping, as they come off the hot coke when it is removed from the oven, and as they combine with steam when the coke is quenched to cool it. The untreated gases are extremely toxic, and one group of their components, coal tars, is recognized as containing many potent carcinogens.

Identifying the individual substances that render coke oven gases toxic is extremely difficult, however. The gases change with the composition of the coal, and the process cannot be duplicated in a laboratory. Thus the most toxic substances are measured in aggregate terms, either as coal tar pitch volatiles (CTPV) or benzene soluble organics.

Laboratory studies are of relatively little help in investigating the potency of CTPV because the gases emanating from heating bituminous coal cannot be produced either uniformly or inexpensively in a laboratory setting. Rather, various components of the gases have been tested separately, uncovering a number of carcinogens. Epidemiological studies have produced conflicting results concerning the effect of coke oven gases on lung cancer and other types of cancer. The initial full-scale study of coke oven workers done in Great Britain failed to discover any excess rates of lung cancer. However, an American study did find significant increases in lung and other cancers. Thus the British and American studies must be contrasted to evaluate study design, implementation, and the methods of analysis. In each aspect the British study is considered either less satisfactory or too vague to evaluate; the U.S. study generally is accepted as the more accurate indication of health effects. It finds excess cancers increase with the period and level of exposure (as indicated by the type of job the worker performs).

History of the Standards

In 1969, under powers granted him by the Contract Work Hours Standard Act of 1962,[1] the secretary of labor adopted a CTPV threshold limit value of 0.2 milligram per cubic meter of air for worker exposure in federally funded employment. When the Occupational Safety and Health Administration (OSHA) was created in 1970, it adopted this standard, along with many other preexisting standards, for all workers.

In June 1971 the American Iron and Steel Institute (AISI) petitioned the secretary of labor to develop a less stringent standard specifically applicable to coke oven emissions. A month later the United Steelworkers of America filed a petition requesting a more stringent standard. Both petitions were denied by the Department of Labor in September 1971, pending further research by the National Institute of Occupational Safety and Health (NIOSH), the research arm of OSHA.

NIOSH gathered information from studies on excess mortality and exposure levels and performed a quantitative risk assessment. Extensive data analyses were developed and presented at rule-making hearings, including estimates of the number of workers affected and the expected number of excess deaths, as well as data on the cost and feasibility of engineering controls to meet the standards. A NIOSH report was published in February 1973,[2] and a Standards Advisory Committee was subsequently established in August 1974. The committee's report was submitted to the secretary of labor in May 1975. Two months later a proposed standard was published in the *Federal Register*.[3] OSHA

1. 83 Stat. 96.
2. National Institute for Occupational Safety and Health, "Criteria for a Recommended Standard: Occupational Exposure to Coke Oven Emissions."
3. 40 Fed. Reg. 32267 (1975). The proposed standard was 0.3 milligram per cubic meter of air. It must be noted, however, that the basis for measurement and the chemical components in CTPV targeted for regulation were changed before the final standard was promulgated. Thus the apparent differences between the proposed and final standards are not accurately represented by a simple comparison of numbers.

conducted hearings on the proposed standard between November 1975 and May 1976. The final standard of 0.15 milligram per cubic meter was published on October 22, 1976, and became effective January 20, 1977.[4]

Specifically, the standard established a permissible exposure limit of 0.15 milligram per cubic meter of air of the benzene soluble fraction of CTPV, averaged over any eight-hour period. In addition, it required both engineering controls and work practice rules at each coke oven battery, even if the exposure level was below 0.15 milligram per cubic meter. If these specified controls and work practices did not reduce emissions below that level, employers were required to install other (nonspecified) controls as necessary. Employees were to be afforded respiratory protection by personal air filtration devices whenever the exposure limit was exceeded. As promulgated, the standard also required employers to engage in research to develop new technologies to reduce emissions.

In December 1976 the AISI and the American Coke and Chemical Institute applied to the secretary of labor for a stay of the effective date of certain of the standard's provisions. The petition was denied in January 1977.

Then the two institutes and a number of steel companies sought judicial review of the standard in the Third Circuit Court of Appeals. The three principal claims were (1) the exposure limit of 0.15 milligram per cubic meter was invalid because there was no substantial evidence of either health effects requiring this standard or the technical feasibility of attaining this limit, (2) the secretary of labor had exceeded his statutory powers, and (3) there was no substantial evidence to support the need for specified mandated controls and procedures.[5]

The case was argued before the Third Circuit Court of Appeals on January 5, 1978. The court upheld the secretary's determination that coke oven emissions are carcinogenic and thus necessitate development of a standard. It also upheld the standard requiring engineering controls and the exposure limit of 0.15 milligram per cubic meter. However, the court held that the secretary had exceeded his authority by requiring employers to conduct research on engineering and work practice controls, by imposing quantitative fit tests for respirators, and by applying the standard to employees who did not work at coke ovens.[6]

4. 41 Fed. Reg. 46742 (1976); 29 C.F.R 1910:1029.
5. 577 F.2d 825 (3d Cir. 1978).
6. Ibid.

Petitions for a writ of certiorari to the U.S. Supreme Court were filed by the AISI and Republic Steel Corporation in December 1978.[7] The court agreed to hear the appeal, but later the plaintiffs withdrew their petitions, apparently believing they had little chance of winning and fearing an earlier related ruling on benzene would be changed to their disadvantage (see chapter 4).

The Environmental Protection Agency is now in the process of developing its own standard for general population exposures to coke oven gases. A draft risk analysis was published in 1979.[8] EPA staff members indicated during an interview that the agency is engaged in reanalysis to produce a document that corrects flaws contained in the draft analysis, which is based on data compiled in a review of health effects of coke oven emissions and a population exposure assessment.[9]

In July 1980 the Emission Standards and Engineering Division of the EPA Office of Air Quality Planning and Standards published a draft preamble and regulation for coke oven emissions from by-product coke oven charging, door leaks, and topside leaks on wet coal-charged batteries.

Health Effects of Coke Oven Emissions

Coal tar pitch volatiles are a complex mixture of particles, vapors, and gases. Emissions into ambient air occur while charging coal into the ovens, during the sixteen- to twenty-hour coking cycle (from leaks in doors, the top of the oven, and the waste gas stock), during quenching of the coke with water, and during the by-product process.

Chemicals generated during the coking process include recognized carcinogens—benzo(a)pyrene, benzo(b)fluoranthene, benzo(b)anthracene and chrysene. Other toxic emissions are benzene, toluene, and phenol.

These chemicals are present as vapors or are absorbed on particles of carbon, iron oxide, and other oxides of trace elements (for example,

7. *American Iron and Steel Institute* v. *Occupational Safety and Health Administration* (December 9, 1978) (78-919); and *Republic Steel Corporation* v. *Occupational Safety and Health Administration* (December 9, 1978) (78-918).

8. Environmental Protection Agency, Office of Research and Development, "An Assessment of the Health Effects of Coke Oven Emissions."

9. EPA, Office of Research and Development, "Human Population Exposures to Coke-Ovens Atmospheric Emissions."

cadmium, lead, silica). Particle sizes range from 0.1 to 2 micrometers in diameter. Particles in this size range will reach the lungs and many will be deposited in the alveoli.

Methods for Estimating Health Effects

Evidence that exposure to coke oven emissions induces cancer is based on an array of epidemiological, bioassay, and in vitro studies with CTPV and their various components. The EPA and OSHA have relied essentially on the same body of scientific knowledge, although treating it in different ways.

The design and conduct of an epidemiological study of occupational exposure, such as that needed for regulating CTPV, is subject to a number of difficulties. One is the possibly long period between exposure and response (the latency period); another is the relatively small sizes of industrial groups; a third is the poor quality of data concerning work history, personal habits (such as smoking), exposure levels, and cause of death.

An extended period of observation, five years or more, helps to compensate for the latency period and for small sample sizes. Thus persons who have had two or more decades of exposure are especially desirable subjects. Retirees meet this criteria, but such a group presents additional problems of data collection and selection bias.

Nonoccupational factors must be observed as well. Family health histories, genetic susceptibilities, and urban air pollutants contribute to observed mortality. Smoking habits are particularly important in coke oven epidemiological studies since the principal concern is lung cancer.

An additional difficulty is the paucity of data on comparison groups. Ideally the control group should be identical to the exposed one, except for exposure to CTPV. In practice, however, the availability of data on possible control groups rather than the similarity of these groups to the experimental group is the most important criterion for control group selection. The estimation of a dose-response relationship is further complicated by problems of data availability and quality.

The sources from which data are obtained are usually government vital statistics and insurance and industrial personnel records. Problems include difficulty in locating death certificates and a lack of consistency in keeping records about items such as worker classification and cause of death. At best, dose is estimated by the number of years at specific jobs. Since exposure levels differ by plant and age of plant, and records on job classification are poor, only crude surrogates for worker dose are available.

In evaluating an epidemiological study, each of these factors is important: (1) the size of the cohort, (2) the period of observation over which mortality (and morbidity) data are collected, (3) the extent to which nonoccupational factors (for example, smoking and family health histories) are monitored, (4) the characteristics of the comparison group, and (5) the quality of worker histories and data about cause of death.

Review of the Epidemiological Studies

The general notion of CTPV toxicity comes from a number of epidemiological studies with gas retort workers. The analogy is strong because of the similarity of CTPV composition to the composition of gas retort emissions; the major difference is the absence of sulfur dioxide in the latter. Gas retort workers have been studied by Kawai, Kennaway and Kennaway, Doll, and Brussgaard.[10] All of these studies, conducted in Japan, Great Britain, and Norway respectively, point to excess incidence of cancer of the lung, kidney, bladder, pancreas, and skin among gas works employees. Also of relevance is a pair of studies by Palmer and Wade indicating no excess risk of skin lesions in oil refinery workers; poor study design precludes confidence in their results, however.[11] Palmer observed only fifty workers, and Wade did not follow up persons who had left the industry.

Two separate efforts were necessary for the coke oven studies. The first measured ambient concentrations of CTPV. The Pennsylvania Department of Health conducted studies at ten coke plants to determine exposure levels at specific job sites. Air samples were collected with filters mounted in plastic holders attached to workers' shirt collars. Eight-hour daily exposures were found to range from 0.4 milligram per

10. M. Kawai, H. Amanoto, and K. Harada, "Epidemiological Study of Occupational Lung Cancer"; E. L. Kennaway and N. M. Kennaway, "A Further Study of the Incidence of Cancer of the Lung and Larynx"; A. Brussgaard, "The Occurrence of Certain Forms of Cancer Among Employees in Gasworks"; and R. Doll and others, "Mortality of Gasworkers with Special Reference to Cancers of the Lung and Bladder, Chronic Bronchitis and Pneumoconiosis."

11. A. Palmer, "Mortality Experience of Fifty Workers with Occupational Exposure to CHP"; and L. Wade, "Observations on Skin Cancer Among Refinery Workers."

cubic meter for the lowest exposed workers to 3.2 milligrams per cubic meter for lidmen.[12]

A second effort involved studies investigating the cause of death among workers. J. William Lloyd and Carol K. Redmond and their associates conducted a long-term epidemiological study of steelworkers. The results of the first phase of the study began to appear in 1969, and further findings continued to be published during the 1970s. These studies found an increased risk of lung and other cancers compared to the general steelworker population.[13] (See table 5-1.) In contrast, D. D. Reid and Carol Buck's study of British plant workers found no excess risk of cancer to coke plant workers when compared with an unspecified control group.[14] We review these studies in terms of the five factors listed above, and find the Redmond and Lloyd studies have a better experimental design and are a more thorough analysis of the data than the Reid and Buck study.

Redmond and associates found a 150 percent lung cancer excess among both white and nonwhite workers.[15] They also found a 650 percent increase of death from kidney cancers. Later data reaffirmed an excess risk of genitourinary, digestive, and lung cancer.[16]

Size of cohort sample affects the ability to separate random and systematic effects. Reid and Buck randomly selected a sample of 800 workers from the 8,000 employed in all British coke plants from 1949 to 1954. They defined the control group only by remarking that it was drawn from a "large industrial organization"; they did not specify its size. (Reid and Buck provided very limited information on several aspects of the methods, making difficult a firm judgment on the quality of their study.) If the control group were exposed to asbestos or some other carcinogen or were heavy cigarette smokers, coke workers might not show an elevated increase in lung cancer. The same might be true if both

12. N. Fannick, L. T. Gonshor, and J. Shockley, Jr., "Exposure to Coal Tar Pitch Volatiles at Coke Ovens."

13. J. William Lloyd and others, "Long-Term Mortality Study of Steelworkers, V: Respiratory Cancer in Coke Plant Workers"; C. K. Redmond and others, "Long-Term Mortality Study of Steelworkers, VI: Mortality from Malignant Neoplasms Among Coke Oven Workers"; and Sati Mazumdar and others, "The Epidemiological Study of Exposure to Coal Tar Pitch Volatiles among Coke Oven Workers."

14. D. D. Reid and Carol Buck, "Cancer in Coking Plant Workers."

15. Redmond and others, "Long-Term Mortality Study of Steelworkers, VI."

16. C. K. Redmond, B. R. Strobino and R. H. Cypess, "Cancer Experience Among Coke By-Product Workers."

Table 5-1. Summary of Epidemiological Studies of Coke Plant Workers

Author[a]	*Date*	*Experimental design*	*Findings*
Reid and Buck	1956	800 workers employed during 1949–54, categorized by job site; comparison group unspecified "large industrial organization"	No excess risk of lung, bladder, or other cancers
Lloyd and others	1971	Men employed in two steel plants in 1953–61; comparison group composed of 58,828 steelworkers	1.5 excess risk[b] of lung cancer and excess risk of cancer of the genitourinary system
Fannick, Gonshor, and Shockley for Pennsylvania Department of Health	1972	Workers at 10 coke plants in 11 job sites, monitored to determine CTPV concentrations	Exposure ranged from 0.39 milligram per cubic meter for pusher machine operators to 3.05 milligrams per cubic meter for lidmen
Redmond and others	1972	Workers employed during 1951–55 in 12 plants	Relative to other steelworkers, an excess risk of 1.34 for lung cancer, 7.49 for kidney cancers
Mazumdar and others	1975	Workers from 12 plants employed during 1951–66 and 1953–66; comparison group of steelworkers	CTPV levels at top of ovens are 2–3 times the levels at side of ovens; dose-response relationship for nonwhites was developed
Redmond, Strobino, and Cypess	1976	Workers during 1953–66; comparison with steelworkers with no coke plant exposure	15.72 excess risk of lung cancer for full-time topside workers
Land	1976	Used Redmond data	Developed linear and quadratic time-dependent dose-response curves

a. See Bibliography for complete citations of the studies.
b. After standardizing for differences in age, smoking, and other relevant factors in the exposed population compared to a control group, an excess risk of 1.5 indicates an incidence of disease 150 percent greater than in the control group.

coke workers and the control group were heavy smokers because of the lower power of statistical tests to find a significant increase in a prevalent condition. There are a host of possible explanations for the lack of significant results, assuming coke oven gases are carcinogenic; Reid and Buck do not provide sufficient information to evaluate each possibility.

The 1971 Lloyd study was based on 3,530 U.S. coke plant workers and the 1972 Redmond study on 4,661 oven workers.[17] Redmond selected the comparison group on a number of criteria; two were that the worker must have been employed actively for at least thirty days and that he must not have worked in the coal, coke, handling or by-products areas. The comparison group of 25,011 steelworkers was probably comparable to coke workers in terms of income, geographical and socioeconomic background, and initial health status, at least after accounting for race.

Duration of exposure was not discussed in the Reid and Buck study. Their data base consisted of workers who died in 1949–54 while still employed or retired. Since dose is related to the duration of exposure, more information on the work histories would have been helpful.

The Lloyd and Redmond studies were both prospective and retrospective; they included previous workers as well as those newly employed, and made painstaking efforts to follow workers from 1953 throughout the seventeen years of their study. The most difficult data to obtain were notice of death and then cause of death. They studied death certificates from the entire nation for the period, failing to obtain data on only 0.1 percent of workers. The period of study is important in that the data suggest that perhaps twenty-five years elapse between first exposure and death from lung cancer. The Reid and Buck study was retrospective with apparently less care taken to find notice and cause of death.

The relation of job sites to exposure was recognized by Reid and Buck. Their worker cohort was divided into four groups—oven workers, by-product workers, laborers, and foremen—on the basis of the job held in 1949 or the most recent job before retirement.

A paper in the Lloyd and Redmond series divided the worker population into topside, side oven 1, and side oven 2 groups, with further subdivisions into eleven job classifications.[18] Cumulative occupational

17. Lloyd and others, "Long-Term Mortality Study of Steelworkers, V"; and Redmond and others, "Long-Term Mortality Study of Steelworkers, VI."

18. Mazumdar and others, "Epidemiological Study of Exposure to Coal Tar Pitch Volatiles among Coke Oven Workers."

exposure (CE) was calculated as $CE = \Sigma M_i E_i$, where M_i is the number of months at the job and E_i is the exposure at the job. This measure is a reasonable characterization of cumulative dose but does not characterize time of dose or dose rate. Although incomplete, this approach is preferred to that of Reid and Buck.

Reid and Buck used claims made to the U.K. National Union of Mine Workers, Cokemen's Division, or death certificates from the General Register Office to determine cause of death. Complete occupational histories of men who died while employed in the coke plant were available, but the data on age distribution of retirees were incomplete.

Neither study included information on workers' smoking habits. This is especially troublesome for Reid and Buck, since there is no reason to presume that smoking habits of the control group were similar to those of the coke plant workers. In their 1975 paper, Mazumdar and associates assume that "since these two groups [all steel workers and the subset who are coke oven workers] . . . belong to the same stratum of society, . . . on the average they have similar smoking habits, thus minimizing the effect of smoking in the relative risks."[19] Furthermore, Lloyd is able to show for these workers that the death rates of topside oven workers from lung cancer exceed the rate that would be expected even if they were heavy smokers.[20]

The discussion above of these conflicting epidemiological studies yields the following conclusions:

—Both studies lack important data and neither set of findings can be accepted at face value or with confidence.

—The flaws revealed in the Reid and Buck study combine with the sketchiness of the description of methods to cast doubt on any finding of the study. It appears likely that the failure to find a significant increase in the incidence of lung cancer among British workers was due to inadequate sample size, too few years of data, inadequate data on retirees, possibly a poorly chosen comparison group, and possibly a high prevalence of smoking in both populations, combined with other factors hypothesized to raise the incidence of lung cancer.

—The large sample size, many years of observation, apt control group, and care in following workers lend confidence to the Lloyd and Redmond study. Furthermore, they are able to place bounds on the

19. Ibid., p. 389.
20. Lloyd and others, "Long-Term Mortality Study of Steelworkers, V."

effects of important unmeasured factors that indicate these factors cannot be responsible for the observed effects.

—Mortality rate and job site are correlated in both studies. Lloyd and Redmond are able to develop rough dose-response relationships.

—Precise estimation of the elevation in risk is impossible due to the lack of data on cigarette smoking and other important factors.

Laboratory Studies

The carcinogenic effect of CTPV apparent in the epidemiological data is confirmed by a number of animal bioassays and in vitro tests. Since it is not possible to generate CTPV in the laboratory, in vitro and in vivo tests are performed using various constituents of CTPV. The carcinogen most often tested is benzo(a)pyrene. Suspended particulate matter (iron oxide and carbon) and sulfur dioxide have also been tested separately and in combination for synergistic effects. These may be administered by cutaneous application, intratracheal instillation, or by inhalation techniques.

From animal bioassays, it becomes clear that the various components of CTPV interact positively: for example, combinations of benzo(a)pyrene and sulfur dioxide and of benzo(a)pyrene and ferric oxide produce greater effects together than separately.[21] The significance of this result for CTPV concentrations in the vicinity of coke plants is yet unclear. (Composition of the emissions changes with time and diffusion, hence it is not known if the synergistic effects combine to create a stronger or weaker carcinogenic emission as it drifts farther from the plant.)

Integrating Laboratory and Epidemiology Studies

The laboratory and epidemiological data form a coherent picture of the effects of CTPV. Hill proposed a framework for considering such evidence to help decide whether an epidemiological association is a causal relationship.[22] While the criteria he proposed are meant to provide

21. Sidney Laskin, M. Kuschner, and T. Drew, "Studies in Pulmonary Carcinogenesis." Also, Saffioti and others produced tumors in the respiratory tract of hamsters administered mixtures of benzo(a)pyrene and ferric oxide; each chemical alone induced no tumors. U. Saffioti, F. Cefis, and L. Kobb, "A Method for the Experimental Induction of Bronchogenic Carcinoma."

22. A. B. Hill, "The Environment and Diseases: Associations and Causation."

a framework for thinking about the problem, Hill characterized them as neither necessary nor sufficient conditions.

The first criterion is the strength of the association. Lloyd and Redmond found an association of considerable strength but Reid and Buck failed to find any. This criterion is partly satisfied. The second criterion is consistency. Since there are contradictory results between the only two sets of epidemiological studies, this criterion is not satisfied. As shown above, however, the studies are of quite different quality. The third criterion is specificity. As hypothesized, the principal effect of inhaling coke oven gas is an increase in lung cancer, with increases in other cancers related to inhalation. This criterion is satisfied. The fourth criterion, temporality, is satisfied since the excess lung cancer is manifested only two or more decades after first exposure. The fifth criterion, the existence of a gradient response, is satisfied by the dose-response relationship estimated by both Mazumdar and Land (see below).

The sixth criterion is plausibility. Is the observed effect consistent with biological expectations? The demonstration that many coal tars are carcinogenic serves to satisfy this criterion. The seventh criterion is coherence. Do results from chemistry, biology, toxicology, and epidemiology present a coherent picture? Bioassay results, previous epidemiological studies of the constituent chemicals, and the Lloyd and Redmond studies appear to satisfy this criterion.

The eighth criterion concerns experimentation. The laboratory results appear to support the epidemiological results and vice versa, thus satisfying this criterion. The ninth and last criterion has to do with analogy. Do previous investigations of related disease or of this disease in other contexts support this association? Epidemiological studies of gas retort workers and cigarette smokers demonstrate a link between coal tars and lung cancer.[23] The latency period in these studies appears consistent with that demonstrated for coke oven workers.

Hill's criteria suggest that the relationship between coke oven gases and lung cancer is causal. The principal qualification is the failure of Reid and Buck to find a significant association. As discussed earlier, however, this failure appears to be due to problems with their study, in contrast to the more careful studies of Lloyd and Redmond. Thus there

23. See supporting evidence cited in the final standard promulgation (41 Fed. Reg. 46742 [1976]); Kennaway and Kennaway, "A Further Study of the Incidence of Cancer"; and Doll and others, "Mortality of Gasworkers."

is a strong case that lowering exposure to coke oven gases would result in a decrease in the incidence of lung and other cancers.

OSHA's Quantitative Risk Assessment

OSHA's attitude toward risk assessment and cost-benefit analysis has been skeptical. In the preamble to its inflationary impact statement in 1975, OSHA concluded that quantification of risk would be so arbitrary as to be meaningless.[24]

Nevertheless, when the final standard was published in October 1976, calculations by OSHA of the number of excess lung cancer deaths per year were presented, as was the risk analysis of the Council on Wage and Price Stability, which was based on OSHA data. The council's analysis concluded that the regulation would prevent between eight and thirty-six deaths a year.[25] OSHA's calculation was 240 excess lung cancer deaths a year.[26]

The method of the OSHA calculation was discussed briefly in the publication of the final standard. The population at risk and the excess mortality were calculated as follows:

$$\begin{aligned}\text{Population exposed} &= [\text{present work force}] \\ &\quad \times [\text{turnover per year}] \times 45; \\ \text{excess mortality} &= [\text{total population exposed}] \\ &\quad \times [\text{mortality rate}] \times \text{excess risk} \times 2.\end{aligned}$$

Data on the number of workers in coke plants were not readily available and had to be estimated from testimony presented during the hearings. OSHA estimated the 1976 work force in all coke plants to be 29,600. This figure, however, includes white-collar workers and other supervisory staff who were exposed to 200 milligrams per cubic meter-months or less. Mazumdar and associates found that "for all ages combined, workers having less than 200 milligrams per cubic meter-months exposure experience almost the same mortality as men who never worked in coke ovens."[27] Therefore OSHA should have used only

24. Occupational Safety and Health Administration, *Inflationary Impact: Coke Oven Emissions*, p. 7.

25. J. F. Morrall, testimony before the Occupational Safety and Health Administration, in Docket H-017A (OSHA, May 11, 1976).

26. 41 Fed. Reg. 46742 (1976).

27. Mazumdar and others, "Epidemiological Study of Exposure to Coal Tar Pitch Volatiles among Coke Oven Workers," p. 386.

the labor force employed in the coke oven operations, estimated at 22,200 in the inflationary impact statement.[28]

OSHA calculated the labor turnover rate by assuming that most workers stayed in coke plants less than five years, and that those employed more than five years worked an average of ten years, based on Redmond's finding that one-third of the workers in her cohort stayed more than five years. A value of 10 per 1,000 for the mortality rate and an excess risk of 9 percent of all causes (all worker classifications) were obtained from the Redmond epidemiological data.

OSHA also estimated that implementation of the standard would result in an increase of 4,300 workers in all job classifications, and thus an increased risk.[29] Because of market dynamics, it is uncertain whether employment actually would rise or fall. However, more important than this somewhat arbitrary assumption is that it was not used consistently; the same set of assumptions should be used in calculating both control costs and benefits. Finally, the unpublished supplement to the inflationary impact statement also addressed the question of morbidity, suggesting that "there is at least as much excess morbidity as mortality."[30] In deference to the numerous difficulties in attempting to identify and define morbidity, the statement did not attempt to quantify the reduction of morbidity to be achieved by the standard.

Critique of OSHA Methods

In reviewing the OSHA risk assessment, a number of questions arise. Were sufficient data available at the time to perform an adequate risk assessment? Did the OSHA assumptions and method of calculation produce a reliable risk assessment?

The data collected by Lloyd and Redmond and associates appear to be an adequate base. Many data are missing and further analysis is desirable, but these would refine the estimates, not make qualitative changes. If these data had been combined with other available labor statistics, a sufficient data base existed on which to make an adequate risk assessment, but it was not fully utilized. For example, OSHA could have utilized available labor statistics to measure actual labor turnover,

28. OSHA, *Inflationary Impact*, p. 27.
29. Ibid.
30. Ibid., unpublished supplement, p. 67.

rather than making assumptions. As indicated, the figure used for the population exposed was not calculated with care.

OSHA implicitly assumed that the risk to all workers in all job classifications is the same (or that workers rotated through job classifications). It would have been more helpful if the mortality rate had been tied to exposure levels. To do this would have required knowledge of the number of workers employed in various locations of the coke plant and the risk associated with each job site. The first set of data could have been obtained from participants in the hearings, and the second could have been deduced from the Redmond paper and testimony by Charles Land.

OSHA had employed Land, of the National Cancer Institute, to estimate dose-response relationships. In his testimony he presented linear and quadratic dose-response curves. To account for latency periods, lag models for zero years, five years, ten years, and fifteen years were estimated. For example, if the exposure level for workers was 0.1 milligram of CTPV per cubic meter, Land's estimated excess risk of death would be 0.001 for the quadratic model with zero lag and 0.010 for the linear model with zero lag.[31] These values of excess risk could have been applied to the workers categorized by level of exposure. An analysis by job classification is important because turnover rates are likely to differ by jobs, as are the reductions in exposure levels.

OSHA's calculation assumes that the standard will relieve all excess lung cancer deaths. The assumption is contradicted by Land's analysis, where even low concentrations of CTPV result in some excess lung cancer.

In an attempt to quantify the range of uncertainty, high and low estimates should have been obtained by using the dose-response models. (An example of this approach is the Council of Wage and Price Stability estimate of eight to thirty-six deaths.)

Choice of the final standard was based on a mix of "feasibility criteria" and a quasi risk assessment. For example, levels of 0.56 milligram per cubic meter and 0.30 milligram per cubic meter were rejected because of high excess risk,[32] as shown by the Redmond and Land analyses. The 0.15 milligram per cubic meter level was chosen because (1) it represented a decrease in excess and relative risks from the established standard of

31. Charles E. Land, "Presentation to OSHA Hearings on Coke Oven Standards."
32. 41 Fed. Reg. 46742 (1976).

Table 5-2. Estimates of Lifetime Excess Risk of Lung Cancer Mortality Due to Occupational Exposure to Coal Tar Pitch Volatiles[a]

Dose model	CTPV level (milligrams per cubic meter of air)	Linear dose-response		Quadratic dose-response	
		Excess risk	Relative risk[b]	Excess risk	Relative risk[b]
Zero lag	0.05	0.005	1.103	0.000	1.004
	0.10	0.010	1.206	0.001	1.015
	0.20	0.019	1.408	0.003	1.062
	0.30	0.029	1.608	0.007	1.138
	0.40	0.038	1.804	0.012	1.245
Five-year lag	0.05	0.005	1.113	0.000	1.005
	0.10	0.011	1.225	0.001	1.019
	0.20	0.021	1.446	0.004	1.077
	0.30	0.031	1.664	0.008	1.173
	0.40	0.041	1.878	0.014	1.306
Ten-year lag	0.05	0.006	1.132	0.000	1.006
	0.10	0.012	1.263	0.001	1.024
	0.20	0.024	1.521	0.005	1.095
	0.30	0.036	1.774	0.010	1.212
	0.40	0.048	2.021	0.018	1.375
Fifteen-year lag	0.05	0.008	1.160	0.000	1.008
	0.10	0.015	1.318	0.002	1.033
	0.20	0.029	1.628	0.006	1.131
	0.30	0.044	1.930	0.014	1.292
	0.40	0.057	2.224	0.024	1.514

Source: Adapted from Charles E. Land, "Presentation to OSHA Hearings on Coke Oven Standards," May 4, 1976, table 3.

a. Based on a hypothetical individual occupationally exposed to a constant (or average) CTPV concentration from age twenty to age sixty-five (or death).

b. Total risk of lung cancer mortality as compared with the "normal" lifetime risk of 0.0469, obtained from U.S. mortality statistics for nonwhite males. Relative risk = 1 + excess risk/0.0469.

0.20 milligram per cubic meter, based on Land's estimation (see table 5-2); and (2) more important, it was regarded as technically and economically feasible.

In conclusion, the basic data for a quantitative risk assessment were available in 1976 to OSHA. The number of lives saved per year as calculated in the inflationary impact statement was not used in support of the final rule. Land's testimony was used to support the idea that the 0.15 milligram per cubic meter standard would involve less risk of lung cancer than higher levels.

The EPA's Risk Assessment

In 1977 the EPA began a study of coke oven emissions and prepared an assessment of the health effects of coke oven emissions, a document on human population exposures to coke oven atmospheric emissions, and a summary document based on the first two. The risk assessment, prepared by the EPA's Carcinogen Assessment Group, was released on March 24, 1978.[33]

The Redmond epidemiological data and the Land estimates were relied on in the EPA risk analysis for information on dose levels (worker exposure) and mortality rates, correlated by age, job site, and length of exposure. Estimates of the number of persons exposed in the vicinity of coke plants and the ambient CTPV levels were provided by the Stanford Research Institute. Air quality measurements were made using benzene soluble organics and benzo(a)pyrene indicators of CTPV. Exposure data were collected by monitoring forty locations nationwide, including cities without coke ovens and rural areas.[34]

Data recorded in the vicinity of coke plants were analyzed to develop a general mathematical relationship of benzo(a)pyrene concentration as a function of distance from the coke plant.

The function selected was:

$$C(d) = Pd^x + B,$$

where C is the atmospheric concentration of benzo(a)pyrene, P is some fraction of the total amount of coal processed annually, B is the background exposure at the plant, and d is the distance from the plant. Least squares regression techniques were used to fit the data to this mathematical function. Estimated coefficients for x were found to range from 0.5 to 1.0. Exposures were found to be 0.04 to 1.6 nanograms per cubic meter, depending on location.

The largest source of error arises because of the small sample size available for each plant. Sampling was usually conducted for four or five days (continuously) for each plant. Changes in meteorological conditions during the sampling period introduced variations in the data. Selection

33. EPA, Carcinogen Assessment Group, "Preliminary Report on Population Risk to Ambient Coke Oven Exposures."

34. EPA, "Human Population Exposures to Coke-Ovens Emissions," p. 5.

of a sampling site in relation to the plant site could also have been a source of variation in the data.

This method permitted calculation of concentration rings around the plants. Average concentration and concentration ranges were calculated for all plants for five concentric rings of 0–0.5, 0.5–1, 1–3, and 3–15 kilometers. Actual monitoring data were available for twenty coke plants, while the general mathematical model was applied to the other plants.

Resident populations for each of the geographic rings were obtained from data taken from the 1970 census. Residents were considered to be at risk if their average annual benzo(a)pyrene exposure was 0.1 nanogram per cubic meter. The study concludes that 15 million people are exposed to levels of CTPV greater than background. The risk analysis indicated an excess of 150 deaths a year, at the then prevailing conditions.

The 66,000 people exposed to the highest concentration (6.5 micrograms per cubic meter and above) would have an excess risk of lung cancer death of 0.0033 to 0.0060. The remainder of the exposed population experienced a 0.0006 to 0.0015 excess risk (background risk = 0.0329) (see table 5-3).

The lack of epidemiological studies for the general population necessitates the use of coke oven worker data. These data are generalized to the entire population with the use of the Weibull probability model, which corresponds to an instantaneous-probability, single-hit biological model in which the risk of death is proportional to dosage raised to some power, x. The form of the Weibull model is given as

$$h(t) = Y(A + B\delta^{x})t^{Y-1},$$

where h is the risk, t is the duration of exposure, δ is the dose; and A, B, Y and x are parameters.

The values of A, B, Y and x were obtained by a nonlinear least squares analysis of the data on coke oven workers. The EPA assumed a linear no-threshold dose-response relationship ($x = 1$), although Land's least squares analysis on worker exposure suggests a value of 1.21. The assumption, which is not discussed, is that the parameters A, B, and Y obtained at workplace doses of 1 to 3 milligrams per cubic meter are applicable to population exposures of 0.004 to 0.01 milligram per cubic meter. The EPA estimates assume that the instantaneous-probability, single-hit model is precisely correct over a thousandfold range. Given the uncertainties surrounding a biological model of cancer development,

Table 5-3. Estimated Effects of Coke Oven Emissions on U.S. Population[a]

Exposure to benzene soluble organics (micrograms per cubic meter of air)[b]	*People in exposure group (thousands)*	*Lifetime probability of lung cancer*[c]	*Increase in lung cancer due to coke oven emissions*	*Number of lung cancer deaths per year due to coke oven emissions*
4.5	13,900	0.0335	6.37×10^{-4}	125.0
5.5	1,034	0.0344	1.49×10^{-3}	22.0
6.5	54	0.0362	2.33×10^{-3}	1.8
7.5	8	0.0360	3.18×10^{-3}	0.4
8.5	2	0.0369	4.02×10^{-3}	0.1
10.9	2	0.0389	6.04×10^{-3}	0.2

Source: Adapted from Environmental Protection Agency, Carcinogen Assessment Group, "Preliminary Report on Population Risk to Ambient Coke Oven Exposures" (EPA, March 1978), p. 14.

a. Estimated using the Weibull probability model.

b. Background level assumed to be 3.75 micrograms per cubic meter of air.

c. Lifetime probability 0.0329 at background exposure level.

it is understandable that the EPA based its choice of a mathematical model at least partially on the availability of input data.

Equations for excess risk of death and for life expectancy were developed from the Weibull model as functions of dose. The average years of lifespan lost for lung cancer victims were calculated to be 12.44 to 12.34 years for the highest to the lowest exposed groups (background exposure included). The calculation assumed an average lifetime of 70.96 years.

Errors of estimation are inherent, especially in inferring population exposures and expected lung cancers. For example, the EPA estimates that the standard error of the overall U.S. estimated exposure doses is 10–100 percent of actual concentration. The level of uncertainty would have been made more explicit if in table 5-3 a dose range had been used, with a resulting range of excess deaths.

Critique of EPA Methods

Assuming the accuracy of the worker risk estimates; the calculation of the population at risk; the calculation of ambient exposure levels as a function of distance from the coke plant; and the assumption of an instantaneous-effect, one-hit model for developing lung cancer from CTPV, then the calculation of 150 excess deaths a year would be accurate. How valid are these assumptions?

The major difficulties are the validity of the dose-response curve for workers and its application to the general population. The assumption of an instantaneous one-hit model is crucial. Allowing for a latency period, especially one as long as twenty-five years for coke workers, would lower the estimates markedly. It is evident that there is a latency period. Failure to account for this lag in the estimation procedure means that the EPA risk estimation is much larger than can be defended. The assumption of a linear functional form is also crucial: if effect rises more rapidly than linearly as Land estimated, the estimated population effects would be small or even zero at these low doses. Until more is learned about the mechanisms by which CTPV cause or aggravate lung cancer, the choice among models will be arbitrary; linearity is a standard, conservative assumption.

Many considerations influence whether the dose-response curve for workers is adequate for the general population. For example, the healthy worker effect suggests the incidence of lung cancer might be higher in the general population. Other reasons for believing the worker risk estimate is conservative are the intermittent nature of worker exposure and the ability to end exposure when alarming symptoms appear. A more important factor is the physical-chemical changes in coke oven emissions as they diffuse. Heavy particles fall to the ground, and chemicals are absorbed or degraded. After twenty-four hours in the atmosphere, the toxicity of coke oven emissions might be quite different.

A second section of the EPA risk assessment in which error should be examined explicitly is the calculation of ambient exposure levels. As discussed, the EPA applied a general mathematical model to each individual coke plant. The validity of this method is questionable. No plant is likely to be "average," and the model embodies none of the physical and demographic characteristics of each site. Certainly it is necessary to have some such extrapolation of data from monitored plants to plants that are not monitored. The uncertainty affects the accuracy of the parameters developed for this particular model.

The calculation of the size of the population at risk is also subject to considerable uncertainty. The accuracy of background measurements is crucial to this calculation. Benzo(a)pyrene is released into the atmosphere from coal, gas, and other fossil fuel combustion. Background concentration (that is, concentrations that would exist if there were no coke plants present) must be measured at locations far away from the plant site. The data obtained from monitored sites is of uncertain quality because of meteorological fluctuations and geographic variables.

Conclusion

Amid major controversy and uncertainty, OSHA and the EPA have produced useful analysis of the risk of exposure to coke ovens that enlighten the regulatory decision process. Nonetheless, controversies at the scientific level (for example, the shape of the dose-response relationship) and at the regulatory decision level (for example, engineering controls versus work rules and protective devices) continue to dominate the analysis. Still, the analysis has managed to narrow the range of possible effects and to dismiss many concerns as irrelevant. More sophisticated future analyses should be even more successful both in isolating the crucial issues and in exploring the implications of alternative assumptions.

CHAPTER SIX

Regulation of Ionizing Radiation

RONALD J. MARNICIO

THE TOXICITY of ionizing radiation became apparent soon after the discovery of and experimentation with radium in the 1890s. Since they took no care to shield themselves, many early workers suffered burns and developed cancerous lesions. A particularly egregious example was that of workers who painted radium on watch faces to provide luminescence; the radium they ingested while licking their paintbrush tips to form finer points often caused bone cancer. In 1927 Hermann J. Muller, a geneticist, discovered that X rays produced heritable changes in fruit flies and that the number of mutations in the exposed insects increased proportionally with the radiation dose (see appendix A for a glossary of terms). Since then the safety and protection of persons exposed to radiation has been a major concern. A chronology of events relating to radiation protection is provided in appendix B. Growing knowledge about the health effects of ionizing radiation has led to progressively more restrictive exposure standards. Moreover, the public desire to be protected against radiation has led to ever more subtle and complex examination of the potential hazards from ionizing radiation. Recent examinations have attempted to quantify explicitly the trade-offs between the costs and benefits of exposure to ionizing radiation.

The author wishes to acknowledge the contributions of the individuals whose personal communications have been cited in the footnotes to this chapter, and also the following: Indira Nair, Carnegie-Mellon University; Miller Spangler, U.S. Nuclear Regulatory Commission; Edward Radford, University of Pittsburgh; and Edward Kaplan, Brookhaven National Laboratory.

The EPA Regulation

This chapter explores the use of quantitative risk assessment by the Environmental Protection Agency in 1974–76 in support of 40 C.F.R. 190, a regulation concerning the safety and protection of individuals in the general population exposed to ionizing radiation discharged during the normal operation of nuclear power generation and support processes. The authority for this regulation stems from the Atomic Energy Act of 1954 and subsequent amendments.[1] In December 1970 Reorganization Plan No. 3 transferred the function of establishing "generally applicable environmental standards for the protection of the general environment from radioactive material" from the former Atomic Energy Commission and Federal Radiation Council to the administrator of the EPA. The reorganization plan defined these standards as "limits on radiation exposures or levels, concentrations or quantities of radioactive material outside the boundaries of locations under the control of persons possessing or using radioactive material."[2] Responsibility for the implementation and enforcement of these EPA standards lies with other agencies, however. For commercial nuclear power operations, it is vested in the Nuclear Regulatory Commission, which issues and enforces regulations and licenses individual facilities.

In October 1973 the EPA's Office of Radiation Programs produced an environmental analysis of the uranium fuel cycle.[3] The EPA published an advance notice of intent to propose environmental radiation protection standards for the uranium fuel cycle in May 1974, invited public participation in the formulation of this proposed rule, and in May 1975 proposed regulations setting forth such standards.[4] The agency received numerous written comments, and a public hearing was held in 1976.[5] Comments received at this hearing helped identify a number of areas in which the development of additional information was deemed necessary by the EPA. A supplementary analysis to the 1973 environmental analysis of the uranium fuel cycle was published by the EPA in July 1976 and on

1. 68 Stat. 919.
2. 35 Fed. Reg. 15623 (1970).
3. Environmental Protection Agency, Office of Radiation Programs, *An Environmental Analysis of the Uranium Fuel Cycle,* parts 1, 2, and 3.
4. 39 Fed. Reg. 16906 (1974); 40 Fed. Reg. 23420 (1975).
5. 41 Fed. Reg. 1124 (1976); 41 Fed. Reg. 5349 (1976).

December 28, 1976, the regulation was promulgated in final form.[6] It has not been challenged in court.

The EPA noted that before the regulation, radiation protection guidance applicable to the nuclear power industry was incomplete. The agency cited a failure to include the long-term impact on humans of long-lived radionuclides; the unacceptable practice of deriving population standards from occupational standards (generally resulting in insufficiently stringent guidelines); and a failure to balance both the cost of effluent controls and their resulting population exposures. The EPA promulgated the regulation to assure the public that an acceptable level of radiation protection would be maintained even with a major expansion of the nuclear power industry.[7]

The regulation contains a combination of exposure and emission standards. It sets a maximum annual whole-body dose from normal releases from the uranium fuel cycle and doses to other specified organs and also seeks to limit the environmental burden of long-lived radioactive materials that may accumulate by setting maximum emission levels of krypton-85, iodine-129, and other long-lived transuranics. The numerical dose and emission levels established by the regulation are shown below.[8]

Individual dose limits

Whole body	25 millirems per year
Thyroid	75 millirems per year
Other organs	25 millirems per year

Limits for long-lived radionuclides

Krypton-85	50,000 curies per gigawatt-year
Iodine-129	5 millicuries per gigawatt-year
Transuranics	0.5 millicurie per gigawatt-year

Variances are allowed at the discretion of the regulatory agency for temporary and unusual operating circumstances to ensure orderly delivery of electrical power. The effective date of the standards was 1978, except for krypton-85 and iodine-129, which become effective in 1983.

6. EPA, *Environmental Radiation Protection Requirements for Normal Operations of Activities in the Uranium Fuel Cycle;* 40 C.F.R. 190; 42 Fed. Reg. 2857 (1976).

7. EPA, *Environmental Radiation Protection Requirements,* vol. 1, p. 17.

8. "Other organs" refers to any human organ except the dermis, epidermis, or cornea and the explicitly specified thyroid. Transuranics are limited to alpha-emitters with half-lives greater than one year. EPA, *Environmental Radiation Protection Requirements,* vol. 1, p. 70.

The EPA's analysis was done with exemplary care and thought. Public fears of ionizing radiation led the EPA to conduct a careful, almost overwhelmingly comprehensive study. Where uncertainty remained, the EPA erred on the side of being conservative. However, the analysis seems to have lost sight of the objective of reducing risk at a reasonable cost; it tended to focus on areas that were analytically tractable rather than on areas that appeared most important. Various changes in the analysis could have achieved the same level of protection at much lower cost.

The Quantitative Risk Assessment

The first step in quantitative risk assessment is to identify the point of origin of each effluent and the magnitude of its emission. The second stage involves tracking the radioactive effluents through the biosphere over as wide an area and for as long a period of time as they might interact with human populations. The third stage involves determining the pathways by which the radionuclides contact people. The fourth stage involves calculating the resulting absorbed doses to the whole body and then conversion to the dose to particular tissues or organs. The final step involves applying a best estimate of the number of somatic and genetic health effects attributable to absorbed doses of radiation to critical body organs in order to obtain estimates of the number of ensuing health effects.[9]

The Uranium Fuel Cycle

The regulation defines the uranium fuel cycle as "the operations of milling of uranium ore, chemical conversion of uranium, isotopic enrichment of uranium, fabrication of uranium fuel, generation of electricity by a light-water-cooled nuclear power plant (LWR) using uranium fuel, and reprocessing of spent uranium fuel, to the extent that these directly support the production of electrical power for public use utilizing nuclear energy."[10]

The uranium milling process consists of grinding and treating uranium ore (which contains approximately 0.2 percent uranium) to produce

9. Ibid., p. 37.
10. 42 Fed. Reg. 2857 (1976).

"yellowcake," a compound containing about 85 percent uranium oxide. A uranium conversion facility purifies and converts the uranium oxide to gaseous uranium hexafluoride. The uranium enrichment plant increases the concentration of U-235 (a fissile isotope) in the uranium hexafluoride from about 0.7 percent to 2–4 percent. At the next stage in the fuel cycle the enriched uranium hexafluoride is converted back into a solid and formed into uranium fuel pellets, which are subsequently loaded into thin Zircaloy or stainless steel tubing. This tubing is then fabricated into individual fuel element bundles in the form and configuration required for a particular reactor. At the power reactor the nuclear energy in the uranium is converted into thermal energy and used to raise steam to generate electricity. After burn-up in the reactor the contents of the spent fuel rods are processed to remove radioactive waste products and reclaim valuable fissile material for reuse.[11]

Defining the Effluents

The discharge of effluents from a processing facility depends largely on the inputs. Richer or more refined resources are typically handled more efficiently, resulting in lower levels of discharge. Lower-quality inputs and feedstock generally require processing more material to obtain a given quantity of output, resulting in greater effluent releases. The composition of inputs also affects the nature of effluents and whether they appear in solid, liquid, or gaseous form.

The naturally occurring radionuclides uranium, radium, and thorium and their decay products are discharged from the prefission fuel cycle facilities for milling, conversion, enrichment, and fuel fabrication. In fission roughly thirty different radionuclides are formed that do not occur naturally. Because of their abundance and decay half-lives, however, only one or two dozen of these are generally important in postfission discharges.

The methods of plant operation also affect the levels of radioactivity that enter the environment. Assuming that effluent levels under normal operating conditions can be ascertained, a knowledge of the frequency and magnitude of foreseeable fluctuations in discharges due to process adjustment is also required.

11. Major controversy surrounds the reprocessing of spent fuel. President Carter scrapped all plans and President Reagan has revived them. Although reprocessing takes place in other countries, spent fuel is not currently reprocessed in the United States.

In sum, the ideal specification of effluents from facilities requires knowledge of the characteristics of inputs, techniques, and conditions of operation, technical plant design and incorporated cleanup features, and the composition and forms of outputs.

When the regulation was being developed, there was a paucity of effluent data. Apparently less attention was paid to the emissions of natural uranium and its daughter products from prefission support facilities than to the emissions from reactors and reprocessing facilities. The Nuclear Regulatory Commission was not then legally bound to comply with the procedural directions of the National Environmental Policy Act of 1969, which required the filing of environmental impact statements. Another consideration was that only a small number of support facilities were operating, and this meant relatively limited operating experience. Effluent data were more available for power reactors (because of their numbers) and to a lesser degree for reprocessing plants.

As a result of these deficiencies, levels and types of radioactive discharges were estimated using generic model facilities patterned largely on models developed by the Atomic Energy Commission. By necessity, great reliance was placed on the personal views and estimates of nuclear industry experts. The models were believed to be representative of real facilities, averaged over time and number.

Because power reactors outnumber any other type of facility in the uranium fuel cycle, relatively more data are available on their operation. However, due to the number of architect-engineering firms and reactor vendors in the industry, each applying its own engineering and design preferences, many component configurations have been employed. This has led to significant variability in the quantities and types of effluents. The EPA relied on effluent data from operating plants, estimates submitted to the Atomic Energy Commission plants under construction, and other cost and discharge information supplied by the commission. The resulting discharge estimates included projections for control failures and departures from optimally designed operation. Specific identification of these expected abnormalities and their frequency and magnitude was not undertaken since these occurrences were assumed to be reflected in the data.[12]

The EPA emphasized that current and past experience was not

12. Allan Richardson (EPA, Office of Radiation Programs), personal communication, August 1980.

sufficiently documented to permit an average discharge value to be adopted with confidence. It specified a number of design parameters to characterize the LWR facility so that the magnitude and composition of reactor effluents could be estimated. Among these were the process flow rates, leakage rates, partition factors involving various phase changes, and internal reactor system cleanup decontamination factors.[13] The EPA attempted to make use of generally accepted estimates of parameters reflecting operating experience. LWRs are usually located near large centers of population and display a wide variation in site layouts, local populations, and climates. In addition to these variations, there is variability in design and radionuclide production; thus the uncertainty about the model reactor emissions is large, perhaps a factor of ten or more.

Effluent Tracking

Radioactive effluents were assumed to disperse by both air and water pathways, with the resulting population exposure coming through ingestion, inhalation, and immersion and from the uptake of irradiated plants and animals in the human food chain. Discharges can be tracked from their point of origin to eventual human destinations using a variety of models that simulate the patterns of air and water dispersion to assumed populations[14] (see table 6-1). Since air-dispersed radionuclides are thought to be the principal source of human exposure, the EPA's model for estimating them will be reviewed here.

The EPA used a standard Gaussian plume model, a mathematical representation of air dispersion. Among the many physical mechanisms or constraints that can be incorporated into such air dispersion models are diffusion, overall plume rise, aerodynamic turbulence, particle size, particle settling and deposition, plume reflection at the mixing height and the ground, and the aerodynamics induced by complex terrain formations and structures projecting into the plume region. The inputs to such models can include many details of meteorology (such as wind direction as a function of altitude, thermal gradients, pressure gradients, wind fluctuation, humidity, and the physical and chemical composition of the air); the characteristics of the emitting source (such as height of

13. EPA, *An Environmental Analysis of the Uranium Fuel Cycle*, pt. 2, p. 39.

14. William Rish (Brookhaven National Laboratory), personal communication, August 1980.

Table 6-1. Population Models for Air and Water Pathways

Pathway	*Area of concern*	*Population (millions of people)*	*Biological effects*
Air	Within 80 kilometers	1.5	Somatic
		0.8	Genetic
	Within 80 kilometers	0.05	Somatic
	of mills	0.01	Genetic
Water	Within 300 kilometers	0.6	Somatic
		0.3	Genetic
	Within 300 kilometers	0.04	Somatic
	of outfall for mills	0.02	Genetic

Source: Environmental Protection Agency, *An Environmental Analysis of the Uranium Fuel Cycle*, pt. 1: *Fuel Supply* (EPA, 1973), p. A-7.

release, chemical state and composition of effluents, likelihood of their chemical or radioactive state change during dispersion, and their schedule or periodicity of release); and other boundary constraints or initial conditions (such as times or distances). Depending on the complexity of the model chosen, a subset of these inputs would have to be specified. Errant data in any of the inputs to such a model would of course handicap it from the outset.

Another factor that influences the appropriate level of complexity of a model is the cost of its use and application relative to the information it provides. Complex and sophisticated atmospheric tracking models are costly but are considered essential since air-dispersed effluents have been found to be more important than water-dispersed effluents in terms of doses to humans.[15]

The remaining consideration in model selection is the time period and spatial range over which projections are to be made. Time periods can be from one hour to one year (or more in special cases). Spatially, a model can be designed to predict concentrations over a few kilometers or a few hundred. One cannot confidently extrapolate beyond the design limits of space and time imposed by a model.

The goal of the EPA's atmospheric modeling exercises and this stage of the quantitative risk assessment is to determine the concentration of radioactivity in the air to the most exposed person and to an average

15. EPA, *Environmental Radiation Protection Requirements*, vol. 1, p. 66; and Reginald Gotchy (Nuclear Regulatory Commission), personal communication, August 1980.

person in the population as a function of the magnitude of the source term. To do this a quantity called the meteorological dispersion factor, χ/Q, was developed as an average across sites (see equation below).

Two distances are generally important to atmospheric modeling calculations. The first is the distance from the source (the plant's stack) to the plant boundary, the point where the maximum ambient concentrations, and hence the maximum individual doses, are likely to be encountered. After examining facilities in operation, the EPA assumed that this distance was between 0.5 kilometer and 1.5 kilometers. The second important distance is the radius to the system boundary that defined and conceptually limited the population exposed to a particular source. The EPA chose this distance to be eighty kilometers because it was large enough to include nearby large population centers, yet small enough to be considered a local area. This distance was also believed to be the limiting range for reliable results from the diffusion equations used to characterize the effluent's dispersion.[16]

The basic diffusion equation used is as follows:[17]

$$\frac{\chi}{Q} = \left(\frac{2}{\pi}\right)^{1/2} \frac{f \exp(-h^2/2\sigma_z^2) \exp(-\lambda t)}{\bar{u}\sigma_z 2\pi r/n},$$

where

χ = ground-level airborne concentration in curies per cubic meter;
Q = source release rate in curies per second;
f = fractional wind frequency in a sector;
r = distance from the stack in meters;
h = effective stack height in meters;
n = number of sectors;
$2\pi r/n$ = sector width at distance r in meters;
σ_z = standard deviation of the vertical distribution of an assumed Gaussian cloud, in meters;
$\bar{u}$ = average wind speed in the sector in meters per second;
λ = decay constant of radionuclide in inverse seconds;
t = transit time from the stack to distance r, in seconds ($t = r/\bar{u}$).

This equation was solved repeatedly for each radionuclide and meteorological stability classification for the downwind distances of interest.

The utility of the meteorological dispersion factor is that the atmospheric radioactivity concentration at any specified distance from a source within a given sector can be calculated by multiplying the source strength, Q, by the value of χ/Q for that distance in that sector. To predict the maximum radioactivity concentration to which the general population would be exposed, a value for χ/Q at the boundary had to be estimated. A ten-meter stack height and a mixing height appropriate to the meteorological stability were assumed. Based on the data for roughly fifty reactor sites, χ/Q values for river, lakeshore, and seashore facility locations were estimated for each of the three assumed stack-to-boundary distances (that is, 0.5 kilometer, 1.0 kilometer, or 1.5 kilometers). The arithmetic average of these nine values was taken to be χ/Q. The parameter required to determine the maximum individual exposure, χ/Q max, was taken to be twice χ/Q to approximate χ/Q for the sector with the maximum concentrations. The standard deviation was roughly estimated to be one-sixth the range of the values. Hence the value for χ/Q max for all fuel supply facilities (not only the LWRs on which they were based) was taken to be $(6 \pm 4) \times 10^{-6}$ seconds per cubic meter.[18] The concentration in picocuries per cubic meter at the model facility boundaries could then be calculated by multiplying that site's effluent output rate (in picocuries per second) by χ/Q max.

Since the average annual radiation concentration to which the general population is exposed is also of interest, a method for estimating this quantity was developed using a ratio of the average concentration of radioactivity within eighty kilometers of the plant to the maximum concentration at the plant boundary. Using the diffusion equation given earlier in conjunction with the population distribution and meteorological characteristics for fifty reactor sites, an average value of this ratio was calculated to be 2.3×10^{-4}. This value was also adopted for each type of uranium fuel supply facility.[19] Thus to estimate the average concentration of radioactivity within the eighty-kilometer radius of a facility, the facility's total emissions would be multiplied by χ/Q max and then by 2.3×10^{-4}.

18. Ibid., pt. 1, p. A-2.
19. Ibid., pt. 1, p. A-4.

The criteria for evaluating air dispersion models have not been universally agreed upon. One criterion is the degree of agreement between the model's projections and actual measured effluent concentrations. Another theory contends that comparable concentrations do not provide an adequate measure of the performance of a model since compensating errors could yield the "right" answer, masking flaws in the theory or inputs. Thus interim calculations of the model would have to be verified along with final predictions. Another criterion, termed "verification by parts," requires that each step of the model's performance be measured against real world conditions. A third important check is to compare model parameters and input data to recent independent measurements. Thus, to be considered accurate, the model must be tested by contextual use.[20] At present the only formal attempts at verification compare predicted and observed concentrations at various locations. Better model verification is a growing concern in the field and many recognize the need for estimating confidence intervals for predicted concentrations, especially in regulatory applications.[21]

These models lack a high degree of accuracy. For example, the Gaussian models predict only to within a factor of two or three of observations under simple conditions. For complex terrains and climatological settings, model results are often not within a factor of ten of measured values.[22]

Pathway Transfer to Humans

The next stage in the quantitative risk analysis involves determining the nature of human radioactivity intake as a function of radioactivity concentrations present in the air and water environment. Effluents can result in external exposure or enter the body and cause internal doses via a number of pathways.

Airborne effluents can cause doses in four ways: whole-body exposure, inhalation and transpiration through the skin, transferral of deposited radionuclides from the soil into vegetables and fruit consumed by

20. D. Bruce Turner, *Workbook of Atmospheric Dispersion Estimates*.

21. Ibid.; Frederick C. Hamburg, "Atmospheric Dispérsion Modeling"; and J. D. Spengler, "Atmospheric Dispersion Modeling."

22. V. A. Mirabella, "Atmospheric Dispersion Modeling."

people, and similar uptake by plants later eaten by animals that provide meat and milk for human consumption.

Waterborne effluents can result in radiation doses to humans through the ingestion of contaminated drinking water or contaminated aquatic or marine life and submersion in and exposure to contaminated waters (such as during fishing, boating, or swimming). The pathway transfer factors depend on a variety of parameters, including dietary and recreational habits of the population, biological mechanisms at work in both plants and animals, physical mechanisms of transmission and deposition, and the temporal patterns of radioactivity transferral and decay. A discussion of one air pathway transfer factor, that for whole-body exposure, follows as an example.

WHOLE-BODY EXPOSURE FROM PLUME AND DEPOSITED RADIONUCLIDES. For dose calculations, the plume of dispersed effluents is modeled as a photon-emitting cloud positioned in three-dimensional space with a human as a point collector on the ground. Using geometrical considerations and accounting for transmission attenuation and scattering in the air, the flux of photons of each energy level reaching the receptor from each point in the plume can be ascertained. By performing this projection and summing for each photon energy level and plume configuration possibility (in the proper proportions as determined by observed frequency), the total radiation dose from the plume can be estimated. Calculations of this type are performed on computers with standard programs.

To calculate doses from radionuclides deposited on the ground's surface, it is assumed they create a "radioactive sheet," which emits a flux of radioactivity to a receptor located on the ground. The projection method used is similar to that for the overhead plume, except that the source of radioactivity here is modeled as a flat plane rather than a three-dimensional cloud. Projecting particle settling downwind of the source gives an estimate of the accumulated deposit of radioactive material on the ground. However, a variety of factors such as rain or snow wash-off, wind, and plant growth can cause deposition inhomogeneities and generate effects that cannot be accounted for in the simple model.

The EPA did a painstaking job of identifying and estimating the extent to which radioactivity in the air and water come into contact with people. Fortunately only a few pathways contribute significantly to general population doses.

Dose Conversion

The next stage of the quantitative risk analysis involves the dose conversion factors relating absorbed internal or whole-body doses to absorbed doses to particular organs, biologically weighted for carcinogenic effectiveness. This single parameter embodies a great many biophysical mechanisms, including (1) the mechanism by which radionuclides penetrate the body and migrate to and concentrate in the body's tissues; (2) the metabolic mechanisms of organs relative to the radionuclides for which they have an affinity; (3) the body's clearance mechanisms that remove foreign substances; (4) the irradiation distribution of cells within an organ; and (5) the effect of radiation quality and varying cell sensitivities on the carcinogenicity of doses.

Radiation is fairly uniformly distributed throughout the body in the case of whole-body exposure and is initially deposited in the respiratory or digestive tract in the case of internal doses. In the latter case, chemical-biological activity allows some fraction of the radionuclides to be transferred into the bloodstream and circulated to other organs where they are absorbed and accumulated. Another fraction of the radionuclides will be removed from the body via clearance mechanisms, such as sneezing, exhaling, or defecation. The remaining radioactivity may become lodged in a certain site or migrate within an organ for some period of time before absorption or excretion.

The estimation of dose conversion factors is basically an exercise in input-output bookkeeping for a particular site, which accounts for a number of physical and biological transfer processes.[23] The dose conversion factor is characterized by the type of radionuclide, its intake and migratory modes, its target organ(s), and the organ's self-radiation and radiation effects to other proximate organs. Knowledge of the biological mechanisms involved has come primarily from studies done with animals, although a small amount of human experience has been gained through follow-ups on people exposed to inadvertent doses.[24] Information on some radionuclides has been fairly well established, while estimates for others are still under revision.

A complete discussion of the biophysical process involved in each

23. J. Nagy (Brookhaven Laboratories), personal communication, August 1980.

24. N. Wald (Graduate School of Public Health, University of Pittsburgh), personal communication, August 1980.

possible radionuclide-organ deposition pair would fill volumes. Shown below are radionuclide-organ pairs that have been found to be of greatest importance in uranium fuel cycle analyses.[25]

Effluent	*Principal critical organ*
Noble gases	Whole body
Radioiodine	Thyroid
Tritium	Whole body
Carbon-14	Whole body
Cesium and other metals in liquids	Whole body, gastro-intestinal tract
Plutonium and other transuranics	Lung
Uranium and daughter products	Lung, bone
Gamma and neutron radiation	Whole body

LUNG DOSE CONVERSION FACTORS. To provide some perspective of the level of complexity and uncertainty involved in the determination of dose conversion factors, a description of the considerations and mechanisms in the case of the lung may be helpful. The lung dose conversion factor is applied sequentially after the inhalation pathway transfer factor, which quantifies the amount of radioactivity of a certain type entering the lungs per unit of time. The chemical and physical form of the inhaled radionuclides influences the eventual resting place of particles. Radionuclides inhaled in a soluble form dissolve in the lungs' moisture, causing a diffuse dose to the peripheral lung,[26] or they are absorbed into the bloodstream, finally setting in the blood-forming regions of the bones. Radionuclides inhaled in an insoluble form typically undergo no chemical changes. These particles stay where they are initially deposited or where they are moved to by the lungs' clearance mechanisms.

Particles so large that they cannot negotiate the many turns in the airway's branching network become trapped in the mucous lining and are removed by the ciliary escalator clearance mechanism. Some particles are so small they rarely touch any surface and are eventually

25. EPA, *Environmental Radiation Protection Requirements,* vol. 1, p. 36.

26. A. R. Kennedy and J. B. Little, "Radiation Carcinogenesis in the Respiratory Tract," p. 209.

exhaled. An intermediate size range of radionuclides can enter and remain in the lung, causing problems.

The particles that elude the lungs' primary filtering system are deposited on the walls of some part of the respiratory tract. Much of the radioactivity deposited in the lower lung is carried to the upper lung and then to the throat, where the transporting mucus is either swallowed or rejected. The process is fairly rapid, estimated to take less than twenty-four hours in humans.[27] Most deposited radionuclides are constantly in motion and their energy release can be distributed over many regions of the lung. Radionuclides with long half-lives (much longer than one day) may be cleared from the lungs before much energy has been released, or their doses will be delivered to regions of the lung far from their point of deposition. Thus initial deposition and temporal clearance and migratory patterns in the lung must all be modeled.

The quality of radiation emitted from the inhaled radionuclide influences dose distributions within the lung. The quality is a fundamental characteristic specified by comparative levels of particles' linear energy transfer (LET).[28] High-intensity, high-LET radiation results in intense exposure to cells in the immediate vicinity of the deposited particle. A few cell diameters away, however, cells may receive no exposure at all. This occurrence has come to be called the "hot particle" phenomenon and there has been much controversy over whether hot particles are more carcinogenic than diffuse radiation. The current consensus is that hot spots are not more carcinogenic than more uniformly distributed doses, and the concept that radiation is "wasted" in "cell overkill" or that hot spots do not generate such concentrated doses has been proposed to support this observation.[29]

27. Ibid.

28. LET is a measure of the amount of energy lost by a particle per unit of distance traveled through the absorbing material. Low-LET ionizing radiation produces ionizing events that generally are not close together in space or time. It is responsible for most of the absorbed doses received by the general population. Alpha radiation from internally deposited radionuclides is the most important directly ionizing high-LET radiation. Neutron radiation, producing recoil protons, has been found to be the principal form of indirectly ionizing high-LET radiation. Low-energy electrons, produced by directly or indirectly ionizing radiation, can have any level of LET. (National Academy of Sciences, Advisory Committee on the Biological Effects of Ionizing Radiation, *The Effects on Populations of Exposure to Low Levels of Ionizing Radiation* [1980].)

29. Kennedy and Little, "Radiation Carcinogenesis in the Respiratory Tract," p. 220; and J. H. Diel, "Local Doses to Lung Tissue from Inhaled $^{238}PuO_2$ Particles," p. 367.

Low-intensity, low-LET radiation has a greater range of penetration in tissues. This radiation generally has sufficient range and energy to irradiate the whole lung regardless of where it is initiated. Thus low-intensity radiation from radionuclides results in more uniform doses to the peripheral and upper airway regions of the lung.

In summary, inhaled radionuclides can have a variety of effects once inside the lung. Some fraction of them is cleared from the lung while another fraction is passed on to other parts of the body through the blood. The fraction that remains can be deposited in varying parts of the lung depending on the chemical and physical characteristics of the particles. Radionuclides, having been deposited in the lung, are not generally stationary and tend to migrate upward. The doses imparted by these particles depend in part on this migratory behavior and on the nature of the radiation emitted from them.

Health Effect Coefficients

BASIC CONCEPTS IN RADIATION CARCINOGENESIS. Ionizing radiation can alter the molecular structure of cells. These alterations can be amplified by biochemical and biological processes and result in clinically observable effects. The probability of these developments depends not only on the total absorbed dose of ionizing radiation but also on the ionization density, or quality of the radiation.

Ionizing radiation has been found to interact with absorbing matter along more or less straight tracks or trajectories, but the deposition of energy is not uniform. Irradiation of the nuclei of cells in the human body, which are the loci believed to be most affected by ionizing radiation at low doses, results in greatly varying quantities of absorbed energy to specific nuclei sites.

The finding that certain kinds of radiation produce more effects than others at equal doses led to attempts to quantify the differences, expressed as relative biological effectiveness (RBE). One kind of radiation is usually compared with another chosen as a standard (typically X rays or gamma rays); the RBE is defined as the ratio of the doses of the standard radiation to the specified radiation producing the same biological effect, when all other conditions are similar. This condition dictates that the varied biological and physiological mechanisms must respond in the same way at varying doses and dose rates. The lack of understanding concerning these mechanisms precludes any verification or controlling for these many factors. The RBE is an imprecise characterization of the ability of a specific particle or energy level to produce a specific disorder. The RBE of low-LET radiation is generally considered to be one; the RBE of high-LET radiation is greater.[30]

The link between energy transfer to the cells and the induction of malignant transformations and ensuing health effects is not precisely known. A controversial theory is the dual radiation action theory,[31] which provides a framework in which to consider how radiation causes cancer.[32] Essentially it is postulated that sublesions are produced within cells at a rate proportional to the energy deposited, and a biological effect results if two sublesions are produced close enough in both time and space. The double-strand DNA molecule is thought to be the critical site of radiation-induced damage. Since other chemical and environmental agents may produce sublesions either before or after cellular irradiation, it is thought that a single radiation event could be sufficient to produce a biological effect. In addition, factors such as age and hormones and habits such as smoking could modify the effect of radiation on cells. Carcinogenesis is a complex process, and cell transformation alone does not necessarily result in a cancer.

After irradiation, a latency period is experienced, followed by the period of expression (when biological effects are manifested), and then by a postexpression period after which the effect subsides. More is known about the duration of the expression period than about the postexpression period.[33] Factors affecting the expression and inhibition of cellular effects are also important for their influence on the shape of dose-response curves. This then confounds the estimation of radiation risk. It should be emphasized that different cancers in different organisms exhibit different dose-response relationships. Nevertheless, theoretical considerations of this sort suggest that the basic mechanisms of cell damage that give rise to cancer, chromosome aberrations, cell death, and point mutations are proportional to the first and second power of the amount of energy deposited in cells.[34]

There is little theoretical justification for the selection of a dose-

30. John D. Boice and Charles E. Land, "Ionizing Radiation," p. 246.

31. A. M. Kellerer and H. H. Rossi, "A Generalized Formulation of Dual Radiation Action."

32. Boice and Land, "Ionizing Radiation," p. 246.

33. G. W. Beebe, "What Is Considered Certain Regarding Human Somatic Effects of Ionizing Radiation?"

34. Boice and Land, "Ionizing Radiation," p. 247.

response model, and no body of human data is adequate to determine the shape of the dose-response function with certainty. This function is instead estimated as a family of curves. At low doses the resulting estimates are lowest for a pure quadratic expression and highest for an expression purely linear in dose. The "best estimate" relationship contains contributions from both the dose and dose-squared terms.[35] The pure linear model is generally adopted for radiation protection purposes because it is believed to be generally conservative.[36] The pure linear model was supported by the National Academy of Sciences Advisory Committee on the Biological Effects of Ionizing Radiation in 1972 and was adopted by the EPA for application in the analysis for the regulation. However, another NAS committee supported a linear-quadratic model in 1980 after prolonged acrimonious debate.

For specified forms of cancer and types of radiation, there are practical thresholds below which the effect cannot be observed clinically. In general, however, nothing indicates that thresholds limit the carcinogenic response to ionizing radiation. The no-threshold assumption has come to be adopted for estimates of radiation risk, although the assumption cannot be proved or disproved without knowing the mechanisms by which radiation induces cancer.[37]

Researchers have expended significant time and effort to identify and characterize the types of uncertainties associated with the causation and incidence of cancer. Dose rate, for example, has been found to influence the effectiveness of a given radiation dose in causing adverse health effects in animal studies. The manner of this influence appears to depend on the type of radiation exposure. Low-LET radiation delivered at low dose rates does less biological damage per unit of absorbed dose than low-LET radiation delivered at high dose rates. It is hypothesized that this is due to the opportunity for repair of cell injury before a second hit, or a lower resulting probability of two or more sublesions; this explanation is offered by proponents of the dual radiation theory.[38] For high-intensity, high-LET radiation, the effects of dose rate appear to be more complex and less conclusive, even in laboratory settings. Studies have

35. BEIR, *The Effects on Populations of Exposure to Low Levels of Ionizing Radiation* (1980).

36. Beebe, "What Is Considered Certain Regarding Human Somatic Effects of Ionizing Radiation?"

37. Ibid.

38. BEIR, *The Effects on Populations of Exposure to Low Levels of Ionizing Radiation* (1972).

typically found the effectiveness of high-LET radiation to be insensitive to dose rate,[39] while others have warned against drawing any conclusion due to confounding and masking influences.[40] It is thought that the RBE of high-LET radiation may increase at low doses.

Dose fractionation can have an impact on the effectiveness of specified levels of exposure in causing adverse health effects.[41] The direction of the effect appears to depend on the intensity of radiation. For low-LET radiation, the effectiveness of a given dose appears to decrease with fractionation and long protraction.[42] This observation is consistent with the theories postulating that biological mending and repair of the damage caused by sparsely ionizing radiation is possible when sufficient time is available between successive ionizing events. The available human data is inconclusive, but considered by some to be "strongly suggestive."[43] High-LET radiation has shown an increased effectiveness with dose fractionation.[44] Reasons offered for this observation include increased numbers of irradiated cells, less killing of "premalignant" cells, prolonged stimulus for cell division, and little repair of the more extensive local damage.[45]

An important consequence of radiation accounting for the symptoms of large doses of whole-body irradiation is the suppression of cell division.[46] The ultimate biological effects of cell killing and suppression of cell division depend markedly on the fraction of cells affected. At low radiation doses only a small fraction of the cells undergoing division may be damaged, and this damage may lead to no detectable change in the function of the tissue. In tissues with rapid cell turnover, normal function will be impaired only when the affected cells make up a large fraction of those available for replenishment of cell stores. Thus these effects are

39. Ibid.

40. Boice and Land, "Ionizing Radiation," p. 247.

41. Fractionating or protracting a specified dose of radiation is dividing that total dose into a series of smaller doses of the same cumulative magnitude and spreading them out over some period of exposure at regular or irregular intervals. Fractionation of radiation exposure is generally contrasted with one-shot, acute irradiation of the same total dose.

42. BEIR, *The Effects on Populations of Exposure to Low Levels of Ionizing Radiation* (1980); United Nations Scientific Committee on the Effects of Atomic Radiation, *Sources and Effects of Ionizing Radiation*.

43. C. W. Mays, H. Spiess, and A. Gerapach, "Skeletal Effects Following Ra-224 Injections into Humans."

44. UNSCEAR, *Sources and Effects of Ionizing Radiation*.

45. Mays, Spiess, and Gerapach, "Skeletal Effects."

46. N. Wald, "Radiation Injury."

generally attributed to high doses of radiation, where more damage is expected. However, the low-dose irradiation of a developing fetus, especially during organogenesis early in pregnancy, may be quite damaging since normal development may depend on the integrity of relatively few cells from which tissues will develop.[47]

Host factors, namely the biological and environmental characteristics of individuals, can also modify the risk of radiogenic cancer in humans. Some factors that influence risk are immune competence, hormonal status, capacity for DNA repair, genetic composition, age (probably the most important factor), sex, and ethnic background.[48] The importance of environmental risk factors in radiation carcinogenesis lies in the possibility of positive interaction, where the combined effect of radiation and the other risk factors exceeds the sum of the effects that each would be expected to exert independently. For example, synergistic effects between irradiation and cigarette smoking have been observed in studies of lung cancer development in uranium miners.[49] A strong interaction between asbestos and cigarette smoking has also been found.

UNCERTAINTIES INHERENT IN EPIDEMIOLOGICAL STUDIES. Detection and attribution of the incidence of radiogenic cancer is a complex task. One major reason is that a cancer caused by ionizing radiation is no different from a cancer caused by other environmental agents. Thus even though the existence of a causal connection between radiation exposure and cancer risk is no longer in dispute, there is still uncertainty in the attribution of a particular effect to irradiation, other agents, or natural causes. As a result, incidences of excess cancers due to irradiation must be enumerated statistically. A necessary dependence on relatively imprecise statistical methods has created a number of associated difficulties and opportunities for bias that can influence estimates.

The power of a statistical sample is a measure of its ability to identify abnormal effects as statistically significant. The sample size required to identify an increase in the incidence of a certain cancer depends on the natural or background incidence rate of that cancer type. Since lower doses translate to fewer cases of cancers, large sample sizes are required to find statistically significant effects at low doses. The importance of

47. BEIR, *The Effects on Populations of Exposure to Low Levels of Ionizing Radiation* (1980).

48. Beebe, "What Is Considered Certain Regarding Human Somatic Effects of Ionizing Radiation?"

49. Kennedy and Little, "Radiation Carcinogenesis in the Respiratory Tract," p. 234.

sample size on the significance of results was emphasized by Land, who estimated that a sample of 10 million people would be needed to test the effects of a one-rad exposure.[50]

In assessing the somatic effects of ionizing radiation, the approach adopted by most experts is to place primary emphasis on studies of exposed human populations. In contrast, estimates of the risks of hereditary effects on humans have been based primarily on evidence from animal experiments. This approach reflects the difficulty of obtaining firm evidence of hereditary changes in human populations exposed to ionizing radiation or any other environmental agent. Some human data have been obtained concerning somatic abnormalities induced in utero by ionizing radiation, but animal data are still heavily relied upon.[51]

It is well recognized in the field of environmental toxicology that results obtained in animal experiments are not necessarily directly translatable to humans. The kinds of human studies that have been done vary greatly but can be classified on the basis of the source of radiation as follows: (1) accidental/disaster, (2) therapeutic, (3) occupational, and (4) diagnostic.[52] Problems associated with all four classifications of studies have led to the softening of conclusions and increased uncertainties.

Atomic bomb survivor studies (accidental/disaster) are atypical in that the exposed populations (the inhabitants of Hiroshima and Nagasaki) were unusually large and encompassed a wide range of doses. The type of irradiation experienced by the inhabitants may have been different for the two cities. Original estimates indicated that the survivors in Nagasaki received radiation that was about 99 percent low-LET and 1 percent high-LET neutrons, whereas the dose received at Hiroshima consisted of approximately 80 percent low-LET and 20 percent high-LET radiation. These figures are currently being reexamined.[53] For the

50. Charles E. Land, "Estimating Cancer Risks from Low Doses of Ionizing Radiation," p. 1197.

51. BEIR, *The Effects on Populations of Exposure to Low Levels of Ionizing Radiation* (1980).

52. Carnegie-Mellon University, Department of Engineering and Public Policy, School of Urban and Public Affairs, "Selected Strategies for Reducing Risks from Diagnostic X-Radiation."

53. These estimates are currently being challenged by new evidence indicating that the doses in both cities were due primarily to low-LET radiation. See appendix B; Eliot Marshall, "New A-Bomb Data Shown to Radiation Experts"; Edward Radford, "Radiation Dosimetry"; and W. E. Loewe and E. Mendelsohn, "Revised Dose Estimates at Hiroshima and Nagasaki."

task of estimating low-dose, low-LET radiation risks, the high-LET component of the Hiroshima dose has confounded the process. Attempts have been made to account for this difference by applying RBE factors, but it is not yet agreed whether the RBE should be fixed at a particular value or vary with dose. These efforts have been made to "salvage" the data since the Hiroshima group was so large. The Nagasaki group, however, had relatively pure low-LET radiation but was smaller in number; hence these data possess relatively less statistical power. The data have additional bias in that the Japanese people have been found to react differently to radiation than other ethnic or racial groups. Moreover, survivor study results are implicitly based on high-dose and partial-body exposure, while estimates are sought for low-dose, whole-body exposure. The definition of a control group was also necessarily uncertain, especially for Nagasaki. Because the conditions of exposure were far from those found in laboratories, the estimation of doses to all the individuals was a difficult task. The primary consideration was radial distances from the detonation center, but the effects of body position and shielding by structures and terrain had to be accounted for. Because the survivor studies were done retrospectively, as were most other human studies, dose determination was a significant problem.[54]

Therapeutic studies are plagued by the generic problems of exact dose determination, control group identification, and insufficient sample size. Furthermore, medical exposures of this type may occur because of a cancer or related factor, rather than the other way around.[55] The influence of the disease being treated and other host factors on the effects of radiation are often uncertain.

Occupational exposure studies are potentially useful in that they generally involve low-dose, low-LET radiation. A common problem is that occupational groups are rarely representative of the population as a whole. This relative lack of heterogeneity could bias resulting risk estimates.[56] Workers may also be exposed to other workplace environmental factors that could mask effects and bias the estimates. Sample size generally is also a problem.

54. J. I. Fabrikant (Donner Laboratory, University of California, Berkeley), personal communication, August 1980.

55. Boice and Land, "Ionizing Radiation," pp. 238–39.

56. BEIR, *The Effects on Populations of Exposure to Low Levels of Ionizing Radiation* (1980), p. 34.

Diagnostic exposure studies also typically involve low-dose, low-LET radiation. Nonetheless, the problems of dose estimation, sample size, and the confounding effects of the suspected disease are again potentially significant.

A concern common to all classifications of studies is the length of the latency period for the manifestation of cancer relative to the length of follow-up time available for the sample population being studied. The maximum amount of information from an epidemiological study of this kind is not obtained until all the members of the sample have died. Even then, the full effects of cancer may not have been recognized.[57] Average latency periods for the various types of cancers range from around two years to approximately twenty to twenty-five years, vary between individuals for a given cancer type, and are influenced by such host factors as age at exposure. Studies in the early stages of follow-up cannot distinguish between a person who will not develop a cancer and one who will. Older exposed persons may die of other causes before the end of the latency period. Insufficient consideration of latency may lead to insufficient follow-up time and result in underestimates of risk. Human studies must generally span four decades from the time of exposure to provide meaningful radiation data.

While bias is a problem with most studies, a given bias tends not to apply universally to all studies of a single cancer type. Thus consistency of results among studies involving populations irradiated under different circumstances is the best and strongest argument that reported radiation-related risks are real.[58]

EPA HEALTH EFFECT COEFFICIENTS. The health effect coefficients used by the EPA in the risk analysis for the regulation were derived using assumptions consistent with the 1972 report of the National Academy of Sciences Advisory Committee on the Biological Effects of Ionizing Radiation (BEIR-I).[59] The health risk coefficients presented by BEIR-I and used by the EPA were based on a linear dose-response relationship with the added assumption of no dose threshold. The EPA analysis further assumed that health effects observed at high dose rates are indicative of radiation effects at low dose rates. The EPA believed the

57. Fabrikant, personal communication.

58. Boice and Land, "Ionizing Radiation," p. 249.

59. BEIR, *The Effects on Populations of Exposure to Low Levels of Ionizing Radiation* (1972).

BEIR-I health risk estimates to represent upper limits of risk, insofar as any biological repair of the radiation damage from low-dose radiation was neglected.

As the EPA noted and the BEIR-I report pointed out, a nonthreshold linear dose-response relationship hypothesis is not in itself sufficient for the prediction of health risk. It is also necessary to assume that all members of the exposed population have equal sensitivity to the radiation insult so that the expression of health risk is independent of how individual exposures are distributed. This requirement is never wholly satisfied, but the EPA noted two considerations that might tend to validate the application of the available mortality data to a consideration of health effects from uranium fuel cycle operations.

Some of the data used in the derivation of the BEIR-I estimates were taken from the atomic bomb survivors of the cities of Hiroshima and Nagasaki. Thus to a limited extent these data reflect the exposure of a relatively heterogeneous population. The EPA considered that even though the number of health effects would depend on the exact makeup of the population at risk, the relative order of importance of the various pathways of exposure would not be very sensitive to the particular population characteristics near a fuel cycle facility. The EPA also pointed out that the health risk estimates used in the regulation assumed that the expected radiation effects were independent of other environmental stresses or host factors that may have been unique either to the populations surrounding uranium fuel cycle facilities or to the exposed groups considered in the BEIR-I report.[60] Depending on the details of the risk model used, the BEIR-I Committee's relative risk estimate was 160–450 annual deaths per million person-rems. From this it can be seen that the precision of these estimates is at best a factor of two or three, even when applied to sample populations studied on the basis of the same dose rates. The application of the BEIR-I risk estimates to exposures at lower dose rates and to population groups more heterogeneous than those studied further increases the uncertainty in the risk estimate.[61]

The BEIR-I report calculated the cancer mortality risk (including leukemia from whole-body radiation) by two quite different models. The absolute risk model predicted about 100 cancer deaths per million person-rems, while the relative risk model predicted 160–450 fatalities. Using

60. EPA, *Environmental Analysis of the Uranium Fuel Cycle*, pt. 2.
61. Ibid.

BEIR-I recommendations, the EPA adopted a coefficient for total cancer risk of 400 cancers per million person-rem exposure.

The range of risk estimates for genetic effects set forth in the BEIR-I report was so large that the EPA believed that such risks were better considered on a relative basis for different exposure situations rather than in terms of absolute numbers. The range of uncertainty was tenfold in the dose required to double the natural mutation rate; additional uncertainties in the fraction of currently observed genetic effects due to background radiation and the fraction of deleterious mutations eliminated per generation lead to an overall uncertainty of a factor of about twenty-five.[62] To arrive at a genetic risk health effect coefficient, the EPA took a geometric average of the 60–1,500 range offered by BEIR-I, yielding 300 effects per year for a gonadal dose of a million person-rems per year. This coefficient was considered to be applicable only for persons up to thirty years of age.

The EPA went on to consider coefficients for exposure to the lung, thyroid, skin, and other organs. The results and uncertainties are similar to those described above.

The Environmental Dose Commitment

The release of radioactive material from a uranium fuel supply facility causes an immediate radiation dose to members of the general population in the vicinity of the facility. This dose is delivered when the radioactive effluents, moving quickly through the air and water pathways, are taken up by individuals at the time the effluents are released. Health effects resulting from these doses of radiation were estimated using quantitative risk assessment in the manner just described.

The same radioactive material upon release to the biosphere may, over longer periods of time, find its way back to humans through slow secondary pathways such as resuspension inhalation and food chains. These exposures can cause additional radiation doses and health effects. Although the dose rates of these secondary pathways are usually small, the number of people exposed may be large. Because of the linear nonthreshold health effects model employed, the number of predicted health effects can become significant.

The determination of doses committed by the release of a radioactive

62. Ibid.

material to the environment involves a multitude of factors. The environmental dose commitment, however, is particularly dependent on the radioactive half-life of the nuclide under consideration, since this will determine the nuclide's availability for widespread dispersion in the environment and the total number of persons potentially exposed over space and time. For short-lived radionuclides the environmental dose commitment (EDC) would theoretically consist only of the short-term exposure of a limited population group. There would effectively be no environmental buildup of these radionuclides since the actual amount available at any time would represent a balance between incremental additions and incremental removals by radioactive decay, producing an equilibrium achievable in a short span of time.

For long-lived radionuclides, such an equilibrium condition would not be reached for many generations. These radionuclides continue to accumulate in the environment and, even if all further additions were halted, would persist for extended time spans as a potential source of cumulative exposures to successive generations. For some radionuclides this time period may be of the order of thousands or millions of years. Theoretically their total impact would have to be evaluated over the entire time period. In practice, however, it is difficult if not impossible to make predictions over such extremely long time periods. For the EPA analysis an arbitrary cutoff time of 100 years was chosen. This time span includes very nearly the entire potential impact of radionuclides with half-lives of up to about ten years, such as tritium and krypton-85, and provides at least some evaluation of the impact of the much longer-lived radionuclides such as plutonium-239 and iodine-129.[63]

The first attempt by the EPA to calculate the cumulative radiation dose and health effects resulting from a single year's releases of radioactive effluents was the 100-year environmental dose commitment study. The effect of thirty years of facility operations was obtained by summing the 100-year EDC for each year. These resulting health effects are predicted in addition to the effects that occur from the exposure to, or immediate uptake of, radioactive effluents by people during the year of release.[64]

The potential health impacts resulting from the 100-year EDC were evaluated for all the major radionuclides associated with discharges from

63. EPA, Office of Radiation Programs, *Environmental Radiation Dose Commitment: An Application to the Nuclear Power Industry*.

64. Ibid.

the uranium fuel cycle. Although some calculational specifics varied for the various radionuclides, the logic of the EDC evaluation was similar for all radionuclides.

THE URANIUM EDC EVALUATION. The uranium EDC evaluation will be discussed briefly to provide some perspective on the EDC determination process and the nature of assumptions employed. The total emissions were identical to those used in the immediate dose calculations. Natural uranium was assumed to have been released from the model facilities of the fuel cycle in liquids and washed into the ocean or deposited in the silt along the riverbed. It was assumed that these locations could absorb all uranium releases. Hence liquid releases were assumed not to contribute to the 100-year EDC.[65]

Airborne releases of natural uranium in the form of soluble gases or insoluble particulates were assumed to settle out. About 20 percent of the uranium airborne releases were assumed to be uniformly distributed within eighty kilometers of the model facility, with the remaining 20 percent uniformly distributed across the eastern half of the United States. It was further assumed that the deposited uranium would be uniformly distributed throughout the top fifteen centimeters of soil. The major pathway was assumed to be ingestion of uranium through the food chains.

Next, it was assumed that the increase in concentration of uranium in the soil above natural levels due to releases from uranium fuel supply facilities caused a proportional increase in the average daily intake of uranium. Radiation dose from background levels of uranium had been calculated; hence this assumption allowed the additional dose due to uranium discharges to be estimated.

The EPA calculated the additional doses due to the deposition of a one-curie release from a model facility. It multiplied the background doses due to naturally occurring uranium by the ratios of incremental soil concentration to naturally occurring uranium soil concentration for the two areas. A quality factor (RBE) of ten was applied to convert the critical organ dose to biological dose equivalent. These doses were then multiplied by the same health effect coefficients used in the immediate dose calculations.

The population within eighty kilometers of a model facility was assumed to be 0.7 percent of the total U.S. population and was assumed

65. EPA, *Environmental Analysis of the Uranium Fuel Cycle*, pt. 1, p. A-25.

Table 6-2. Health Effects Resulting from the Immediate and the 100-Year Dose Commitment from Uranium, Thirty-Year Facility Operations

Model facility	*Total air-borne emissions (curies per year)*	*Number of health effects per facility from immediate dose commitment*	*Number of health effects per facility from 100-year dose commitment*	*100-year dose effects as percent of immediate*
Mill	0.1	0.05	0.006	10.0
Conversion				
Wet solvent	0.023	0.40	0.002	0.5
Hydrofluor	0.057	0.20	0.005	3.0
Enrichment	0.045	0.10	0.004	4.0
Fabrication	0.005	0.10	0.0005	0.5

Source: Adapted from EPA, *An Environmental Analysis of the Uranium Fuel Cycle*, pt. 1: *Fuel Supply*, p. A-30.

to grow as the U.S. population grew. An exception was the population in the vicinity of a model uranium mill that was assumed to remain constant at 54,000 people. The population of the eastern half of the United States was assumed to be 80 percent of the total U.S. population and was also assumed to grow as the U.S. population grew.

Table 6-2 gives the number of potential health effects resulting from the 100-year uranium dose commitment for thirty years of fuel supply facility operations. For comparison, the health effects expected to result from the immediate doses from thirty years of facility operations are also included.

As can be seen, for all types of fuel supply facilities the 100-year dose commitment was estimated to cause less than 10 percent additional health effects when compared with the immediate dose commitment for uranium discharges.

The EPA stressed that any calculation of environmental dose commitment is subject to great uncertainty. The projections outlined here were considered to be indicative only of current best estimates of possible consequences, indicating only potential future trends. Despite the inherent uncertainties involved with projections of populations and dispersions over so wide a range and so long a period of time, the EPA considered the concept of the EDC as a useful basis for making policy decisions concerning the protection of people and the environment.[66]

66. EPA, *Environmental Radiation Dose Commitment*.

Critique of the Quantitative Risk Assessment

Performing a risk assessment for every design and type of facility, through all conceivable dispersion pathways, and for every possible target organ would have been prohibitively costly. The opposite extreme would be a calculation for a single facility, considering one set of pathways and target organs. The EPA attempted to obtain sufficient coverage yet retain simplicity by the use of generic modeling. It chose average rather than actual facilities and a "best estimate" of each parameter (which tended to be conservative). Insofar as the analysis uses this type of estimate, the chain of calculations produces a conservative estimate but will give no measure of uncertainty or stochastic variation.

Few data were available to estimate the parameters of the quantitative risk assessment for source and dispersion modeling, especially for prefission support facilities. The EPA was forced to use design projections and check them with only limited data, both inherently unsatisfactory practices. Population and meteorological data were available for the existing sites and were assumed to characterize support facilities, for which data were not available.

Only two uranium mills and one fuel reprocessing facility were operating at the time of the EPA analysis. Furthermore, all three facilities were built during a period of lower concern for radioactive emissions. Indeed, the reprocessing facility was shut down due to radiological and operational problems that contributed to unacceptable emissions and was never reopened. Thus the previous data on these three facilities are certain to overstate what could be expected of a new plant, but the alternative, reliance on design data, must also be regarded with skepticism.

Data for LWRs show substantial differences in effluents across facilities and over time within each facility. The variation arises from the type of measurements taken, changes in release guidelines, fuel cladding defects, changes in waste treatment systems, operational difficulties, and equipment problems.[67] Notable findings from an examination of such data include (1) pressurized water reactors are relatively more variable in their quantities of discharges, but their discharges are

67. T. R. Decker, ed., "A Summary of Radioactive Material Releases from Nuclear Power Plants."

much smaller in absolute magnitude than those of boiling water reactors; (2) interfacility variation is typically greater than temporal variation for a specific facility; and (3) ranges of values often span four orders of magnitude.

The distribution of the annual meteorological airborne dispersion factor for LWRs generally fell within a range spanning a factor of ten or less for a given type of site. Application of the LWR factor (based on a wide range of meteorological sites) to all facilities in the uranium fuel cycle appears reasonable.

An approach similar to the one used to arrive at a "best estimate" meteorological dispersion factor was used to determine a standard population. A new consideration is that the total emissions, the meteorological dispersion factor, and the facility's local population may not be independent parameters, as implicitly assumed. Should facilities with meteorological conditions causing higher ambient concentrations also tend to have larger surrounding populations, the estimates run the risk of being two to three orders of magnitude too low.

Atmospheric dispersion models have been found to predict the concentrations of contaminants for short ranges and simple terrains to within a factor of two to four. For the actual terrains surrounding fuel cycle facilities and for distances out to eighty kilometers, accuracy probably deteriorates by a factor of twenty.[68] This level of uncertainty detracts significantly from the overall confidence given to estimates of health effects because of the linear nonthreshold model. Projected health effects resulting from small doses to large populations at the outer distances from the source are difficult to either justify or discount. Site-specific models and inputs would reduce this uncertainty.

Pathway transfer factors are constructed from a number of separate parameters. Not until recently has an uncertainty analysis been rigorously attempted for this stage of the overall risk analysis. In an examination of the Nuclear Regulatory Commission default values, which are comparable to the EPA values, the analysis conducted by the Oak Ridge National Laboratory indicated that for a given deposition rate of the radionuclide iodine-131, the commission's estimated annual mean dose was approximately a factor of six greater than the estimated most probable dose. The assumptions of critical importance to the results were stated to be that (1) the available data for input parameters are

68. Chris Nelson (EPA, Office of Radiation Programs), personal communication, August 1980.

representative of the true population of parameter values; (2) the model parameters are statistically independent; and (3) the structure of the model was an appropriate simulation of reality.[69] A reduction in model output uncertainty would be expected with the use of site-specific input parameters; however, this source of uncertainty appears small compared with other sources associated with generic modeling. Studies such as the Oak Ridge report could help identify critical parameters in the pathway calculations and suggest instances and applications when the use of generic values might yield undesirable results.

The most commonly used internal dose model and data base for dose conversion factors over the past twenty years have been those presented by the International Commission on Radiological Protection.[70] This model assumes a single-exponential retention function for radioactive materials deposited in reference organs, and it further assumes that the radioactivity is concentrated in the center of a spherical organ. This model does not account for dose contributions from cross irradiation from radionuclides deposited in neighboring organs. The ICRP concept also assumed a simple lung model that was later revised by the ICRP Task Group on Lung Dynamics (TGLD). The TGLD model is more complex than its predecessor and requires more extensive input data. This revised model represented the state of the art at the time the EPA was making its analysis and was adopted by the EPA.

Internal doses, even for inhalation exposure, are not estimated with the lung model alone. Comprehensive internal dose estimation requires a set of models to simulate radionuclide behavior within the body. These models are typically adopted from recognized sources or developed from documented default data. For many radionuclide-organ combinations, the internal dose conversion factors calculated with the more recent models and data bases do not differ significantly from the older values developed on the basis of ICRP principles; for other combinations, however, the differences are very significant.

Dose conversion factors are typically presented with no indication of the error associated with their application. For instance, dose conversion factors for children frequently include considerations for variation in

69. F. Owen Hoffman and Charles F. Baes, III, eds., "A Statistical Analysis of Selected Parameters for Predicting Food Chain Transport and Internal Dose of Radionuclides," p. 45.

70. ICRP, *Recommendations of the International Commission on Radiological Protection.*

organ mass but default to adult values for other age-dependent parameters in the absence of specific data. Within an assumed homogeneous population subgroup, considerable variation among people exists. To place a bound on this variability, the Federal Radiation Council suggested the use of the arbitrary assumption that in an appreciably homogeneous population group the majority of individuals do not vary from the average by more than a factor of three.[71] This magnitude of variability should be kept in mind when calculating and interpreting individual dose estimates based on dosimetric parameters such as those tabulated in ICRP documents.[72]

There was strong precedent for the EPA's decision to adopt the models and dose conversion factors of the ICRP groups. The field is continuously under revision by this group, with most "best estimate" values remaining fairly stable. The ICRP is the dominant but not the sole voice on this topic. Recently a radioecological assessment of a nuclear power plant in West Germany used some non-ICRP dose conversion factors that resulted in higher estimates of health risks.[73]

Uncertainties did not arise in determining health effect coefficients for lack of a sufficiently detailed model or representative set of input parameters, but rather from a genuine lack of understanding of the problem. The EPA used the limited findings of the respected BEIR-I committee in a way consistent with its needs and current knowledge. A major criticism of the EPA procedure was the application of high-dose data to low-dose situations. However, health effect coefficients were needed, so the simplest justifiable approach, a linear response, was assumed. In light of the subsequent judgments of the BEIR committee, as it was constituted in 1979, this approach would be considered conservative but still appropriate for the purposes of protecting human health.[74] The best estimate of the dose-response relationship is now considered to be one containing contributions from both linear and quadratic terms, but this possibly could change owing to the new atomic bomb dose calculations. Future guidelines should explicitly account for

71. Federal Radiation Council, *Background Material for the Development of Radiation Protection Standards,* Report no. 1.

72. Oak Ridge National Laboratory, "Proceedings of a Workshop on the Evaluation of Models Used for the Environmental Assessment of Radionuclide Releases."

73. Nuclear Regulatory Commission, "Summary of NCRC Staff Review of Radioecological Assessment of the NYHL Nuclear Power Plant."

74. BEIR, *The Effects on Populations of Exposure to Low Levels of Ionizing Radiation* (1980).

this varying degree of conservatism if the linear model is retained for regulatory purposes. It appears that the EPA's choice of health effect coefficients was made in a reasonable manner.

The concept of an environmental dose commitment was a new and meritorious addition to the considerations of radiation protection. At the time of the promulgation of the EPA regulation, the EDC was newly conceived and, as was evident from its description, based on a number of plausible but arbitrary assumptions. Information of the kind provided by the EDC calculations is necessary to an acceptable assessment of the risks of discharges from the uranium fuel cycle. Long-term population and particle deposition projections, spanning 100 years or more, are at best tenuous. Quantifying the uncertainties involved would not be a trivial undertaking, if it is possible at all. However, until efforts toward this end are made, EDC calculations should at best be considered order-of-magnitude while providing some insight into the impact of the long-lived radionuclides.

An issue distinct from the stage-by-stage critique of the quantitative risk analysis is the performance of the analysis as a unit. The EPA reported that, based on field experience, the estimated doses "fairly accurately represent the actual doses that would be received by a hypothetical individual located at a reactor site boundary in the prevailing wind direction, year-round, and unshielded by any structure."[75] It also noted that actual maximum doses to real individuals would be "substantially lower." A goal for future analyses of this type would be to be able to quantify such phrases as "fairly accurately" and "substantially." When this has been achieved, the results of a quantitative risk analysis can be applied in a more robust way.

The appropriateness of the form of the EPA models is extremely difficult to judge, but two very different questions do arise: were the models appropriate at the time of the promulgation of the regulation, and are they appropriate now? The existence of previously noted problems of model verification, the models' strong dependence on quality inputs, and an overall inability to quantify uncertainty in all parameters raises the problem of finding other criteria to judge appropriateness. One highly unsatisfactory basis is precedent. The EPA models were similar to the Nuclear Regulatory Commission's models for the source, dispersion, and uptake stages of the quantitative risk assessment. This probably

75. EPA, *Environmental Radiation Protection Requirements*, p. 62.

resulted from an effort to keep the two agencies consistent with one another rather than from independent development. This type of consistency is desirable in that licensing requirements and operational performance will be measured in the same terms, but it could produce a wrong answer twice. However, both the EPA and the commission derivations were thorough and careful; they represent the state of the art.

An important point is the delay between initial analysis and implementation of the regulation. The bulk of the analysis for the regulation was done before October 1973, yet the regulation did not become effective until about 1980, with review scheduled in 1985. However, the atomic bomb doses have been challenged, new uranium conversion dose factors have appeared, and the linear-quadratic dose-response curve is displacing the linear dose-response curve. In a field of science where so much research is taking place, these lags are unforgivably long. Unfortunately the difficulty and cost of reevaluating regulations precludes rapid revision.

The Role of the Quantitative Risk Assessment

The quantitative risk assessment described in the previous sections allowed the EPA to estimate the number of potential health effects for each quantity and type of radioactive discharge. These estimates were then used to specify health benefits in a cost-effectiveness analysis.

The promulgated standard bears a somewhat puzzling relationship to the quantitative risk assessment. It is clear from this brief review of the EPA's work that the agency made a heroic attempt to achieve a best estimate of the potential health effects from radionuclides. In no other case has so much information on a single type of environmental pollutant been amassed and interpreted. After a study aiming so steadily at quantification, one would hope for regulatory standards that laid out a clear path for the industry to follow. Instead, the EPA's decisions represent at best a rough trail.

Standard by standard, a consistent pattern of debate and decision emerges in which the single most important determinant appears to be the cost-effectiveness of the chosen control levels. In at least one instance, however, a stricter than necessary standard was chosen because it was relatively cheap to achieve. In other cases, two or more standards march together, not because the risks, as measured by analysis, were exactly the same, but because a single set of controls could bring both effluents within an acceptable range of risk.

The analysis identified control technologies. Each operating or planned plant had specific treatment systems; these systems and their associated costs were used in the analysis to estimate the "lowest practicable effluent discharges" as required by regulations.[76] There was a wide variety in the control systems for each effluent pathway, and also in the ways control options were combined in individual plant systems. This multiplicity complicated the selection of cost-effective systems. The EPA attempted to model add-on components in a logical sequence. However, in actual operating experience, the order of addition of systems may differ greatly from the sequence the EPA used.[77]

The EPA sought the control point in the fuel cycle that would result in the greatest reduction in the number of potential health effects from the whole cycle for the least cost. It constructed efficiency frontiers showing the cheapest methods of progressively lowering population exposure to ionizing radiation, as illustrated in figure 6-1. The next question was what goal should be set for population exposure, or the equivalent question, how much is society willing to spend to save a person-rem?

The EPA looked for "breakpoints" or "knees" in the curves that would indicate logical stopping places. These were found at a point representing a cumulative net present cost of about $3 million per gigawatt of power capacity for pressurized water reactors (about $8 million for boiling water reactors), with an implied cost of $1 million per cancer averted. Beyond this level, the costs of averting further health effects rise sharply.

These breakpoints defined only the starting points for the EPA's determination of the levels of doses and discharges to be promulgated. Total emissions were once again estimated for all uranium fuel cycle facilities, assuming imposition of the controls identified before the breakpoints in the cost-effectiveness analysis. Maximum acceptable doses to individuals were then estimated for each facility. The maximum remaining quantities of radionuclides released to the environment per gigawatt were also determined.

Two further criteria were considered at this point by the EPA in

76. 10 C.F.R. 50, Appendix I.

77. EPA, *An Environmental Analysis of the Uranium Fuel Cycle*, pt. 2, p. 38.

Figure 6-1. Risk Reduction versus Cost in a Light Water Reactor[a]

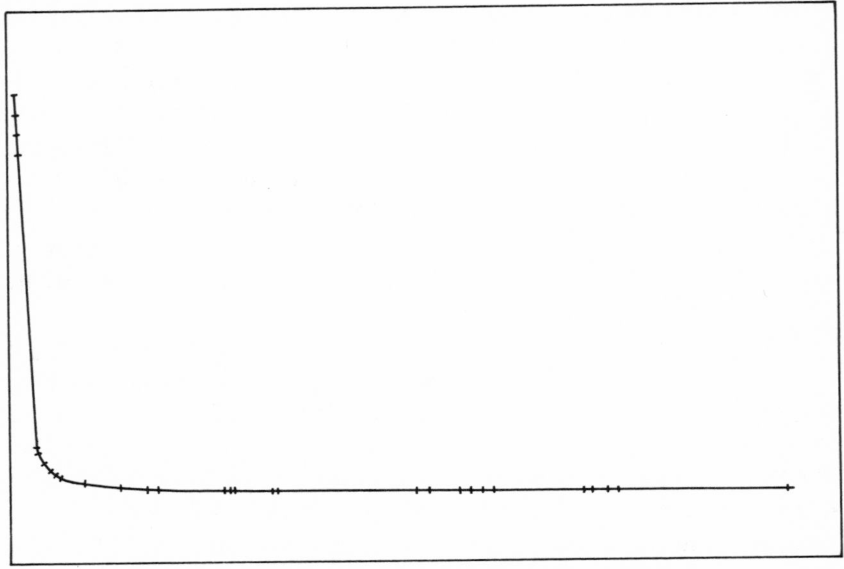

a. Assuming a 1,000-megawatt light water reactor operating for thirty years; the risk measure is equivalent to a measure of population exposure to ionizing radiation from the reactor. The points on the curve indicate the adoption of particular control technologies. See Environmental Protection Agency, *Environmental Radiation Protection Requirements for Normal Operations of Activities in the Uranium Fuel Cycle*, vol. 1 (EPA, 1976) for elaboration.

addition to the cost-effectiveness criterion (based on the quantitative risk analysis). They were (1) the equity of distribution of radiological impact, and (2) the existing use of control technology by the industry as the result of nonradiological considerations. On the basis of the first criterion, the EPA decided to augment the levels of radioiodine controls at pressurized water reactors and boiling water reactors to lower the anticipated doses to those in the population living very near the reactors. The second criterion indicated that the strong economic incentive to retain valuable uranium dust made it standard practice to apply high-efficiency filters at fuel fabrication facilities even though this practice did not appear to be cost-effective merely as a safety measure. The EPA thus decided to assume that these facilities would use filters as a matter of course. Consistent with normal Nuclear Regulatory Commission licensing practices, the EPA added a margin to these levels to provide operating flexibility to accommodate minor deviations from anticipated performance levels, differences in specific parameters of actual sites, and the impact of multiple facilities on larger sites.

The EPA set a standard of twenty-five millirems per year for maximum annual whole-body dose from short-lived gaseous and liquid effluents and gamma radiation originating from all operations on the fuel cycle. It was estimated that this standard was attainable at cost-effective control levels and that the standard was achievable at all sites for which environmental impact statements had been filed. The EPA believed, on the basis of operating experience at existing sites, that the standard could be readily achieved in practice. This value was chosen to provide a reasonable margin of operating flexibility beyond the one to five millirems per year projected for most sites, including those with more than two reactors. Finally, the additional impact of a fuel reprocessing facility on the reactor site was judged achievable under cost-effective levels of control, even though the single site with mixed facilities was considered a "worse case" setting.

The standard for a maximum annual thyroid dose was not as easy to select.[78] On the basis of existing field measurements, a more relaxed standard appeared to be appropriate than had been proposed. The level of control the Nuclear Regulatory Commission assumed to be necessary was more stringent than a cost-effectiveness assessment of risk reduction for the whole population justified. This was because a small number of hunters and fishermen might consume large quantities of game caught in the proximity to the facility, thus being subject to relatively high doses. But the final standard was not derived from field measurements or commission recommendations; instead, it reflected a level of biological risk comparable with that represented by the standard for a whole-body dose. This level (seventy-five millirems per year) was believed to be readily achievable by all sites using no more control equipment than was required by normal licensing procedures.[79]

Doses to other organs were judged to be maintainable below twenty-five millirems per year using economical and readily available controls for limiting environmental releases. These doses, arising principally from lung and bone exposure through airborne effluents, affected small populations near many fuel supply facilities. Even though control for such facilities appeared not to be a cost-effective measure, the low cost

78. EPA, *Environmental Radiation Protection Requirements*, vol. 1, p. 71.
79. Ibid., p. 72.

of the remedial control measures was the justification for the standard of twenty-five millirems per year.

The standards for long-lived materials fell into two categories: those that could have been achieved using control methods available at that time and those that required the use of methods that had been demonstrated but had not come into routine use. In the former case, exemplified by the standard for plutonium and other transuranics, the standard limited the environmental burden to a level consistent with that reasonably achievable using the best available control methods. This level of control also satisfied the criteria for cost-effectiveness. In the latter case, that of the proposed standards for krypton-85 and iodine-129, the limiting levels of environmental burdens specified were not those achievable by best currently available technologies, but instead the best performance of new systems. Again, the costs of these systems were judged to be justified by the reduction of potential health impact achieved at these levels of performance.[80]

Conclusion

The pragmatic approach appears to have produced a serviceable set of standards. But questions remain. Did the exhaustive accumulation of detailed information really help? If cost-effectiveness is the determining criterion, why not rely on that alone? Does the decision pattern really provide the public with optimal protection, or is it merely expedient? These are disturbing questions, given the high premium the American public places on avoiding exposure to radioactivity and susceptibility to cancer.

Whatever its imperfections, the EPA model gives the most comprehensive analysis of potential risks now available. Indeed, the apparent exhaustiveness and refinement of the model may result in excessive confidence in the results. Uncertainty still abounds. There is also some question of whether the analysis was too detailed and thus too expensive. Probably the total expenditure was not unwarranted, given public concern about ionizing radiation. But the funds could have been better spent by concentrating on the areas of greatest importance rather than pursuing the areas that seemed most tractable. For example, the analysis

80. Ibid., p. 73.

quickly showed that some pairs of radionuclides and pathways were relatively unimportant; this should have been a signal to switch effort to those of greater importance. Using the available resources more wisely would have done much to reduce uncertainty.

The quantitative risk assessment's benefits go beyond an assurance that the Nuclear Regulatory Commission has not permitted the nuclear industry to expose society to undesirable risks. The analysis has been helpful in showing the implications of alternative controls for each aspect of the emissions and diffusion process. Cost-effectiveness analysis works extremely well at the ends of the range of choices—some tasks are obviously worth doing while others are obviously foolish. In the middle range, the risk assessment provides detailed information about implications; while it is unlikely to be conclusive, it can prove extremely helpful.

Both the cost-effectiveness framework and the quantitative risk assessment act as an impartial conscience, keeping the regulatory decisionmaking honest. For example, the decision to stay with a standard of twenty-five millirems per year had to be justified on the basis of a small incremental cost because it clearly failed the cost-effectiveness test. If the public demands particularly stringent controls on a particular radionuclide-pathway combination, the analysis can provide a quantitative measure of the additional cost and reduced risk, with estimates of how much the risk could be reduced for the same expenditure.

The EPA analysis was complicated and detailed, but it was well organized and seems to have met the EPA's goals for the analysis. After reviewing it, one does not have the feeling that ionizing radiation from the routine operation of the nuclear fuel cycle presents risks appreciably larger than those estimated.

Two aspects of the analysis are worth further comment, however. The first is the EPA's decision to adopt conservative assumptions whenever there was uncertainty. The resulting estimates are not easily interpreted. It is not clear how conservative they are. For example, rather than making a "most likely" estimate, it is conceivable that the EPA could be overestimating risk by a factor of more than one hundred. The analysis would be more enlightening if it carried through two estimates. The first would be a genuine best estimate that used the best guess at each stage; the second would be the sort of conservative estimate that the EPA has derived. It would be enlightening to know what is the most likely estimate and how much of a difference the conservative assumptions make.

Second, the initial assumptions in the analysis are highly arbitrary. The earlier goals of 500 or 170 or 25 millirems per year are completely arbitrary. Yet the cost-effectiveness analysis makes it clear that very large costs result from selecting one assumption versus another. The analysis needs a further stage that feeds back the cost and health implications of the first stage into the initial assumptions. With the inclusion of such internal reexamination, it would be clear that the EPA has attempted to provide a level of protection in excess of those provided for other risks of cancer and mutation. It is evident that some relaxation in the arbitrarily selected initial goals could vastly decrease costs and quite possibly decrease overall health risks by freeing resources for use in other aspects of the nuclear fuel cycle, such as preventing risks from accident or sabotage.

Appendix A: Glossary

Body burden: An equilibrium concentration of radioactivity in a person measured in curies, representing a balance of the rate of intake of a radionuclide, its radioactive decay, and the rate of its biological concentration, metabolism, and excretion by the body. Body burdens of certain radionuclides that are not preferentially concentrated in any single organ of the body result in essentially uniform, whole-body doses. The body burdens of radionuclides that are preferentially concentrated, such as iodine in the thyroid, result in much more localized, generally organ-specific doses.

Curie: The special unit of activity. One curie equals $3{,}700 \times 10^{10}$ nuclear transformations per second.

Genetic effect: An effect that is passed on through biologic mechanisms of inheritance to the descendants of a parent who was exposed to radiation or some other insult.

Linear energy transfer (LET): The average energy lost by a directly ionizing particle per unit distance of its travel in a medium. A high LET is generally associated with protons, alpha particles, and neutrons, while a low LET is associated with X rays, electrons, and gamma rays.

Material in this glossary was adapted from "Risks of Nuclear Energy and Low-Level Ionizing Radiation," report of an American Medical Association Advisory Panel to the Council on Scientific Affairs of the AMA (February 1981), pp. 41–49.

Person-rem: A unit of population dose of radiation exposure. The number of person-rems a group receives equals the product of the number of persons in the group and the average radiation dose equivalent (rem) received by persons in the group.

Quality factor: The LET-dependent factor by which absorbed doses are multiplied to obtain (for radiation protection purposes) a quantity that expresses, on a common scale for all ionizing radiations, the effectiveness of the absorbed dose.

Rad: The special unit of absorbed dose of ionizing radiation equal to 0.01 joule per kilogram in any medium. A dose of one rad corresponds to the absorption of 100 ergs of radiation energy per gram of absorbing material.

Relative biological effectiveness (RBE): The RBE is a factor used to compare the biological effectiveness of absorbed radiation doses (rads) due to different types of ionizing radiation. It is the experimentally determined ratio of an absorbed dose of the radiation in question to the absorbed dose of a reference radiation required to produce an identical biological effect in a particular experimental organism or tissue. The RBE is the ratio of rem to rad.

Rem: Radiation Equivalent Man; the special unit of dose equivalent. The dose equivalent in rems is numerically equal to the absorbed dose in rads multiplied by the quality factor, the distribution factor, and any other necessary modifying factors. For example, one rad of x-radiation equals one rem, while one rad of neutron radiation might equal ten rems.

Roentgen: The special unit of radiation exposure equal to 2.58×10^{-4} coulombs per kilogram of air.

Somatic effects: An effect that is manifested in the body over the lifetime of the individual.

Transuranics: Those elements with an atomic number greater than 92. All are radioactive and not naturally occurring.

Appendix B: Chronology of Radiation Protection

1928: An international unit of radiation measurement, the roentgen, was adopted.

The chronology is adapted from Lauriston S. Taylor, "The Development of Radiation Protection Standards," submitted as public comments to the Interagency Task Force on the Health Effects of Ionizing Radiation, Document no. 21 (U.S. Department of Health, Education and Welfare), June 1979, p. 12.

1934: The U.S. Advisory Committee on X Ray and Radium Protection [now the National Council on Radiation Protection (NCRP)] recommended a permissible dose of 0.1 roentgen a day. The International Committee on Radiological Protection (ICRP) recommended a permissible daily dose of 0.2 roentgen.

1941: The NCRP established a maximum permissible body burden of 0.1 microcurie of radium.

1949: The NCRP adopted new permissible dose standards for radiation workers (0.3 rem a week) as well as for population groups containing children (one-tenth occupational limits). The recommendation that exposure to radiation be kept to the lowest practicable level in all cases regardless of the quantities established by the standards was also developed at this time.

1948–53: In a series of tripartite conferences, England, the United States, and Canada adopted the general principles developed by the NCRP, and later by the ICRP, for atomic energy operations.

1950: The standards recommended by the NCRP in 1949 were adopted by the ICRP.

1952: The NCRP developed detailed lists of maximum permissible concentrations and body burdens for some seventy-five radionuclides.

1956: The Atomic Energy Commission (AEC) promulgated a rule (10 C.F.R. 50) pertaining to the licensing of nuclear production and utilization facilities. Appendix I (added a few years later) provides guides for design objectives consistent with the "as low as is reasonably achievable" philosophy of limiting radioactive effluents. Working more or less independently, the U.S. National Academy of Sciences, the British Medical Research Council, the NCRP, and the ICRP reduced the basic permissible exposure level for radiation workers to 5 rems a year to the whole body, the blood-forming organs, and the gonads. The permissible dose to other individual organs was left at either 15 rems a year or 26 rems a year. A permissible dose of 0.5 rem a year was recommended for the general population. Limiting the average dose to one-third of this individual value, or 170 millirems a year, was considered reasonable to ensure that no person in the general population would receive an annual dose exceeding 0.5 rem.

1957–59: The Joint Committee on Atomic Energy held a series of hearings about radiation protection standards that led to the establishment of the Federal Radiation Council by executive order and an amendment to the Atomic Energy Act of 1954 (73 Stat. 690). The new FRC standards differed little from the 1949 NCRP standards.

1959: The NCRP established an ad hoc committee to examine the question of somatic effects of radiation on large population groups. A set of recommendations concerning general radiation protection philosophy was developed.

1960: The Federal Radiation Council presented the president with a list of recommendations concerning radiation protection guidelines for federal agencies. A regulation (10 C.F.R. 20) and its amendments were promulgated by the Atomic Energy Commission to protect against radiation hazards arising from activities under the commission's license.

1971: The NCRP completed a ten-year study and review of the basic radiation protection criteria.

1972: The report of the National Academy of Sciences Committee on the Biological Effects of Ionizing Radiation (BEIR-I) provided a major review of the health effects of low levels of ionizing radiation and the role of such information in public protection efforts.[81] A report by the United Nations Scientific Committee on the Effects on Atomic Radiation (UNSCEAR), similar in scope to the BEIR-I study, identified the sources and effects of ionizing radiation.[82]

1975: The NCRP issued a review of current radiation protection philosophy, which included a critique of the two 1972 reports by BEIR and UNSCEAR.

1976: EPA issued the final promulgation of a regulation (40 C.F.R. 190) designed to protect the public against radiation releases from the uranium fuel cycle.

1977: A second UNSCEAR report was published on the topic of sources and effects of ionizing radiation, updating the 1972 report.[83] The BEIR committee published a report on considerations of health benefit-cost analysis for activities involving ionizing radiation exposure and alternatives.[84]

81. BEIR, *The Effects on Populations of Exposure to Low Levels of Ionizing Radiation* (1972).

82. UNSCEAR, *Ionizing Radiation: Levels and Effects*, vol. 2: *Effects*.

83. UNSCEAR, *Sources and Effects of Ionizing Radiation*.

84. BEIR, *Considerations of Health Benefit-Cost Analysis for Activities Involving Ionizing Radiation Exposure and Alternatives*.

1980: The BEIR committee published an updated report on the health effects resulting from ionizing radiation exposures.[85]

1981: New studies of the radiation released from the atomic bomb blasts at Hiroshima and Nagasaki indicated that the human doses calculated for the high-LET component of the radiation may be in error. Preliminary work suggested that the previous assumption of a significant neutron contribution to the causation of health effects at Hiroshima may be unfounded, indicating that low-LET radiation may have a greater capability to cause health effects than had been previously thought. Should preliminary studies be affirmed, radiation risk coefficients, such as derived by the BEIR committees, may need to be revised. Work is continuing at the time of this writing.[86]

85. BEIR, *The Effects on Populations of Exposure to Low Levels of Ionizing Radiation* (1980).

86. Loewe and Mendelsohn, "Revised Dose Estimates at Hiroshima and Nagasaki."

CHAPTER SEVEN

Risk Assessment of Chlorobenzilate

THOMAS R. BARTMAN

THE Environmental Protection Agency's regulation of chlorobenzilate represents an exemplary regulatory response to a toxic pesticide. The EPA analysis of the health effects of the miticide carefully explored the issues and the risks and benefits. Sorting out conflicting studies and benefit claims was far from a trivial task. This case should serve as a model for other EPA programs as well as for other federal agencies regulating risk.

Events Preceding EPA Regulation

Chlorobenzilate is a pesticide widely used on citrus fruits and other products such as nuts, trees, and cotton. Ninety percent of its use in the United States is for the control of the citrus rust mite on oranges, grapefruits, and lemons. It is applied primarily with a tractor-pulled speed sprayer. An estimated 700 workers employed as applicators constitute the group at the highest risk through dermal and inhalation exposure. Pickers are exposed to an unknown level of the toxin on entering the groves after spraying has occurred. General population exposure results from chlorobenzilate residues in fruits and fruit products. Additionally, the treated pulp of sprayed citrus is used as animal feed in Florida, exposing local populations to chlorobenzilate through meat and milk. Little is known about the metabolism of chlorobenzilate in humans and other organisms or about its degradation in soil or water.[1]

1. Its half-life has been determined to be 1.5–5 weeks in soil persistence studies. Environmental Protection Agency, "Chlorobenzilate: Position Document 3."

While assessing the tumorigenic effects of 120 pesticides, J. R. M. Innes found that chlorobenzilate caused tumors in the two strains of mice studied.[2] Relying on this research, the Commission on Common Pesticides of the secretary of health, education and welfare recommended that human exposure to chlorobenzilate be reduced to a minimum.[3] In 1970 chlorobenzilate became a candidate for the Suspect Chemical Review Process administered by the U.S. Department of Agriculture, and in 1976 became the first subject of the EPA's Rebuttable Presumption against Registration (RPAR) process for pesticide regulation on the basis of these earlier listings.[4]

On May 26, 1976, EPA announced the RPAR for chlorobenzilate,[5] citing three studies that had found chlorobenzilate to be oncogenic in rats and mice through oral exposure.[6] This notice solicited rebuttal evidence from applicants seeking to register products containing chlorobenzilate and comments from agencies and the public. A subsequent notice on July 14, 1976, reported additional applications.[7]

On July 11, 1978, the EPA announced the availability of its position document, which presented the scientific basis of the chlorobenzilate regulation, and announced as well its preliminary response to evidence submitted to rebut the RPAR. The agency had concluded that the RPAR had not been rebutted.[8] While determining that two of the studies on which the RPAR was based were unreliable,[9] it did cite evidence,

2. J. R. M. Innes and others, "Bioassay of Pesticides and Industrial Chemicals for Tumorigenicity in Mice: Preliminary Note."

3. Department of Health, Education and Welfare, *Report of the Secretary's Commission on Common Pesticides and Their Relation to Environmental Health.*

4. A rebuttable presumption arises when a pesticide meets or exceeds risk criteria set out in 40 C.F.R. 162.11 in a pre-RPAR preliminary risk profile. To rebut, respondents may try to show that the agency's initial determination of risk was in error; that actual human exposure levels to a particular pesticide are unlikely to have a significant adverse effect; or that economic, social or environmental benefits of using the pesticide outweigh the risk [40 C.F.R. 162.11(a)(5)]. More detailed reviews of the RPAR process and chlorobenzilate chronology are available in National Academy of Sciences, Committee on Prototype Explicit Analyses for Pesticides, *Regulating Pesticides;* and EPA, "Chlorobenzilate: Position Document 3."

5. 41 Fed. Reg. 21517 (1976).

6. Innes, "Bioassay of Pesticides"; H. J. Horn, R. B. Bruce, and O. E. Paynter, "Toxicology of Chlorobenzilate"; Woodard Research Corporation, "Chlorobenzilate Safety Evaluation by Dietary Feeding to Rats for 104 Weeks: Final Report."

7. 41 Fed. Reg. 29015 (1976).

8. 43 Fed. Reg. 29824 (1978).

9. Horn, Bruce, and Paynter, "Toxicology of Chlorobenzilate"; and Woodard Research Corporation, "Chlorobenzilate Safety Evaluation." See EPA, "Chlorobenzilate: Position Document 3," p. 9.

including a new National Cancer Institute study,[10] concerning both oncogenic and adverse testicular effects in rats. The EPA concluded that these risks were significant enough in view of the estimated human exposure, particularly for pesticide applicators, to warrant action. Consequently the agency suggested modifications in the registered uses of the pesticide to facilitate significant risk reduction. At the same time it affirmed certain benefits of chlorobenzilate use, including the substantial cost-effectiveness of using it instead of likely substitutes. Thus the EPA canceled registration of chlorobenzilate for all noncitrus uses, limited its use to three states (Florida, Texas, and California), promulgated clothing and work rules to protect applicators, and required registrants to submit additional exposure studies. It also solicited comments on the preliminary rule.

The EPA announced the final decision of the RPAR process on February 13, 1979.[11] The agency reviewed comments on its preliminary announcement and altered its proposed regulation in response to comments (adding Arizona to the states in which chlorobenzilate use was permitted), thus confirming its decision to modify the terms of chlorobenzilate registration. On April 9, 1979, the EPA noted objections to its proposed action and requests for a hearing by the Environmental Defense Fund and registrants.[12] An agency administrative law judge denied petitions for rehearing; this decision was upheld by the Circuit Court of Appeals for the District of Columbia Circuit on July 17, 1980.[13]

Scientific Basis of the Regulation

In the Innes study, chlorobenzilate was administered orally to two hybrid strains of mice.[14] The study found tumors of the liver in 52.9 percent (9 out of 17) of the male mice ingesting chlorobenzilate at a concentration of 603 parts per million; the incidence in the controls was only 10.1 percent (8 out of 79). The female mice showed no liver tumors. The studies done by Horn and the Woodard Research Corporation found tumors in some animals after ingestion of chlorobenzilate.[15]

10. National Cancer Institute, *Bioassay of Chlorobenzilate for Possible Carcinogenicity*.
11. 44 Fed. Reg. 95118 (1979).
12. 44 Fed. Reg. 21069 (1979).
13. 10 Environmental Law Reporter 20585.
14. Innes, "Bioassay of Pesticides."
15. Horn, Bruce, and Paynter, "Toxicology of Chlorobenzilate"; and Woodard Research Corporation, "Chlorobenzilate Safety Evaluation."

Irreducible elements of uncertainty affect the evaluation of these and all other positive findings. One is that types of carcinomas may occur that fall between clearly defined categories; thus classifying and recording them involves subjective choices. Further, results of animal bioassays depend on laboratory controls for many variables such as the choice of animal or dose that may vary between studies. Finally, the extrapolation of effects of high doses in animals to low doses in humans is dubious.[16]

Registrants seeking to rebut the presumption against registration questioned the validity of the results of these bioassays. They pointed out the extremely small size of Innes's sample. While acknowledging the small size of the sample of exposed animals, the EPA noted that the limitation in size affects the sensitivity, not the statistical significance, of the test; these results were statistically significant. The agency emphasized that the excess incidence occurred in both strains of mice. It was also suggested that since most of the test animals did not die before sacrifice, the pesticide could not be a potent carcinogen. The threshold criteria that trigger the RPAR process, however, are met by even the slightest showing of oncogenic effects. Finally, the EPA responded to the criticism of the use of newborn (seven-day-old) mice, which may have incompletely developed immune systems, instead of older mice by noting that the younger animals would offer a sensitive test more likely to correspond to human susceptibility.

The EPA's reevaluation of the results of the Horn study found that an insufficient number of animals was examined, that the tumor incidence in controls often exceeded that in the exposed group, and that the results may have been distorted by the examination of only representative organs. Thus the EPA concluded that the study might not be a reliable indicator of oncogenicity. The study by Woodard Research Corporation, while indicating an increased incidence of liver tumors at the highest dose (400 ppm), had similar statistical deficiencies that also limited its reliability as an indicator of oncogenicity. Consequently the results of two of the studies on which the RPAR was based were found to be of questionable validity.

As rebuttal evidence, a number of studies showing no significant response to chlorobenzilate were presented. The EPA also noted that

16. For a more detailed discussion, see EPA, "Chlorobenzilate: Position Document 3"; and National Academy of Sciences, *Regulating Pesticides,* app. 1.

evidence showing that chlorobenzilate was not mutagenic did not necessarily contradict a finding of tumorigenicity. Finally, the agency found preliminary results of an epidemiological study of employees in a chlorobenzilate manufacturing facility to be inconclusive.[17]

In the face of this barrage of criticism, the National Cancer Institute offered evidence that justified the RPAR. A two-year bioassay tested the oncogenicity of chlorobenzilate in mice and rats.[18] Long-term oral administration of the pesticide to mice at a concentration of 4,000 ppm resulted in a 67 percent (32 in a sample of 48) incidence of hepatocellular carcinomas in male mice; at 8,000 ppm the incidence was 49 percent (22 in 45). These findings correspond to a rate of 21 percent (4 in 19) in controls. Female mice showed an incidence of 22 percent (11 in 49) and 26 percent (13 in 50) after doses of 3,200 and 5,900 ppm respectively; no carcinomas developed in the twenty controls. The EPA noted a statistically significant increase in total tumors ($p = 0.017$) and in hepatocellular carcinomas ($p = 0.0001$). The rats exposed to chlorobenzilate, however, showed no statistically significant effects.

In an announcement concluding the RPAR process, the EPA introduced a new area of adverse effects associated with chlorobenzilate that the agency uncovered in reevaluating the studies on which the RPAR was based. The Horn study had found a dose-related increase in small or soft testes in 69 percent of mice (9 in 13) ingesting 50 ppm for two years and adverse testicular effects in 100 percent (14 in 14) of mice exposed to 500 ppm; there was a 25 percent incidence in controls.[19] The Woodard Research Corporation study found testicular effects in 33 percent (2 in 6) of animals ingesting 125 ppm, 60 percent (3 in 5) exposed to 400 ppm, and 20 percent (1 in 5) at 40 ppm; no such effects showed up in the five controls. However, the small sample size limits the significance of these results.

In the National Cancer Institute study, 66 percent (33 in 50) of rats fed either 1,600 or 3,200 ppm for seventy-eight weeks showed testicular effects (particularly gonadal atrophy); 18 percent (9 in 49) of controls showed such effects.[20] No effects were shown in mice. In comparison, a ninety-nine day subacute study of various dose levels found sper-

17. R. T. Murphy, "Rebuttal Submission to Chlorobenzilate RPAR," cited in EPA, "Chlorobenzilate: Position Document 3."

18. National Cancer Institute, *Bioassay of Chlorobenzilate*.

19. Horn, Bruce, and Paynter, "Toxicology of Chlorobenzilate."

20. National Cancer Institute, *Bioassay of Chlorobenzilate*.

miogenetic injury and gonadal atrophy in 25 percent of rats ingesting 2,500 ppm of chlorobenzilate, the highest dose.[21]

The EPA noted that the biological significance of the adverse testicular effects is unknown. While no significant difference in fertility between treated and untreated animals has been shown, and while no studies have evaluated the significance of such effects, the occurrence of testicular effects in five studies is cause for concern. The EPA's Position Document 3 noted that given a no-observable-effects level of 40 ppm (citing a memo by R. F. Potrepka), the margin of safety for an unprotected applicator would be 55–160 ppm.[22]

In summary, there is evidence of chlorobenzilate's carcinogenic effects in male mice at exposures of 600 ppm and above. Additional studies that were held to be unreliable found such effects at lower levels. Five studies showed a correlation between chlorobenzilate exposure and adverse testicular effects. In the National Cancer Institute and Potrepka studies, the exposure level was 1,600 ppm and above.[23] These studies are summarized in table 7-1.

The EPA Quantitative Risk Assessment

The Federal Insecticide, Fungicide, and Rodenticide Act[24] requires a manufacturer to demonstrate that an insecticide performs its intended function without causing unreasonable adverse effects on people or the environment, taking into account the pesticide's economic, social, and environmental costs and benefits. Thus the EPA established the Rebuttable Presumption against Registration for the gathering and evaluation of such information in identifying the risks and benefits of a pesticide. Chlorobenzilate was the first pesticide regulated under the act.

The Special Pesticide Review Division of the EPA's Office of Pesticide Programs issued a quantitative risk assessment in its Position Document 3 for chlorobenzilate on July 11, 1978. The risk assessment comprised an exposure estimate and risk calculation and was used to weigh risks and benefits on which the choice of a regulatory option was based.

21. R. F. Potrepka, "Testicular Atrophy in Rats From Chlorobenzilate," EPA memorandum to J. B. Boyd (June 5, 1978), cited in EPA, "Chlorobenzilate: Position Document 3."

22. EPA, "Chlorobenzilate: Position Document 3," p. 38.

23. The human population at highest risk is exposed to about 12 ppm. EPA, "Chlorobenzilate: Position Document 3."

24. 7 U.S.C. 135.

Table 7-1. Summary of Effects of Chlorobenzilate in Animals

Study[a]	*Oral dose (parts per million)*	*Oncogenic findings*	*Testicular effects*
Innes (1969)	603	Liver tumors in 52.9 percent of male mice of two hybrid strains; 10.1 percent in controls; no effects in females	
National Cancer Institute (1978)	4,000	Liver tumors in 68 percent of male mice	In 66 percent of males at 1,600 ppm and 3,200 ppm, 18 percent of controls
	6,000	Liver tumors in 49 percent of males and 21 percent in male controls	
	3,200	Liver tumors in 23 percent of female mice	
	6,400 (for 78 weeks)	Liver tumors in 26 percent of females; no effects in female controls; no significant effects in exposed rats	
Horn (1955)[b]	40, 125, 400	Increased incidence of liver tumors in rats at highest dose	20 percent at 40 ppm, 33 percent at 125 ppm, 60 percent at 400 ppm, none in controls
	Three-generation study: first generation, 50; second and third, 50 or 25		Decreased testicular weights at 50 ppm, significantly reduced ($p = 0.05$) compared with controls at 25 ppm
Woodard (1966)[b]	40, 125, 400	Increased incidence of liver tumors in mice	20 percent at 40 ppm, 33 percent at 125 ppm, 60 percent at 400 ppm, none in controls
Potrepka (1978)	20, 100, 500, 2,500 (for 99 days)		Spermiogenetic injury and gonadal atrophy in 25 percent of rats at highest dose

a. See Bibliography for complete citations of the studies.

b. The EPA considered these studies possibly unreliable indicators of oncogenicity and suggested that independent analysis of the testicular effects data was appropriate. Environmental Protection Agency, Special Pesticide Review Division, "Chlorobenzilate: Position Document 3" (EPA, 1978), pp. 22–25.

In view of the lack of data on actual dietary exposure levels, the calculation of dietary exposure was based on the extent of chlorobenzilate use on food crops for which it was registered, on residue data, and on estimated human consumption of the foods produced. Because concentrations of chlorobenzilate in certain foods are below the limit of detection (0.1 ppm) of the analytical method used, the EPA assumed an upper limit of 0.1 ppm for chlorobenzilate contained in orange juice and 5 ppm in apples, explaining that when faced with a range of assumptions, it used conservative values. Based on the residue of chlorobenzilate in the citrus pulp fed to Florida beef and dairy cattle, the EPA estimated concentrations of between 1 and 3 ppb in milk and a range of up to 40 ppb in beef.

Using exposure and absorption data for other pesticides, the EPA estimated dermal and inhalation exposure, and then calculated a total daily exposure for applicators of 6.2–19.8 ppm. The EPA averaged this exposure over a forty-year occupational life, arriving at an average daily dose of 0.39–1.3 ppm. This calculation assumes that both exposure and its related effects are cumulative over a lifetime, though actual exposure involves only forty days a year. The EPA estimated the worst-case occupational exposure to involve 714 workers exposed for forty days a year.

No data were available on the exposure of the 25,000 to 30,000 citrus pickers, but the agency assumed that since the workers would enter the groves after spraying and be exposed dermally, their exposure would be less than that of the applicators.

In calculating risk, the EPA Carcinogen Assessment Group and agency consultants used the findings of the Innes study because it showed a response five times greater than the National Cancer Institute study.[25] Similarly, from several mathematical models for extrapolating the high animal test exposures to expected human exposure levels, they selected the one-hit model because it gave the highest estimate of risk. The risk calculations of this method are summarized in table 7-2.

Finally, in assessing the risk of testicular effects the EPA computed the dietary and occupational exposure estimates and compared them with the no-observable-effects level of 40 ppm found by Potrepka. The agency subsequently arrived at a safety margin of 15,000 ppm for men exposed to chlorobenzilate in the diet and between 55 and 169 ppm for

25. See EPA, Carcinogen Assessment Group, "Evaluation of the Carcinogenicity of Chlorobenzilate."

Table 7-2. The Potential Cancer Risk of Chlorobenzilate[a]

Type of exposure and population	*Maximum lifetime probability of tumor formation*	*Maximum mathematical expectation of number of tumors in a lifetime*[b]
Occupational, ground applicators, citrus only[c]	400–1,400 in 1 million	0.3–1.0
Dietary, Florida population (8 million)[d]	2.7–6.5 in 1 million	22–52
Dietary, U.S. population (except Florida) (212 million)	2.1 in 1 million	445

Source: Adapted from EPA, "Chlorobenzilate: Position Document 3," tables 6, 7, and 8.

a. Risk figures given here are based on J. R. M. Innes and others, "Bioassay of Pesticides and Industrial Chemicals for Tumorigenicity in Mice: Preliminary Note," *Journal of the National Cancer Institute*, vol. 42 (1969). For comparison, the EPA also gives the data from National Cancer Institute, *Bioassay of Chlorobenzilate for Possible Carcinogenicity* (HEW, 1978). Figures are for tumors occurring in addition to the spontaneous rate and represent an estimate of observed tumors. The extent of the EPA's reliance on the one-hit linear model of risk is indicated by the low number of cancers expected in the most highly exposed group (applicators) and the high number in the population exposed to nondetectable levels of the pesticide.

b. "Since lifetime animal studies were used to make risk estimates, the probability of cancer in humans is estimated as a lifetime probability and should therefore be interpreted as an index or 'mathematical' expectation rather than a 'clinical' expectation." EPA, "Chlorobenzilate: Position Document 3," p. 35.

c. Assumes that applicators' daily exposure is equivalent to 0.39–1.3 ppm.

d. Assumes that dietary exposure occurs at the level of exposure expressed as a reasonable upper limit (0.0025–0.0061 ppm daily throughout lifetime).

unprotected applicators. In addition, the Carcinogen Assessment Group stated in the conclusion of its assessment that "the weight of evidence indicates that chlorobenzilate is a possible human carcinogen."[26]

The EPA's formulation of regulatory options and its final choice were ultimately based on an assessment of benefits associated with the use of chlorobenzilate; the quantitative risk assessment entered into a general balancing of risk against the costs of cancellation. Such benefits include chlorobenzilate's selectivity, which is important to integrated pest management programs that use a combination of natural predators and parasites of the insects with this compatible miticide. Uncontrolled mites affect fruit size, appearance, and crop yield. Position Document 3 includes information on the costs of pesticides and programs that would most likely be used in place of chlorobenzilate as well as their effectiveness, cancer risk, and cost per acre, but does not quantify risks by comparing these other pesticides to chlorobenzilate.

The regulatory options considered included continued registration of chlorobenzilate, cancellation of all uses, and modified terms of registration. Specifically, EPA chose to limit registration of chlorobenzilate

26. EPA, "Chlorobenzilate: Position Document 3," p. 31.

citrus use to certain states and to cancel its noncitrus uses, since the benefits of the latter did not outweigh the risks. Moreover, limiting the pesticide to certain states would prevent proliferation of its use. Thus the maximum risk incidence under the chosen option was estimated to be 2.6 to 6.4 cancers per million lifetimes for Florida citrus consumers and 4 to 278 cancers per million lifetimes for pesticide applicators.[27] The cost was estimated to be $4.4 million to $19.1 million for the modified citrus use and $200,000 a year for cancellation of noncitrus use.

A Critique of the Assessment

A central source of uncertainty in the chlorobenzilate risk assessment results from the paucity of exposure data. The EPA's methods of estimating applicator exposure, using exposure levels and absorption rates derived from data on other pesticides, is reasonable. But the agency should explicitly acknowledge the lack of exposure data and thus the conjectural nature of its exposure estimates. Similarly, instead of reducing these uncertain exposure estimates to single figures, the EPA should indicate the range of possible exposure and resulting risk. A detailed National Academy of Sciences review of the RPAR examination of chlorobenzilate recommended that this range be represented by figures for the most probable and maximum plausible levels of risk.[28]

The NAS study proposes two modifications for the calculation of human exposure. It notes that pesticides have a limited life on the market. Consequently the NAS assumes a maximum ten-year exposure in calculating average worker exposure instead of the EPA's forty-year, occupational lifetime exposure. This modifying assumption would likewise reduce the lifetime estimate of the amount of chlorobenzilate ingested by the general population. The NAS study also attempts to account for expected worker noncompliance with respiratory regulation. Only 50 percent compliance with the work rules is expected, and this

27. This compares with a risk if all uses of chlorobenzilate were continued of 2.6–6.4 cancers per million lifetimes for Florida citrus consumers, 2 per million for the remainder of U.S. consumers, 400–1,400 per million for applicators, and 0.1 million for noncitrus applicators.

28. NAS, *Regulating Pesticides*. The NAS report presents a comprehensive critique of the RPAR process, to which reference is made in the following discussion.

would therefore suggest that the EPA's calculation of the risk reduction resulting from its regulation might be an overestimate.[29]

The EPA's use of quantitative risk assessment in choosing a regulatory option through a balancing of risks and benefits would be complemented by assessments of the risks associated with alternatives that would be used if chlorobenzilate were canceled.[30] Under the RPAR, a registrant bears the burden of coming forward with evidence, and if he fails to do so, the alternative is not considered. The agency unduly narrows its options to various modifications of continued chlorobenzilate registration by eliminating alternatives that are not registered for pesticide use. The NAS study, however, proposes a system for establishing priorities for pesticides for a full RPAR review and provides that alternatives to the substance under study receive simultaneous coverage.[31]

The EPA reported and evaluated the scientific data on chlorobenzilate's oncogenicity in detail. Given its final choice between the Innes and National Cancer Institute studies, the agency decided on the Innes report precisely because it showed higher oncogenic risks. Such a conservative choice was based in part on the continued uncertainty of the toxin's effects on the most sensitive populations, such as older people and infants. In addition, the EPA believed a conservative view was warranted due to chlorobenzilate's effects when in synergistic combination with other toxic substances.

29. The NAS study makes detailed modifications in the calculation of dietary exposure, most importantly suggesting that estimates be based on the observed accumulation of residue in meat as compared to the amount of pesticide ingested by the cow (the "accumulation ratio"), instead of assuming a residue level based on the technical limits of analytical sensitivity. In calculating the dietary exposure due to noncitrus fruits, the NAS combines the modifying assumption that these fruits are not generally consumed whole and the finding that residues are not measured in all fruits examined. The NAS arrives at a substantially lower dietary exposure for noncitrus fruits (which constitute a minority of chlorobenzilate-treated fruits).

30. The NAS study criticizes the EPA benefit analysis with regard to its higher estimate for the cost of alternatives to chlorobenzilate control of snow scale and the EPA's failure to consider studies showing no difference in yield between sprayed and unsprayed groves.

31. The committee demonstrates a benefit-risk balancing for dicofol, an alternative pesticide, to make a general comparison of chlorobenzilate's toxicity to that of alternatives. The NAS proposes a complete system for evaluating regulatory options based on the use of a carcinogenic activity indicator instead of on a quantitative risk assessment like that produced by the CAG.

The EPA proposed in September 1982 to modify its rule requiring submission of data on the efficacy of a pesticide, proposing to rely instead on the market to eliminate ineffective products (47 Fed. Reg. 40661 [1982]). The availability of information on efficacy presumably would affect the calculation of benefits.

CHAPTER EIGHT

Regulating Food Additives and Contaminants

CHRISTOPHER H. MARRARO

THE REGULATION of food additives and those contaminants that possess a carcinogenic potential is an issue of high public emotion with important social consequences. However, regulation is difficult because the risk to the public health of ingesting carcinogens in small doses is unknown. Further, some suspected carcinogens confer substantial health and economic benefits when added to food in small quantities. Other contaminants occur naturally in the environment and cannot be eliminated with current technology.

Statutory Framework

The Food and Drug Administration (FDA) has perhaps the clearest mandate of any federal regulatory agency to protect the health of the general population from toxic substances and carcinogens. This mandate is supported by the complex statutory framework.

The governing authority is the federal Food, Drug and Cosmetic Act of 1938,[1] which has been amended several times. Section 402 of the original act declared any food to be adulterated that "bears or contains any poisonous or deleterious substance which may render it injurious to health."[2] Section 406 empowered the FDA to establish tolerance levels for "added poisonous or deleterious substances" whose occurrence in food "cannot be avoided" or whose use is "required" to produce food.

1. 21 U.S.C.301.
2. 21 U.S.C.342(a)(1).

This section authorized the FDA to permit the occurrence of some potentially toxic substances in food because of the utility of the substance or importance of the food.[3]

In 1958 Congress enacted the Food Additives Amendments (section 409).[4] The amendments require that substances that through processing or packaging "can reasonably be expected" to become components of food must be proved safe through rigorous scientific testing procedures. These amendments mark an important benchmark in the evolution of food safety regulation. The burden of proof was originally on the agency to show that an intentionally added food substance may be injurious to health. In contrast, the amendments provide that the burden of establishing the safety of the food additive be shifted to the manufacturer.

The Delaney clause was added to the act as part of the Food Additives Amendments. The clause provides that:

> No additive shall be deemed to be safe if it is found to induce cancer when ingested by man or animal, or if it is found, after tests which are appropriate for the evaluation of the safety of food additives, to induce cancer in man or animal.[5]

It is critical, however, to understand that the Delaney clause is applicable only to substances that fall within the definition of food additives and that it does not apply to all substances found or used in food. Further, Congress has excepted two categories of food additives: (a) substances whose use in food is "generally recognized as safe by qualified experts" and (b) "prior sanctioned substances" that the FDA or the U.S. Department of Agriculture (USDA) formally approved for use before the enactment of the Food Additives Amendment.

In 1960 Congress enacted the Color Additive Amendments,[6] which apply to all substances used for the primary purpose of adding color to food. Under the amendments, a manufacturer of a color additive must demonstrate its safety by rigorous testing before it can be approved by the FDA. There are no prior sanction exceptions, and a second anticancer clause is contained in the amendments.

In 1962 several years of congressional hearings on the drug industry culminated in the Drug Amendments of 1962.[7] The amendments required compounds administered to animals as feed additives to be shown safe

3. 21 U.S.C.346.
4. 21 U.S.C.348.
5. 21 U.S.C.348(c)(3)(A).
6. 21 U.S.C.376.
7. 76 Stat. 785.

before use. As defined in section 201 of the amendments,[8] the term *safe* embraces both human and animal health.

The drug legislation also amended the anticancer clauses to rectify what Congress perceived as the inequity associated with the use of diethylstilbestrol (DES) as a prior sanctioned substance. Under the Food Additives Amendment, certain uses of DES were prior sanctioned. Therefore, continued use of DES consistent with prior sanction was permitted, but the Delaney clause prohibited any new uses. The Drug Amendments of 1962 made the anticancer clause of the Food Additives Amendments inapplicable to chemicals such as veterinary drugs when used in feed if the secretary of Health, Education and Welfare (now Health and Human Services) finds that (1) the drug would not adversely affect the animal and (2) that no residue of the additive could be found in any edible portion of the animal.

The most recent amendments concerning animal drugs build on the 1962 amendments and are applicable to drugs administered directly to animals that "could reasonably be expected" to leave residues in human food. Under the amended act,[9] no drug that is likely to leave residues in edible tissue of livestock may be used, nor may food containing residues be marketed without prior FDA approval. However, the amendments make the anticancer provisions inapplicable to animal drugs "if no residue is found [by methods of examination approved by the secretary] in any edible portion of such animals."

Thus, for the first time amendments were enacted to encourage agency consideration of quantitative risk assessment in the regulatory process for food additives. The agency can determine the acceptable risk for a substance and then mandate the use of particular analytic methods to identify a practical, rather than absolute, no-residue level determined through risk assessment. The agency has described the policy with regard to animal drugs as follows:

> The goal of regulating compounds that are to be used on food-producing animals is to ensure that none is permitted to yield residues in edible tissues at concentrations presenting a risk of carcinogenesis above an acceptable level.[10]

Congress has made several attempts to refine the regulation of food additives. In general, it has required that individual substances be

8. 21 U.S.C.321(u).
9. Animal Drug Amendments of 1968 ("DES Proviso"). 21 U.S.C.360(b), 21 U.S.C.355.
10. 44 Fed. Reg. 17077 (1979).

presented to the FDA for approval prior to use and directed that the agency must find a substance safe for human consumption before approving it. Consequently, Congress has placed the burden of proof on the proponent of the food ingredient. In addition, Congress has placed stringent requirements on the regulation of carcinogens and in three instances has incorporated language that prohibits the FDA from finding a substance safe for human consumption if it is found to induce cancer when ingested by humans or animals.[11] This limitation is not universal; Congress has opened the door for the application of risk assessment to carcinogens in the area of veterinary or animal drugs.

Application of Risk Assessment to Food Substances

The following sections analyze the use of risk assessment in the regulation of three types of substances: sodium nitrite, a food additive; aflatoxin, an environmental contaminant; and DES, an animal drug now banned by the FDA. These sections compare several regulatory schemes with respect to the agency's ability to perceive both the risks and benefits of these different classes of carcinogenic substances.

Sodium Nitrite: A No-Risk Approach

Sodium nitrite is used as a preservative for cured meats; it inhibits the growth of bacteria, particularly *Clostridium botulinium,* which causes the fatal type of food poisoning known as botulism.[12] Nitrite is extremely effective in controlling *Clostridium;* there have been no reports of death due to botulism from cured meats in the United States for several decades. Unfortunately, nitrite combines with amines and amides to produce nitrosamines, which have been identified as potent carcinogens in animals.[13] Thus the issue can be stated simply: nitrite is valuable in controlling *Clostridium* but may itself be a carcinogen.

The statutory framework embodied in the Food, Drug and Cosmetic Act controls the regulation of food additives such as nitrite. Because the

11. Richard Merrill, "Federal Regulation of Cancer-Causing Chemicals," p. 10.

12. Much of the material in this paragraph is from Lester B. Lave, *The Strategy of Social Regulation,* pp. 48–49.

13. D. D. Fine and others, "N-Nitroso Compounds in Air and Water"; Steven R. Tannenbaum and others, "Nitrite and Nitrate Are Formed by Endogenous Synthesis in the Human Intestine"; Donald C. Harvey and others, "Survey of Food Products for Volatile N-Nitrosamines"; and *Food Safety and Quality: Nitrites.*

act is inflexible with respect to carcinogens, it is ineffective in dealing with substances such as sodium nitrite that ironically have strong benefits coupled with potential hazards.

The act provides that a food shall be deemed to be adulterated if it bears or contains an unsafe food additive or color additive.[14] A food additive is considered unsafe unless it is used in conformity with an existing regulation.[15] The Delaney clause provides that an additive shall be deemed unsafe if it is found to induce cancer when ingested by humans or animals. Thus, if nitrites are food additives under the act and induce cancer in man or animal, no regulation for their safe use may be issued and any food containing nitrite is adulterated within the meaning of the act.

The concern that nitrite may be an animal carcinogen was initially recognized as a result of suggestive findings in a study conducted in 1974 by Paul M. Newberne.[16] On the basis of these findings, the FDA commissioned an elaborate study.[17] Newberne used 2,224 rats in eighteen groups to test the carcinogenicity of nitrite. The results generally showed an association between nitrite and cancer and, in the final report, Newberne reported an increased incidence of lymphomas in rats given sodium nitrite in various diets or drinking water. He reported an increased incidence of "immunoblastic cell proliferation" in the spleen of rats receiving nitrite. The results, however, showed little or no association between the level of nitrite in the diet and the proportion of rats with cancer. Newberne also reported that nitrite appeared to be more of a promoter of the neoplastic process than an initiator.

The results of the Newberne study were presented to an FDA committee in May 1978. For unknown reasons, however, the results were withheld from the FDA's senior toxicologists until late July 1978.[18] The findings of the Newberne study were met with heavy skepticism by the senior toxicologists, and it was suggested that a review of the study

14. 21 U.S.C.342.

15. 21 U.S.C.321(s).

16. Paul M. Newberne and R. C. Shank, "Induction of Liver and Lung Tumors in Rats by the Simultaneous Administration of Sodium Nitrite and Morpholine"; R. C. Shank and Paul M. Newberne, "Dose-Response Study of Carcinogenicity of Dietary Sodium Nitrite Morpholine in Rats and Hamsters"; and *Food Safety and Quality: Nitrites,* Hearings before the Senate Committee on Agriculture, Nutrition and Forestry.

17. Paul M. Newberne, "Dietary Nitrite in the Rat"; and Paul M. Newberne, "Nitrite Promotes Lymphoma Incidence in Rats."

18. Interview, Albert C. Kolbye, Jr., associate director of toxicology, Bureau of Foods, Food and Drug Administration (October 1980).

be undertaken. A government interagency working group on nitrite research examined a sample of histologic slides from the Newberne study and found an 85 percent difference in pathologic diagnoses.[19] On the basis of this examination, the FDA requested that a reevaluation of the histopathological findings of the Newberne study be undertaken by the Universities Associated for Research and Education in Pathology, Inc. (UAREP), a nonprofit consortium of fifteen universities.[20]

In essence, the reevaluation found that the Newberne study offered insufficient evidence to conclude that sodium nitrite itself causes cancer in rats. A substantial number of lesions originally diagnosed as lymphomas were not confirmed as such, nor were any of the immunoblastic lesion type originally reported. Instead, many lymphosarcomas were found to represent a different type of sarcoma (mesenchymal, not lymphoid), which is not known to exist in humans.[21]

A major flaw in the experimental design was also discovered. After extensive review, what appeared to be one large experiment was found to constitute groups of animals obtained at different times from the breeder. The groups were not properly randomized and the rats were housed in different rooms with variation in exposure to potential confounding factors. Thus, some experimental groups were not controlled at all by the ostensible control group. The reports conclude that "these sources of uncontrolled variation complicated evaluation of the experiment and rendered certain comparisons invalid."[22] Other potential problems were the possibility of cross-contamination by urethane from some groups to others through vapor-transfer and the possibility of infectious disease in some of the animals, as suggested by the rats in one group who developed pneumonia.

Thus, on the basis of the reevaluation, both the FDA and USDA concluded that there was insufficient scientific evidence to ban sodium nitrite as a carcinogen. In a joint press release dated August 19, 1980, FDA Commissioner Jere E. Goyan and Assistant USDA Secretary Carol Tucker Foreman stated "there is no basis for FDA or USDA to initiate

19. Ibid.

20. Department of Health and Human Services, Food and Drug Administration, *Re-evaluation of the Pathology Findings of Studies on Nitrite and Cancer;* and HHS, FDA, *Report of the Interagency Working Group on Nitrite Research.*

21. HHS, FDA, *Re-evaluation of the Pathology Findings,* pp. 16–17.

22. Ibid., p. 2.

any action to remove nitrite from foods at this time."[23] The result is that nitrite is presently not subject to the anticancer provisions of the Food Additive Amendments or to the Color Additive Amendments.

However, if the reevaluation had supported the Newberne conclusion that nitrite is itself a carcinogen, it would appear that the statutory framework does not permit the FDA to consider the risk or benefits of nitrite and allow its continued use as a food additive despite its potential carcinogenicity. The U.S. Department of Justice, in a recent opinion of the attorney general, has concluded after an extensive legal analysis that:

> It is our opinion that the Secretaries (HHS, Agriculture) do not have the authority to balance the benefits of nitrites against their potential harm and determine that their continued use will be permitted until such time as a feasible substitute is developed and put in place. Upon a determination by the Secretaries that an additive causes cancer in man or animals, the decision whether the statutory ban shall be postponed or eliminated is reserved to the Congress [*Public Citizen* v. *Foreman,* 78-1064 (D.C.C. July 1980)].[24]

The opinion was based on examination of the Food Additives Amendments, the Color Additive Amendments, the Meat Act[25] and the Poultry Act.[26] In rendering its opinion, the Justice Department assumed that the use of nitrites in red meat had a prior sanction by the USDA, and also concluded that nitrites would not have to be considered as color additives in processed meats and would not be subject to the anticancer proviso of the Color Additive Amendments. The USDA did assume, however, that nitrites are "food additives" and therefore subject to the Delaney clause.

The attorney general's opinion states that no indication appears in the legislative history of the Food and Drug Act or the Meat Act that the beneficial effects of a substance may be taken into account. The U.S. Circuit Court of Appeals for the District of Columbia Circuit, in *Schuck* v. *Butz,* supports the prohibition of the balancing approach.[27] In *Schuck,* the plaintiffs sought to require the secretary of agriculture to ban the addition of sodium nitrite and nitrite in meat products on the grounds

23. Karen DeWitt, "U.S. Will Not Seek to Ban Nitrite from Foods as Cause of Cancer," *New York Times* (August 20, 1980).

24. 43 Opin. Att'y Gen. 19 (1979).

25. 21 U.S.C.601 *et seq.*

26. 21 U.S.C.451 *et seq.*

27. 500 F.2d 810 (1974).

that their alleged carcinogenicity rendered the meat adulterated under the Meat Act. After express reference to the USDA's view that these substances prevent botulism, the court noted with approval

> the Department's apparent acceptance, on appeal, of appellant's assertions that *possible beneficial effects are not relevant* to a determination whether a product is adulterated, and that the proper standard of proof is whether there is convincing evidence that the product "contains any poisonous or deleterious substance which may render it injurious to health" [emphasis added].[28]

The opinion of the attorney general is clear. The statutory framework is inflexible in dealing with food additives such as sodium nitrite when there has been a finding of carcinogenicity. The benefits or the risks of the substance may not be considered even where those benefits substantially outweigh the risk.

It is interesting to note, however, that because the government position is that processed red meats are prior sanctioned (that is, not subject to the Delaney clause), the FDA did attempt to do a primitive risk analysis with respect to the addition of sodium nitrite in processed red meats.[29] This attempt to consider the risks of nitrite in processed red meats was done before the opinion of the attorney general was issued and is discussed in the USDA-FDA 1978 report.

Aflatoxin: A Balancing Approach

Aflatoxin is the product of a mold that grows on grain and nuts. Thus it is defined as an environmental contaminant rather than a food additive. Aflatoxin is a potent carcinogen in rats and other animals, and there is suggestive evidence that it causes liver cancer in humans. It is difficult to lower the concentration of aflatoxin in some foods and impossible to eliminate it. Further, there are no known beneficial effects from this mold derivative. Thus it is the responsibility of regulators to define a "safe" tolerance level that is technologically feasible to obtain.[30]

Richard Merrill notes that the FDA has historically given a broad interpretation to the term *added*.[31] In regulations published in 1977, the agency affirmed that any substance that is not an "inherent" constituent

28. 21 U.S.C.601(1)(1); 500 F.2d 812 M.6. (1974).

29. Interviews with Kolbye (October 1980) and Richard Cooper, chief counsel, Food and Drug Administration (October 1980); see also FDA and Department of Agriculture, "FDA's and USDA's Action Regarding Nitrite."

30. Lave, *The Strategy of Social Regulation,* p. 68.

31. The section on aflatoxin is essentially a synopsis of Merrill, "Federal Regulation of Cancer-Causing Chemicals."

of food is an added substance, including contaminants that naturally occur in the environment. Thus, FDA considers aflatoxin to be an added substance but has chosen to regulate this type of substance under section 406 of the food and drug act, instead of the Delaney clause. Section 406 permits the agency to balance risks and benefits in establishing tolerance levels. The FDA apparently desired this flexibility in order to regulate the concentration of some potentially toxic substances on the basis of the importance of the foods containing the contaminants. It is also significant that section 406 does not preclude the marketing of foods that contain substances that have been shown to cause cancer in animals or humans.

Merrill states that the "FDA has taken the position that it may establish a tolerance limit for a contaminant shown to be a carcinogen and thus 'approve' its occurrence in food at levels below the tolerance—if the criteria of Section 406 are met." Although this authorization is difficult to reconcile with the policy set forth in the Delaney clause, Merrill asserts "that the result can be squared if one accepts FDA's conclusion that environmental contaminants are to be considered 'added' substances whose occurrence cannot be avoided."[32]

In setting a tolerance level for a substance under section 406, the statute requires the FDA to consider two criteria: (1) the level at which consumption will pose only an insignificant risk to public health and (2) the extent to which the level can be controlled by good manufacturing processes. Merrill states that the FDA also considers the capability of analytic methods to measure the substance (that is, no agency can set a tolerance level below the detectable limit of the substance).

In 1965 the agency set informal action (tolerance) levels for aflatoxins in several commodities, including corn and peanuts.[33] The level was set at 30 parts per billion (ppb), which reflected the then current limits of detection. This level was later lowered to 20 ppb.

In 1974 the FDA proposed a formal tolerance level of 15 ppb for aflatoxins in shelled peanuts and peanut products.[34] This level was already met by 93 percent of the sampled peanut products; 89 percent met a tolerance level of 10 ppb.[35] Therefore, the agency believed that peanut producers could meet a 15 ppb level without substantial expense.

32. Merrill, p. 1378.
33. Ibid., p. 1403.
34. 39 Fed. Reg. 42751(1974).
35. Merrill, "Federal Regulation of Cancer-Causing Chemicals," p. 1405.

The agency rationale for reducing the level from 20 ppb to 15 ppb, rather than a major reduction, was that the level of aflatoxin present in commercially marketed peanut products had not been found to pose a serious risk to humans: liver cancer rates in the areas of the United States where the climate is conducive to aflatoxin contamination did not differ significantly from liver cancer rates elsewhere.[36]

The FDA also claimed that analytical methods could not accurately detect levels below 15 ppb, and that a reduction to 5 ppb or 10 ppb would result in losses of supply with high increases in price.[37] Merrill comments that the agency's failure to analyze in detail the consequences of lowering the standard to 5 ppb or 10 ppb is troublesome in several respects. He challenges the FDA assertion that analytic techniques do not permit consideration of lower levels, and points out that the 10 ppb level was being met by only 4 percent fewer of the sampled peanut products than those meeting the 15 ppb level.[38]

The FDA reopened its comment period on the proposed 15 ppb tolerance level in response to a study it had completed.[39] The study was an assessment of the health risks of aflatoxin that applied several quantitative risk assessment techniques for extrapolating results from animal experiments and epidemiological studies.[40] The risk assessment addressed the issue of alternative tolerance levels; by quantifying risk, it permitted a balancing approach weighing economic costs against technological feasibility and analyzing the cancer risks attributable to four alternate levels: 20 ppb (current tolerance), 15 ppb (proposed tolerance), 10 ppb, and 5 ppb.[41] This risk assessment was applied to both peanuts and corn.

The results of the risk assessment for peanut products are shown in table 8-1.

The reduction from the current 20 ppb level to the 15 ppb proposed level represents a decline of about 25 percent in the estimated rates of cancer. Further reduction to 10 ppb represents a 33 percent decline in

36. Lave, *The Strategy of Social Regulation,* p. 69.

37. 39 Fed. Reg. 42750 (1974).

38. Merrill, "Federal Regulation of Cancer-Causing Chemicals," pp. 1103–1410. Albert Kolbye supports Merrill's contention concerning analytic capabilities (interview, October 1980).

39. 43 Fed. Reg. 8808 (1978).

40. FDA, "Assessment of Estimated Risk Resulting from Aflatoxin in Consumer Peanut Products and Other Food Contaminants."

41. Since 5 ppb is the lowest detectable level for aflatoxin, it is the functional equivalent of a zero-risk tolerance level.

Table 8-1. Results of Risk Assessment for Peanut Products

Proposed tolerance level (parts per billion)	*Incidence of cancer (per 100,000 people)*	
	Average consumption of peanut products	*Maximum consumption of peanut products*
20	1.1	2.7
15	0.8	2.1
10	0.5	. . .
5	0.3	. . .

Source: Adapted from Richard Merrill, "Federal Regulation of Cancer-Causing Chemicals," draft report to the Administrative Conference of the United States, June 15, 1980.

cancer rates. However, the report concludes that there is little gain in public health from a reduction to 10 ppb or 5 ppb as opposed to the 15 ppb level being considered. No rationale is given for this conclusion.

The final promulgation of a tolerance level has not yet been set by the FDA. The salient point to be made here, however, is that the FDA does have the statutory authority to consider an evaluation of risks and benefits in setting tolerance levels for substances which, although having a carcinogenic potential, present little or no observable risk to the general population. This is in sharp contrast to substances that are classified as food additives under section 409 and subject to the Delaney clause. Albert Kolbye stated that the risks from aflatoxin exceed those of sodium nitrite.[42] Sodium nitrite has special beneficial qualities, while aflatoxin does not. Yet if sodium nitrite had been classified as an animal carcinogen, the FDA would have been required under present law to ban its use. In contrast, the statutory framework used by the FDA to regulate environmental contaminants provides flexibility and enables regulators to weigh risks, benefits, and economic considerations.

DES: Acceptable Risk

Diethylstilbestrol (DES) is a synthetic estrogen used as a drug for humans and, until recently, as a growth stimulant for cattle.[43] DES is employed as a "morning after" drug to prevent pregnancy and was used unsuccessfully to prevent miscarriage. The large doses (often 12–18

42. Interview (October 1980).

43. Much of this discussion is from Lave, *The Strategy of Social Regulation*, pp. 57–58.

grams) given to prevent miscarriage were teratogenic and likely to cause cancer in the fetus.[44] Recent studies suggest that most of the teratogenic effects may be reversible.[45]

The FDA has banned DES as a growth stimulant for cattle and other animals, both as an implant and feed supplement.[46] The drug was prohibited by the FDA as a feed mix in 1972 and as an implant in 1973, but was then reinstated by the court in *Animal Health Institute* v. *FDA*[47] because of procedural failures by the agency in issuing the regulations. The implant ban was finally mandated by the FDA in June 1979 and executed in November 1979. The implant ban was invoked because the industry could not meet its burden under the existing law to prove that the risk of cancer was less than one cancer in a population of 1 million persons.[48]

The DES implant ban was partially justified by the use of risk assessment procedures. The risk assessment approach is arguably authorized by the Drug Amendments to the anticancer clause of the Food, Drug and Cosmetic Act.[49] The "DES proviso" to the anticancer clause, as these amendments are referred to, provides that: "no residue of such drug will be found by methods of examination prescribed or approved by the Secretary by regulations . . . in any edible portion of such animals after slaughter or in any food yielded by or derived from the living animals."[50] The regulations do not require that valid scientific methods be capable of detecting a residue of the drug in food. Rather, they require only that the level of residue produce more than a *de minimis* risk (one cancer in 1 million lifetimes), based on the agency's

44. A. L. Herbst, "Summary of the Changes in the Human Female Genital Tract as a Consequence of Maternal Diethylstilbestrol Therapy"; Marluce Bibbo and others, "Follow-up Study of Male and Female Offspring of DES-Exposed Mothers"; and Bernard Kliman, "Testimony in the Matter of Diethylstilbestrol: Withdrawal of Approval of New Animal Drug Applications," FDA Docket No. 76N-0002 (September 1977).

45. Donald A. Antonioli, Louis Burke, and Emanuel A. Friedman, "Natural History of Diethylstilbestrol-Associated Genital Tract Lesions: Cervical Ectopy and Cervicovaginal Hood."

46. Kliman, "Testimony in the Matter of Diethylstilbestrol."

47. No. 77-806 (D.D.C., February 8, 1978).

48. FDA Commissioner Donald Kennedy concluded that the evidence "does not allow me to determine what level of DES might be low enough to cause less than one cancer in one million persons." Because he could not determine a residue level that had no cancer-causing effect (1 in 1 million risk), he ruled that DES must be banned. See *Wall Street Journal*, July 15, 1980, p. 44.

49. 21 U.S.C.348(c)(3)(A), 360b(d)(1)(H), and 376(b)(5)(B).

50. 21 U.S.C.360b.

interpretation of scientific evidence.[51] Thus the agency will approve carcinogenic compounds for use in animal feeds or as implants on the basis of assays capable of measuring prescribed levels of residues. The procedures and criterion for evaluating and approving assays used to measure the residue levels are known as sensitivity of the method analysis (SOM), and are contained in proposed regulations.[52] These regulations seek to determine the lowest limit of reliable measurement for the regulatory assay required for carcinogenic substances under the "DES proviso." Because of the extensive interest in risk regulation of carcinogens, the agency stated at the same time it published the proposed regulations: "Time is ripe for formulating a comprehensive approach for regulating all chemical carcinogens. Expanding the use of the principles set out in these regulations into other areas regulated by the agency seems desirable from the perspectives of science and public health protection."[53] The agency, therefore, appears to be using the risk assessment element as a basis for a future anticancer policy.

The proposed regulations and their applicability to DES have grown in part out of a concern for a recent trend in the development of analytic science: "spectacular scientific progress in achieving ever-decreasing lowest limits of measure. . . . Depending on the substance or class of substances, this decrease in the lowest limits of measurement during the last 20 years ranges between two and five orders of magnitude."[54] Because the statute allows the approval of drugs only when "no residue" is found, the concern is that analytical methods will detect levels below the carcinogenic potential of the substance. Therefore, the agency approach is to determine the carcinogen potential or risk of a substance and then design regulations to require that an assay's lowest limit of measure be commensurate with the carcinogenic potential.

The acceptable level of risk chosen by FDA in the proposed regulations is one cancer in 1 million over a lifetime. The commissioner has

51. 44 Fed. Reg. 17092 (1979); and interviews with Michael Taylor, special assistant to the FDA commissioner (October 1980); Stuart Pape, FDA attorney (October 1980); and Joseph Rodricks, FDA deputy associate commissioner for health affairs (September 1980). This interpretation is also consistent with case law: *Hess & Clark, Division of Rhodia, Inc.* v. *FDA*, 495 F. 2d 975 (1974); *Chemetron Corp.* v. *U.S. Department of Health, Education and Welfare*, 495 F. 2d 995 (1974); *AHI* v. *FDA;* and *Monsanto Co.* v. *Kennedy*, 613 F. 2d 947 (1979).

52. 44 Fed. Reg. 17070 (1979).

53. Ibid.

54. 44 Fed. Reg. 17075 (1979).

interpreted the statute as permitting the use of carcinogenic animal drugs if there "would be no significant increase in the human risk of cancer from that use" and has concluded that a lifetime risk of one in 1 million imposes no additional risk of cancer to the public.[55] The FDA calculates the risk conservatively.

The regulations further propose to establish a rigorous premarket testing process for sponsored compounds. All sponsored compounds must initially undergo an assessment for carcinogenic potential. The initial assessment is based on a probability of carcinogenesis of the sponsored compound calculated as the product of three factors.[56] If the commissioner makes a determination after applying the previous analysis that a sponsored compound has a carcinogenic potential, the burden then shifts to the proponent to identify the level that meets the one in 1 million requirement.[57] The petitioner will be required under the proposed regulations to undertake a six-step procedure for data collection and evaluation.[58]

On the basis of these data acquisition and evaluation studies, an operational definition of "no residue" is determined. Specifically, the "no residue" definition is established through dose-response testing, followed by extrapolation of the test data using a linear-threshold extrapolation procedure.[59] This process determines the "no residue" dose that corresponds to a lifetime risk no greater than one in 1 million. Once the risk level is below one in 1,000, the different extrapolation models diverge. The linear extrapolation procedure, a no-threshold model, is able to place an upper bound on animal risks.

DES was banned because the industry was unable to show that the lifetime risk of one in 1 million could be satisfied. In assessing the risk associated with the use of DES as an implant, only animal toxicological data was used. The population-dose data on humans is quite poor, according to Joseph Rodricks, who also commented on three basic inadequacies in the data and monitoring techniques. His first criticism is

55. Ibid.

56. 44 Fed. Reg. 17079 (1979).

57. The threshold finding gives the proponent the opportunity to demonstrate that there is no carcinogenic potential, thereby avoiding the burden of costly and rigorous SOM procedures.

58. 44 Fed. Reg. 17078 (1979).

59. The linear extrapolation procedure was selected over several options, including the prior sanctioned Mantel-Bryan procedure. It was considered to be least likely to underestimate risk and to be capable of use without complex computer programs.

that USDA monitoring capability has never been validated and probably underestimates the level of DES residue. Second, he notes that there has never been a true attempt to do systematic toxicology on the effects of DES. Finally, he feels that there should be a complete study of the biochemical effects of DES on feed animals.[60]

The main problem with both the SOM procedures and risk assessment approaches as applied by the FDA to DES (as well as other substances) is that the agency SOM and risk assessment require cumulative conservative assumptions (such as the no-threshold approach).[61] This procedure requires industry to accept costly data acquisition requirements (metabolite studies). This may have the effect of bankrupting an industry, thus defeating the purpose of risk assessment to regulate more systematically. Albert Kolbye has stated that because of too many conservative assumptions, "most drugs in food-producing animals will be banned if the regulations are applied literally."[62]

Further, major controversy surrounds the acquisition and testing requirements. The most controversial and costly requirements are the metabolite studies required in order to obtain information on the residues that occur in edible tissues when a compound is administered to an animal.[63] A substance administered to target animals is not necessarily the substance consumed by persons who consume the edible portions of the animal. The enzymatic system can act upon a compound administered to an animal and produce new compounds (metabolites). The metabolic study requirements are therefore aimed at the identification of those residues. This requirement has been contested because it requires sophisticated testing procedures and economically burdensome multiple testing regimes.

There is agreement among many present and former FDA personnel that the previously permitted uses of DES are not dangerous to humans, but that the substance cannot meet the one in 1 million risk level under the present risk analysis procedures. That is, the previously permitted uses of DES pose only a *de minimis* risk.[64] Kolbye has noted that

60. Interview (September 1980).

61. Interviews with Stuart Pape (October 1980) and Richard Cooper (October 1980).

62. Interview (October 1980).

63. Information provided in interview with Joseph Rodricks (September 1980), who feels the core of the SOM is risk assessment and that the risk assessment extrapolation procedures are not the focus of industry concern.

64. There is some judicial sanction for the concept of *de minimis* risk regulation under section 409 of the act. The opinion in *Monsanto* v. *Kennedy* seems to suggest that where

although DES is a powerful hormone it is not mutagenically active. Concern that DES is a permanent teratogen has been seriously questioned in a recent study that reports that there was a marked regression of structural abnormalities associated with in utero exposure to DES.[65] This regression is biologically plausible and apparently reduces concern that DES is a permanent teratogen.

While DES appears to be a carcinogen at large doses, the dose from DES in meat is 1 million times smaller. Additionally, since some feedlot operators initially ignored the implant ban, the economic value of using DES appears to be great.[66]

The FDA is expected to reexamine its position concerning SOM. New guidelines concerning threshold assessments were announced in February 1982,[67] and there is some thought within the agency and with other persons familiar with SOM that the FDA will eventually promulgate regulations that will lessen the data acquisition requirements for proponents.

The prevailing thought is that the FDA will modify its regulations by concentrating on the initial assessment rather than by modifying the risk assessment extrapolation techniques. The new regulations will reduce the industry burden by allowing proponents to perform simple toxicological studies that will characterize the potential hazards of the residues and exempt the substance from further SOM requirements. A new approach to threshold assessment will impose less burdensome toxicology studies that forgo the economically burdensome chronic testing requirements.

Considering the effects of the DES ban, and the actual risks involved with DES as an implant, this action may promote a more rational approach to the assessment of risks.

---

a substance presents a *de minimis* situation, the agency has discretion not to label it a section 409 food additive (triggering Delaney) and thus to exercise control by regulation rather than by statutory design. The FDA, therefore, would have some control over the classification of a substance possessing a *de minimis* risk, which is critical to the application of a particular regulatory scheme.

65. Antonioli, Burke, and Friedman, "Natural History of Diethylstilbestrol-Associated Genital Tract Lesions."

66. *Wall Street Journal*, July 15, 1980.

67. 47 Fed. Reg. 4972 (1982).

Conclusion

In regulating toxic and carcinogenic substances added or contained in food, Congress has refused to delegate fundamental regulatory policy decisions and basic value judgments. More specifically, Congress has adopted a zero-risk policy toward the use of suspected carcinogens as food additives but has allowed consideration of potential risks and benefits for a limited number of specific uses. Three distinct regulatory schemes have developed.

The first example is the regulation of sodium nitrite as a food additive under the Food Additive Amendments of 1958. The regulation of sodium nitrite is subject to the anticancer provisions of the Delaney clause, which does not permit the assessment of risks or benefits in controlling a substance.

The second is that used in the regulation of aflatoxin, an environmental contaminant. The Food and Drug Administration uses a regulatory scheme that permits the assessment of benefits and risks to control this substance. The regulatory scheme bypasses the Delaney clause in recognition of the importance of the contaminated food and the economic and technologic feasibility of removing the carcinogen.

The final scheme is contained in the "DES proviso" of the Animal Drug Amendments. This regulatory scheme allows consideration of acceptable (*de minimis*) risk and has proposed the use of a formal risk assessment procedure to determine the risk of the substance. This scheme is distinct from that used in the regulation of environmental contaminants in that the agency focuses solely on the potential risk, ignoring beneficial properties or use of the substance.

The classification of a substance by the FDA is critical to the application of a particular regulatory scheme. The Food, Drug and Cosmetic Act prohibits the use of a suspected carcinogen that has been classified as a food additive, whereas a suspected carcinogen that has been classified as either an environmental contaminant or veterinary drug may be permitted in commerce depending on the potential risk or benefit of the substance. An evaluation of risk is immaterial when a food additive is labeled a suspected carcinogen subject to the Delaney clause, because Congress has adopted a zero-risk policy toward carcinogens classified as food additives. This policy is unreasonable when a substance both poses significant risks and confers substantial benefits. A zero-risk policy is also impractical when sophisticated analytic capability has made possible the detection of substances in parts per billion—levels with little or no implications to health. Within the framework of a zero-risk policy, this increasing technological capability forces the FDA to initiate regulatory action for many substances that possess only an insignificant risk of carcinogenicity.

The Supreme Court in the benzene case, *Industrial Union Department, AFL-CIO* v. *American Petroleum Institute*, emphasized the need to consider the level of risk in all health safety regulations. Chief Justice Warren Burger wrote in that case:

> When the administrative record reveals only scant or nominal risk of material health impairment, responsible administration calls for avoidance of extravagant, comprehensive regulation.[68]

The FDA recognizes the importance of determining risk and has used section 406 of the act and the "DES proviso" as mechanisms to promote risk assessment and to develop the concept of *de minimis* risk regulation of carcinogens in food substances. These provisions, however, apply only to specific uses and do not address the vast quantity of substances that are potentially subject to the Delaney clause.

Interviews have indicated that there is a desire within the FDA to extend risk assessment and consideration of *de minimis* risk regulation to the food additive area.[69] Risk assessment is viewed by these FDA policy experts as a mechanism that will preserve the basic congressional policy of protecting the general public from carcinogens added to food while permitting carcinogenic substances that confer benefits to remain in use if the risk level is insignificant.

Thomas P. Grumbly, associate director of the USDA Food and Quality Service, discussed in a recent paper several legislative reform options to accomplish the consideration of risks in food additives.[70] He first suggests that administrative discretion on scientific and regulatory matters in general could be increasingly transferred by Congress to the executive agency. Congress would simply provide a general framework for the regulation of food additives and leave the administrator with the discretion to make the fundamental trade-offs among risk, health, and economics. This approach, embodied in the Federal Insecticide, Fun-

68. 448 U.S. 607 (1980).
69. Interviews with Stuart Pape, Richard Cooper, and Michael Taylor (October 1980).
70. Thomas Grumbly, "Regulatory Science and Public Policy."

gicide and Rodenticide Act, enables the administrator to make risk-benefit judgments.

The second option that the FDA could seek is to preserve the existing legislation and ask Congress to deal with carcinogenic substances that pose insignificant risks on a case-by-case basis. This is essentially the approach adopted during the saccharin debate. Grumbly believes this approach is unrealistic because it ignores the complexity of the food safety laws, including the stringent testing requirements that would result in further stagnation of the regulatory process.

Finally, the FDA could opt for revisions that essentially ask Congress to continue to make the fundamental policy decisions concerning food safety, but to refine these decisions so as to give the administrator discretion to consider the risk to the general public of a suspected carcinogen when added to food. This is the approach of the "DES proviso," which enables the FDA to emphasize the high-risk substances and apply techniques that expedite the regulatory process. This approach, which preserves the basic congressional value judgments with respect to carcinogens, is supported by FDA policy experts because it gives the FDA flexibility in dealing with substances such as sodium nitrite.[71] Further, it allows the agency to regulate a great number of suspected carcinogens within a reasonable time frame.

A final point concerning the application of risk analysis policy is that the agency should be conscious of the benefits and merits of risk assessment. In short, the mechanism of risk assessment can expedite the regulatory process. As a scientific process, it can help regulators distinguish between high-risk substances and those that have both acceptable carcinogenic risks and social and economic benefits. This allows the agency to not overburden the industry with data acquisition requirements but instead concentrate on simple and effective tests for determining threshold carcinogenic potential.

71. Ibid.; and interview with Stuart Pape (October 1980).

Selected Bibliography

THIS BIBLIOGRAPHY is divided into two parts. Complete citations, listed alphabetically, are given in part A; in part B the same publications are listed under subject headings by author and date only.

A. Alphabetical Listing

Aksoy, M. "Leukemia in Shoe-Workers Exposed Chronically to Benzene," *Blood,* vol. 44 (1974).

———. "Leukemia in Workers Due to Occupational Exposure to Benzene," *New Istanbul Centris. Clin. Sci.,* vol. 12 (1977).

———. "Benzene and Leukemia," *Lancet,* no. 1 (1978).

———, and others. "Hematological Effects of Chronic Benzene Poisoning in 217 Workers," *British Journal of Industrial Medicine,*. vol. 28 (1971).

———, and others. "Acute Leukemia Due to Chronic Exposure to Benzene," *American Journal of Medicine,* vol. 52 (1972a).

———, and others. "Details of Blood Changes in Thirty-Two Patients with Pancytopenia Associated with Long-term Exposure to Benzene," *British Journal of Industrial Medicine,* vol. 29 (1972b).

———, and others. "Acute Leukemia in Two Generations Following Chronic Exposure to Benzene," *Human Heredity,* vol. 24 (1974).

———, S. Erdem, and G. Dincol. "Types of Leukemia in Chronic Benzene Poisoning. A Study in Thirty-Four Patients," *Acta Haematologica,* vol. 55 (1976).

———, and S. Erdem. "Follow-up Study on the Mortality and the Development of Leukemia in Forty-Four Pancytopenic Patients with Chronic Exposure to Benzene," *Blood,* vol. 52 (1978).

Albert, Roy E., and Bernard Altshuler. "Considerations Relating to the Formulation of Limits for Unavoidable Population Exposures to Environmental Carcinogens," in C. L. Sanders and others, eds., *Radionuclide Carcinogeneses,* Proceedings of the Twelfth Annual Hanford Biology Symposium. Springfield, Va.: NTIS, 1972.

Altshuler, B., N. Nelson, and M. Kuschner. "Estimation of Lung Tissue Dose from the Inhalation of Radon and its Daughters," *Health Physics,* vol. 10 (1964).

Amdur, Mary O. "Toxicological Guidelines for Research on Sulfur Oxides and Particulates," in *Proceedings of the Fourth Symposium on Statistics and the Environment*. Washington, D.C.: American Statistical Association, 1977.

American Petroleum Institute. *An Evaluation of the Environmental Protection Agency's Risk Assessment Methodology Applied to Photochemical Oxidant (Ozone)*. Washington, D.C.: API, September 1978.

Antonioli, Donald A., Louis Burke, and Emanuel A. Friedman. "Natural History of Diethylstilbestrol-Associated Genital Tract Lesions: Cervical Ectopy and Cervicovaginal Hood," *American Journal of Obstetrics and Gynecology,* vol. 137 (August 1, 1980).

Armitage, P., and R. Doll. "Stochastic Models for Carcinogenesis," *Proceedings of the Fourth Berkeley Symposium on Mathematics, Statistics and Probability*. Berkeley: University of California Press, 1961.

Ashby, John, and J. A. Styles. "Does Carcinogenic Potency Correlate with Mutagenic Potency in the Ames Assay?" *Nature,* vol. 271 (February 2, 1978).

Asher, I. M., and C. Zervos, eds. *Structural Correlates of Carcinogenesis and Mutagenesis: A Guide to Testing Priorities?* Proceedings of the Second FDA Office of Science Summer Symposium, U.S. Naval Academy, Aug. 31–Sept. 2, 1977.

Bartlett, D., C. S. Faulkner, and K. Cook. "Effect of Chronic Ozone Exposure on Lung Elasticity in Young Rats," *Journal of Applied Physiology,* vol. 37 (1974).

Bartsch, H., and others. "Value of Mutagenicity Tests in Predicting the Carcinogenic Effect of Chemicals," in *Carcinogenesis*. Proceedings of the Twelfth International Cancer Congress, vol. 1. Oxford: Pergamon Press, 1979.

Basta, Daniel J., and Blair T. Bower, eds. *Analyzing Natural Systems: Analysis for Regional Residuals—Environmental Quality Management*. Washington, D.C.: Resources for the Future, 1982.

Beebe, G. W. "What Is Considered Certain Regarding Human Somatic Effects of Ionizing Radiation?" Clinical Epidemiology Branch, National Cancer Institute, 1980.

Bell, K., and others. "Respiratory Effects of Exposure to Ozone Plus Sulfur Dioxide in Southern Californians and Eastern Canadians," *American Industrial Hygiene Association Journal,* vol. 38 (1977).

Berg, Robert L., ed. *Health Status Indexes*. Proceedings of a conference conducted by Health Services Research. Chicago: Hospital Research and Educational Trust, 1973.

Bibbo, Marluce, and others. "Follow-up Study of Male and Female Offspring of DES-Exposed Mothers," *Journal of the American College of Obstetricians and Gynecologists,* vol. 49 (January 1977).

Boice, John D., Jr., and Charles E. Land. "Ionizing Radiation" in David Schottenfeld and Joseph F. Fraumeni, Jr., eds., *Cancer Epidemiology and Prevention*. Philadelphia: W. D. Saunders, 1982.

Bora, K. C. "A Hierarchical Approach to Mutagenicity Testing and Regulatory Control of Environmental Chemicals," *Mutation Research,* vol. 41 (1976).

Breslow, Norman. "Design and Analysis of Case-Control Studies" in Norman Breslow, Jonathan E. Fielding, and Lester B. Lave, eds., *Annual Review of Public Health,* vol. 3. Palo Alto: Annual Reviews, 1982.

Bridges, B. A. "Evaluation of Mutagenicity and Carcinogenicity Using a Three-Tier System," *Mutation Research,* vol. 41 (1976a).

———. "Use of a Three-Tier Protocol for Evaluation of Long-Term Toxic Hazards, Particularly Mutagenicity and Carcinogenicity," in R. Montesano and others, *Screening Tests in Chemical Carcinogenesis*. Lyons, France: International Agency for Research on Cancer, 1976b.

Brodsky, Allen. "Radiation Risks: An Historical Perspective." Paper presented at the Radiation and Health Conference, Hershey, Pa., September 14, 1979.

Brook, Robert H., and others. *Conceptualization and Measurement of Health for Adults in the Health Insurance Study,* vol. 8: *Overview*. Santa Monica: Rand Corporation, 1979.

Brown, J. Martin. "Linearity vs. Non-Linearity of Dose Response for Radiation Carcinogenesis," *Health Physics,* vol. 31 (September 1976).

Brown, M. M., and others. "Literature Survey of Bacterial, Fungal, and *Drosophila* Assay Systems Used in the Evaluation of Selected Chemical Compounds for Mutagenic Activity," *Journal of the National Cancer Institute,* vol. 62 (April 1979).

Brussgaard, A. "The Occurrence of Certain Forms of Cancer Among Employees in Gasworks," *Tidsskrift den Norske Laegeforening* [Norwegian Medical Association Journal], vol. 79 (1969).

Buckley, Ramon D., and others. "Ozone and Human Blood," *Archives of Environmental Health,* vol. 30 (1975).

Burton, C. S., and others. "Oxidant/Ozone Ambient Measurement Method: Assessment and Evaluation." San Raphael, Calif.: Systems Applications, Inc., 1976.

The Business Roundtable. *Cost of Government Regulation Study: Executive Study*. New York: The Business Roundtable, March 1979.

Carnegie-Mellon University, Department of Engineering and Public Policy/School of Urban and Public Affairs. "Selected Strategies for Reducing Risks from Diagnostic X-Radiation." Pittsburgh: 1979.

Carroll, R. "Photochemical Oxidants and Human Health: Evaluation of Epidemiological Evidence." Washington, D.C.: American Petroleum Institute, 1977.

Carson, Rachel. *Silent Spring*. Houghton Mifflin, 1962.

Chang, Im Won. "Study on the Threshold Limit Value of Benzene and Early Diagnosis of Benzene Poisoning," *Journal of Catholic Medical College,* vol. 23 (1972).

Chapman, W. H., H. L. Fisher, and M. W. Pratt. "Concentration Factors of Chemical Elements in Edible Aquatic Organisms," Lawrence Radiation Laboratory, University of California, December 1968.

Christian, H. A. "Cancer of the Lung in Employees of a Public Utility," *Journal of Occupational Medicine,* vol. 4 (1962).

Coffin, D. L., and E. J. Bloomer. "Alterations of the Pathogenic Role of Streptococci Group C in Mice Conferred by Previous Exposure to Ozone," in I. H. Silver, ed., *Aerobiology: Proceedings of the Third International Symposium*. New York: Academic Press, 1970.

Cohen, Bernard L. "Society's Valuation of Life Saving in Radiation Protection and Other Contexts," *Health Physics,* vol. 38 (1980).

Cohen, J. J. "A Suggested Guideline for Low Dose Radiation Exposure to Populations Based on Benefit-Risk Analysis." Paper presented at the Sixteenth Annual Meeting of the Health Physics Society, New York, July 1971.

Cornfield, Jerome. "Carcinogenic Risk Assessment," *Science,* vol. 198 (November 18, 1977).

Corvalis Environmental Research Laboratory. *Human Health Damages from Mobile Source Air Pollution: A Delphi Study*. U.S. Environmental Protection Agency, 1978.

Court-Brown, W. *Human Population Cytogenetics*. Amsterdam: North-Holland, 1967.

Crandall, Robert W., and Lester B. Lave, eds. *The Scientific Basis of Health and Safety Regulation*. Washington, D.C.: Brookings Institution, 1981.

Crump, K. S., and others. "Fundamental Carcinogenic Processes and Their Implications for Low Dose Risk Assessment," *Cancer Research,* vol. 36 (September 1976).

Crump, K. S., H. A. Guess, and K. L. Deal. "Confidence Intervals and Test of Hypotheses Concerning Dose Response Relations Inferred from Animal Carcinogenicity Data," *Biometrics,* vol. 33 (September 1977).

Decker, T. R. "A Summary of the Radioactive Material Releases from Nuclear Power Plants." U.S. Nuclear Regulatory Commission, March 1978.

Deichmann, W., W. E. MacDonald, and E. Bernal. "The Hemopoietic Tissue Toxicity of Benzene Vapors," *Toxicology and Applied Pharmacology,* vol. 5 (1963).

DeLucia, A. J., and W. C. Adams. "Effects of Ozone Inhalation During Exercise on Pulmonary Function and Blood Biochemistry," *Journal of Applied Physiology,* vol. 3 (1977).

de Serres, Frederick J., and John Ashby, eds. *Evaluation of Short-Term Tests for Carcinogens*. New York: Elsevier/North-Holland, 1981.

Diel, J. H. "Local Doses to Lung Tissue from Inhaled $^{238}PuO_2$ Particles," *Radiation Research,* vol. 75 (1978).

Dixon, R. L. "Problems in Extrapolating Toxicity Data for Laboratory Animals to Man," *Environmental Health Perspectives,* vol. 13 (February 1976).

Doll, R., and others. "Mortality of Gasworkers with Special Reference to Cancers of the Lung and Bladder, Chronic Bronchitis and Pneumoconiosis," *British Journal of Industrial Medicine,* vol. 22 (1965).

Doniger, David D. *The Law and Policy of Toxic Substances Control: A Case Study of Vinyl Chloride*. Baltimore: Johns Hopkins University Press for Resources for the Future, 1978.

Druckrey, H. "Quantitative Aspects in Chemical Carcinogenesis," in R. Truhaut, ed. *Potential Carcinogenic Hazards from Drugs: Evaluation of Risks*. Berlin: Springer-Verlag, 1967.

Ellett, W. H., and R. M. Humes. "Absorbed Fractions for Small Volumes Containing Proton-Emitting Radioactivity," Medical Internal Radiation Dose Committee, *Journal of Nuclear Medicine,* Supplement 5, Pamphlet 8 (March 1971).

Fannick, N., L. T. Gonshor, and J. Shockley, Jr. "Exposure to Coal Tar Pitch Volatiles at Coke Ovens," *American Industrial Hygiene Association Journal,* vol. 33 (July 1972).

Fine, D. D., and others. "N-Nitroso Compounds in Air and Water." Paper presented at the meeting of the International Agency for Research on Cancer, October 1975.

Fletcher, J. L., and W. L. Dotson. *HERMES—A Digital Computer Code for Estimating Regional Radiological Effects from the Nuclear Power Industry*. HEDL-TIME-71-168. U.S. Atomic Energy Commission, December 1971.

Food Safety Council. "Proposed System for Food Safety Assessment," *Food and Cosmetics Toxicology,* vol. 16 (December 1978).

Forni, A. M., D. Pacifico, and A. Limonta. "Chromosome Studies in Workers Exposed to Benzene, Toluene, or Both," *Archives of Environmental Health,* vol. 22 (1971).

Forni, A. M., and others. "Chromosome Changes and Their Evolution in Subjects With Past Exposure to Benzene," *Archives of Environmental Health,* vol. 23 (1971).

Frank, R., J. Hackney, and P. Mueller. "Report on Visit to Von Nieding Laboratory," U.S. Court of Appeals for the District of Columbia Circuit, *American Petroleum Institute* v. *Costle,* No. 79-1104, Joint Appendix (1977).

Freke, A. M. "A Model for the Approximate Calculations of Safe Rates of Discharge of Radioactive Wastes into Marine Environments," *Health Physics,* vol. 13 (1967).

Garner, R. J. "A Mathematical Analysis of the Transfer of Fission Products to Cow's Milk," *Health Physics,* vol. 13 (1967).

———, and R. Scott Russell. "Isotopes of Iodine," in R. S. Russell, ed., *Radioactivity and Human Diet*. Oxford: Pergamon Press, 1966.

Gaylor, David W., and Raymond E. Shapiro. "Extrapolation and Risk Estimation for Carcinogenesis," in Myron A. Mehlman, Raymond E. Shapiro, and Herbert Blumenthal, eds., *Advances in Modern Toxicology,* vol. 1, pt. 2: *New Concepts in Safety Evaluation*. New York: Halsted Press, 1979.

Gehring, P. J., P. G. Watanabe, and C. N. Park. "Resolution of Dose-Response Toxicity Data for Chemicals Requiring Metabolic Activation: Example—Vinyl Chloride," *Toxicology and Applied Pharmacology,* vol. 44 (1978).

Girard, R., F. Tolot, and J. Bourret. "Hydrocarbure, benzeniques et hemopathies graves," *Archives des Maladies Professionelles de Medecine du Travail et de Securite Sociale,* vol. 31 (1970).

Gittelsohn, Alan. "Evaluation of Hockey Stick Functions Used To Establish

Pollution Health Effect Thresholds.'' Washington, D.C.: American Petroleum Institute, 1977.

Gofmekler, V. A. ''Effect on Embryonic Development of Benzene and Formaldehyde in Inhalation Treatments,'' *Hygiene and Sanitation,* vol. 33 (1968).

Goldstein, Bernard D. ''Hematoxicity in Humans,'' in Sidney Laskin and Bernard D. Goldstein, eds., *Benzene Toxicity: A Critical Evaluation, Journal of Toxicology and Environmental Health,* Supplement 2 (1977).

———. ''Experimental and Clinical Problems of Effects of Photochemical Pollutants.'' New York Academy of Medicine, June 1980.

Goldstein, E., and others. ''Adverse Influence of Ozone on Pulmonary Bactericidal Activity of Lung,'' *Nature* (London), no. 279 (1971).

Gori, Gio Batta. ''The Regulation of Carcinogenic Hazards,'' *Science,* vol. 208 (April 18, 1980).

Graham, John D., and James W. Vaupel. ''The Value of a Life: What Difference Does it Make?'' Paper presented at the Engineering Foundation Conference on Risk-Benefit Analysis in Water Resources Management, Asilomar, Calif., September 22, 1980.

Green, J. D., and others. ''Inhaled Benzene Fetotoxicity in Rats,'' *Toxicology and Applied Pharmacology,* vol. 46 (1978).

Grumbly, Thomas. ''Regulatory Science and Public Policy.'' Paper presented at Animal Health Institute meeting, Key Biscayne, Fla., October 9, 1980.

Guess, Harry, Kenny Crump, and Richard Peto. ''Uncertainty Estimates for Low-Dose-Rate Extrapolations of Animal Carcinogenicity Data,'' *Cancer Research,* vol. 37 (October 1977).

Hackney, J., and others. ''Experimental Studies on Human Health Effects of Air Pollutants: I. Design Considerations,'' *Archives of Environmental Health,* vol. 30 (1975a).

———, and others. ''Experimental Studies on Human Health Effects of Air Pollutants: II. Four-Hour Exposure to Ozone Alone and in Combination With Other Pollutant Gases,'' *Archives of Environmental Health,* vol. 30 (1975b).

———, and others. ''Experimental Studies on Human Health Effects of Air Pollutants: Two-Hour Exposure to Ozone Alone and in Combination With Other Pollutant Gases,'' *Archives of Environmental Health,* vol. 30 (1975c).

———, and others. ''Effects of Ozone Exposure in Canadians and Southern Californians,'' *Archives of Environmental Health,* vol. 32 (1978).

———, and W. S. Linn. ''Experimental Evaluation of Air Pollutants in Humans as a Basis for Estimating Risk.'' Paper presented at Thirteenth International Rochester Conference on Environmental Toxicity, University of Rochester, July 2–4, 1980.

Hamburg, Frederick C. ''Atmospheric Dispersion Modeling—A Critical Review, Discussion Papers—Comments,'' *Journal of the Air Pollution Control Association,* vol. 29 (September 1979).

Hammer, D. I., and others. ''The Los Angeles Student Nurse Study,'' *Archives of Environmental Health,* vol. 28 (1974).

Harnden, D. G. "Relevance of Short-Term Carcinogenicity Tests to the Study of the Carcinogenic Potential of Urban Air," *Environmental Health Perspectives,* vol. 22 (February 1978).

Hartwich, G., and G. Schwanitz. "Chromosomenuntersuchungen Nachchronischer Benzol-Exposition," *Deutsche Medizinische Wochenschrift,* vol. 97 (1972).

Harvey, Donald C., and others. "Survey of Food Products for Volatile N-Nitrosamines," *Journal of the AOAC,* vol. 59 (1976).

Hazucha, M., and others. "Pulmonary Function in Man After Short-Term Exposure to Ozone," *Archives of Environmental Health,* vol. 27 (1973).

———, and D. V. Bates. "Combined Effects of Ozone and Sulfur Dioxide on Human Pulmonary Function," *Nature,* no. 257 (1975).

Herbst, A. L. "Summary of the Changes in the Human Female Genital Tract as a Consequence of Maternal Diethylstilbestrol Therapy," *Journal of Toxicology and Environmental Health,* Supplement 1 (1976).

———, and others. "Clear-Cell Adenocarcinoma of the Vagina and Cervix in Girls: Analysis of 1970 Registry Cases," *Journal of Obstetric Gynecology,* vol. 119 (July 1974).

Hill, A. B. "The Environment and Diseases: Associations and Causation," *Proceedings of the Royal Society of Medicine,* vol. 58 (1965).

Hoffman, F. Owen, and Charles F. Baes, III, eds. "A Statistical Analysis of Selected Parameters for Predicting Food Chain Transport and Internal Dose of Radionuclides." Oak Ridge National Laboratory, Health and Safety Research Division, October 1979.

Holzworth, George C. *Mixing Heights, Wind Speeds and Potential for Urban Air Pollution Throughout the Contiguous United States,* U.S. Environmental Protection Agency, Office of Air Programs, January 1972.

Horn, H. J., R. B. Bruce, and O. E. Paynter. "Toxicology of Chlorobenzilate," *Journal of Agricultural and Food Chemistry,* vol. 62 (1955).

Infante, P. F. "Reply," *Lancet,* no. 2 (1977).

———, and others. "Leukemia in Benzene Workers," *Lancet,* no. 2 (1977).

Innes, J. R. M., and others. "Bioassay of Pesticides and Industrial Chemicals for Tumorigenicity in Mice: Preliminary Note," *Journal of the National Cancer Institute,* vol. 42 (1969).

Interagency Regulatory Liaison Group. "Scientific Bases for Identifying Potential Carcinogens and Estimating Their Risks," Report of the IRLG Work Group on Risk Assessment. Washington, D.C.: 1979.

International Commission on Radiological Protection. *Recommendations of Committee II on Permissible Dose for Internal Radiation,* publication no. 2. New York: Pergamon Press, 1959.

———. *The Evaluation of Risks from Radiation,* publication no. 8. Oxford: Pergamon Press, 1966.

———. *Recommendations of Committee II on Permissible Dose for Internal Radiation,* publication no. 19. Oxford: Pergamon Press, 1972.

———. *Report of the Task Group on Reference Man,* publication no. 23. Oxford: Pergamon Press, 1975.

Jenkins, L. J., Jr., R. A. Jones, and J. Siegel. "Long-term Inhalation Screening Studies of Benzene, Toluene, O-xylene and Cumene on Experimental Animals," *Toxicology and Applied Pharmacology,* vol. 16 (1970).

Jones, H. B., and A. Grendon. "Environmental Factors in the Origin of Cancer and Estimation of the Possible Hazard to Man," *Food and Cosmetic Toxicology,* vol. 13 (March 1975).

Kagawa, J., and T. Toyoma. "Photochemical Air Pollution: Its Effects on Respiratory Function of Elementary School Children," *Archives of Environmental Health,* vol. 30 (1975).

Kagawa, J., T. Toyoma, and M. Nakaza. "Pulmonary Function Tests in Children Exposed to Air Pollution," in A. J. Finkel and W. C. Duel, eds., *Clinical Implications of Air Pollution Research.* Acton, Mass.: Publishing Sciences Group, 1976.

Kawai, M., H. Amanoto, and K. Harada. "Epidemiological Study of Occupational Lung Cancer," *Archives of Environmental Health,* vol. 14 (1967).

Kellerer, A. M., and H. H. Rossi. "A Generalized Formulation of Dual Radiation Action," *Radiation Research* 75 (1978).

Kennaway, E. L., and N. M. Kennaway. "A Further Study of the Incidence of Cancer of the Lung and Larynx," *British Journal of Cancer,* vol. 1 (1947).

Kennedy, A. R., and J. B. Little. "Radiation Carcinogenesis in the Respiratory Tract," in Curtis C. Harris, ed., *Pathogenesis and Therapy of Lung Cancer,* vol. 10: *Lung Biology in Health and Disease.* Harvard University, School of Public Health, 1978.

Kimm, Victor J., Arnold M. Kuzmack, and David W. Schnare. "Waterborne Carcinogens: A Regulator's View," in Robert W. Crandall and Lester B. Lave, eds., *The Scientific Basis of Health and Safety Regulation.* Washington, D.C.: Brookings Institution, 1981.

Kissling, M., and B. Speck. "Chromosome Aberration In Experimental Benzene Intoxication," *Helvetica Medica Acta,* vol. 36 (1972).

Kraybill, H. F. "Conceptual Approaches to the Assessment of Nonoccupational Environmental Cancer," in H. F. Kraybill and Myron A. Mehlman, eds., *Advances in Modern Toxicology,* vol. 3: *Environmental Cancer.* New York: Wiley, 1977.

Kuhn, Thomas S. *Structure of Scientific Revolutions.* University of Chicago Press, 1970.

Land, Charles E. "Presentation to OSHA Hearings on Coke Oven Standards." May 4, 1976.

———. "Estimating Cancer Risks from Low Doses of Ionizing Radiation," *Science,* vol. 209 (September 12, 1980).

Laskin, S., M. Kuschner, and T. Drew. "Studies in Pulmonary Carcinogenesis," in M. G. Hanua, P. Nettlesheim, and J. Gilbert, eds., *Inhalation Carcinogenesis,* Atomic Energy Commission Symposium Series no. 18. AEC, 1970.

Laskin, S., and Bernard D. Goldstein, eds. *Benzene Toxicity: A Critical Evaluation, Journal of Toxicology and Environmental Health,* Supplement 2 (1977).

Lassiter, Donald V. "Occupational Carcinogenesis," in H. F. Kraybill and Myron A. Mehlman, eds. *Advances in Modern Toxicology,* vol. 3, *Environmental Cancer*. New York: Wiley, 1977.

Last, J. A. "Collagen and Mucopolysaccharide Synthesis after Acute and Chronic Exposure to Oxidant Gases." University of California, Davis, California Primate Research Center, 1980.

Lave, Lester B. "Health Benefits of Abating Air Pollutants," *Bulletin of the New York Academy of Medicine,* vol. 54 (1978).

———. "Health, Safety, and Environmental Regulations," in Joseph A. Pechman, ed., *Setting National Priorities: Agenda for the 1980s*. Washington, D.C.: Brookings Institution, 1980.

———. "Conflicting Objectives in Regulating the Automobile," *Science,* vol. 212 (May 22, 1981a).

———. *The Strategy of Social Regulation: Decision Frameworks for Policy*. Washington, D.C.: Brookings Institution, 1981b.

———, and Warren E. Weber. "A Benefit-Cost Analysis of Auto Safety Features," *Applied Economics,* vol. 2 (October 1970).

———, and L. Freeburg. "Health Effects of Electricity Generation from Coal, Oil and Nuclear Fuel," *Nuclear Safety,* vol. 14 (1973).

———, and Eugene P. Seskin. *Air Pollution and Human Health*. Baltimore: The Johns Hopkins University Press for Resources for the Future, 1977.

———, and Gilbert S. Omenn. *Clearing the Air: Reforming the Clean Air Act*. Washington, D.C.: Brookings Institution, 1981.

———, and others. "A Model for Selecting Short-Term Tests of Carcinogenicity," *Journal of the American College of Toxicity* (in press).

Leong, Basil K. G. "Experimental Benzene Intoxication," in S. Laskin and Bernard D. Goldstein, eds., *Benzene Toxicity: A Critical Evaluation, Journal of Toxicology and Environmental Health,* Supplement 2 (1977).

Linn, W., and others. "Health Effects of Ozone Exposure in Asthmatics," *American Review of Respiratory Disease,* vol. 117 (1978).

———, and others. "Effect of Low-Level Exposure to Ozone on Arterial Oxygenation in Humans." *American Review of Respiratory Disease,* vol. 119 (1979).

———, and others. "Short-Term Respiratory Effects of Polluted Ambient Air: A Laboratory Study of Volunteers in a High-Oxidant Community," *American Review of Respiratory Disease,* vol. 121 (1980).

Lloyd, J. William, and others. "Long-Term Mortality Study of Steelworkers: V. Respiratory Cancer in Coke Plant Workers," *Journal of Occupational Medicine,* vol. 13 (February 1971).

Loevinger, R. "Distributed Radionuclide Sources," in F. H. Attix and E. Tochilin, eds., *Radiation Dosimetry*. New York: Academic Press, 1969.

Loewe, W. E. and E. Mendelsohn, "Revised Dose Estimates at Hiroshima and Nagasaki," *Health Physics,* vol. 41 (October 1981).

Louis, Thomas, and Milton Weinstein. "Redesigning Bioassays to Enhance their Contribution to Regulation." Paper presented at First World Congress on Toxicology and Environmental Health, Washington, D.C., May 1982.

Luken, Ralph H., and Stephen G. Miller. "The Benefits and Costs of Regulating Benzene," *Journal of the Air Pollution Control Association,* vol. 31 (1981).

MacMahon, B., T. Pugh, and J. Ipsen. *Epidemiologic Methods.* Boston: Little, Brown, 1960.

Maltoni, C., and C. Scarnato. "The First Experimental Proof of the Carcinogenic Action of Benzene," *Medicina del Lavoro,* vol. 5 (1979).

Mantel, N., and W. R. Bryan. "Safety Testing of Carcinogenic Agents," *Journal of the National Cancer Institute,* vol. 27 (August 1960).

Mantel, N., and others. "An Improved Mantel-Bryan Procedure for 'Safety' Testing of Carcinogens," *Cancer Research,* vol. 35 (1975).

Marshall, Eliot. "New A-Bomb Data Shown to Radiation Experts," *Science,* vol. 212 (May 22 and June 19, 1981).

Martin, J. A., C. B. Nelson, and P. A. Cuny. *AIREM Program Manual—A Computer Code for Calculating Doses and Depositions Due to Emissions of Radionuclides.* U.S. Environmental Protection Agency, Office of Radiation Programs, 1976.

Maugh, Thomas H., II. "Chemicals: How Many are There?" *Science,* vol. 199 (January 13, 1978).

Mays, C. W., H. Spiess, and A. Gerapach. "Skeletal Effects Following Ra-224 Injections into Humans," *Health Physics,* vol. 35 (1978).

Mazumdar, Sati, and others. "The Epidemiological Study of Exposure to Coal Tar Pitch Volatiles among Coke Oven Workers," *Journal of the Air Pollution Control Association,* vol. 25 (April 1975).

McCann, Joyce, and Bruce N. Ames. "Detection of Carcinogens as Mutagens in the *Salmonella*/Microsome Test: Assay of 300 Chemicals: Discussion," *Proceedings of the National Academy of Sciences,* vol. 73 (March 1976).

———. "The *Salmonella*/Microsome Mutagenicity Test: Predictive Value for Animal Carcinogenicity," in H. H. Hiatt and others, eds., *Origins of Human Cancer: Book C. Human Risk Assessment.* Cold Spring Harbor Laboratory, 1977.

McCann, Joyce, and others. "Detection of Carcinogens as Mutagens in the *Salmonella*/Microsome Test: Assay of 300 Chemicals," *Proceedings of the National Academy of Sciences,* vol. 72 (December 1975).

McMichael, A. J., and others. "Solvent Exposure and Leukemia among Rubber Workers, An Epidemiologic Study," *Journal of Occupational Medicine,* vol. 17 (1975).

Menzel, Daniel B., and others. "Heinz Bodies Formed in Erythrocytes by Fatty Acid Ozonides and Ozone," *Archives of Environmental Health,* vol. 30 (1975).

Merrill, Richard A. "Regulating Carcinogens in Food: A Legislator's Guide to the Food Safety Provisions of the Federal Food, Drug, and Cosmetic Act," *Michigan Law Review,* vol. 77 (December 1978).

———. "Regulation of Toxic Chemicals," *Texas Law Review,* vol. 58 (February 1980).

———. "Federal Regulation of Cancer-Causing Chemicals," Draft Report to the Administrative Conference of the United States. Washington, D.C.: Administrative Conference, April 1982.

Miller, Catherine. "Case Study of the Revision of the National Ambient Air Quality Standard for Ozone." John F. Kennedy School of Government, Harvard University, 1980.

Mirabella, V. A. "Atmospheric Dispersion Modeling—A Critical Review, Discussion Papers—Comments," *Journal of the Air Pollution Control Association,* vol. 29 (September 1979).

Mitelman, F., and G. Levan. "Clustering of Aberrations to Specific Chromosomes in Human Neoplasms, III: Incidence and Geographic Distribution of Chromosome Aberrations in 856 Cases," *Hereditas,* vol. 89 (1978).

Morgan, K. Z., and J. E. Turner, eds. *Principles of Radiation Protection.* New York: Wiley, 1967.

Morgan, M. Granger. "Bad Science and Good Policy Analysis." *Science,* vol. 201 (September 15, 1978).

———, M. Hendrion, and S. Morris. "Expert Judgments for Policy Analysis." Report of an Invitational Workshop Held at Brookhaven National Laboratory, July 8–11, 1979. Pittsburgh: Carnegie-Mellon University, 1979.

Mosteller, Frederick, and John W. Tukey. *Data Analysis and Regression: A Second Course in Statistics.* Reading, Mass.: Addison-Wesley, 1977.

Murray, F. J., and others. "Embryotoxicity of Inhaled Benzene in Mice and Rabbits," *American Industrial Hygiene Association Journal,* vol. 40 (1979).

Mustafa, M. G. "Influence of Dietary Vitamin E on Lung Cellular Sensitivity to Ozone in Rats," *Nutrition Reports International,* vol. 11 (1975).

Myers, David K., and Howard B. Nucombe. *Nuclear Power and Low Level Radiation Hazards.* Public Comments on the Work Group Reports: Interagency Task Force on the Health Effects of Ionizing Radiation. U.S. Department of Health, Education, and Welfare, June 1979.

National Academy of Sciences. Advisory Committee on the Biological Effects of Ionizing Radiation. *The Effects on Populations of Exposure to Low Levels of Ionizing Radiation.* Washington, D.C.: NAS, 1972.

———. ———. *Considerations of Health Benefit-Cost Analysis for Activities Involving Radiation Exposure and Alternatives.* U.S. Environmental Protection Agency, 1977.

———. ———. *The Effects on Populations of Exposure to Low Levels of Ionizing Radiation.* Washington, D.C.: NAS, 1980.

———. Committee on Prototype Explicit Analyses for Pesticides. *Regulating Pesticides.* Government Printing Office, 1980.

———. Committee on Toxicology. *Health Effects of Benzene: A Review.* Washington, D.C.: NAS, 1976.

National Cancer Advisory Board, Subcommittee on Environmental Carcinogenesis. "The Relation of Bioassay Data on Chemicals to the Assessment of the Risk of Carcinogens for Humans Under Conditions of Low Exposure," Draft (January 1979).

National Cancer Institute. *Guidelines for Carcinogen Bioassay in Small Rodents.* Carcinogenesis Technical Report Series, no. 1. Government Printing Office, 1976.

———. *Bioassay of Chlorobenzilate for Possible Carcinogenicity.* Department of Health, Education and Welfare, 1978.

Nawrot, P. S., and R. E. Staples. "Embryofetal Toxicity and Teratogenicity of Benzene and Toluene in the Mouse," *Teratology*, vol. 19 (1979).

Nelson, N. "Discussion of Paper by Vaun A. Newill, R. Wyzga and James R. McCarrol," *Bulletin of the New York Academy of Medicine*, vol. 54 (1978).

Newberne, Paul M. "Dietary Nitrite in the Rat." Cambridge, Mass.: Massachusetts Institute of Technology, May 1978.

———. "Nitrite Promotes Lymphoma Incidence in Rats," *Science*, vol. 204 (June 8, 1979).

———, and R. C. Shank. "Induction of Liver and Lung Tumors in Rats by the Simultaneous Administration of Sodium Nitrite and Morphine," *Food and Cosmetics Toxicology*, vol. 11 (1973).

Oak Ridge National Laboratory. "Proceedings of a Workshop on the Evaluation of Models Used for the Environmental Assessment of Radionuclide Releases." Gatlinburg, Tennessee, September 6–9, 1977.

Omenn, Gilbert S., and Robert D. Friedman. "Individual Differences in Susceptibility and Regulation of Environmental Hazards." Washington, D.C.: n.d.

Ott, M. G., and others. "Mortality among Individuals Occupationally Exposed to Benzene," *Archives of Environmental Health*, vol. 31 (1978).

Pagnotto, L. D., and others. "Industrial Benzene Exposure from Petroleum Naphtha. I: Rubber Coating Industry," *American Industrial Hygiene Association Journal*, vol. 21 (1980).

Palmer, A. "Mortality Experience of Fifty Workers with Occupational Exposure to CHP," *Journal of Occupational Medicine*, vol. 21 (1979).

Patrick, D. L., J. W. Bush, and M. M. Chen. "Toward an Operational Definition of Health," *Journal of Health and Social Behavior*, vol. 14 (January 1973).

Picciano, D. "Cytogenetic Study of Workers Exposed to Benzene," *Environmental Research*, vol. 19 (1979).

Pochin, Edward E. "Assumption of Linearity in Dose-Effect Relationships," *Environmental Health Perspectives*, vol. 22 (February 1978).

Poirier, Lionel A., and Frederick J. de Serres. "Initial National Cancer Institute Studies on Mutagenesis as a Prescreen for Chemical Carcinogens: An Appraisal," *Journal of the National Cancer Institute*, vol. 62 (April 1979).

Purchase, I. F. H., and others. "Evaluation of Six Short Term Tests for Detecting Organic Chemical Carcinogens and Recommendations for Their Use," *Nature*, vol. 264 (December 16, 1976).

Raab, Otto G., Steven A. Book, and Norris J. Parks. "Bone Cancer from Radium: Canine Dose Response Explains Data for Mice and Humans," *Science*, vol. 208 (April 4, 1980).

Radford, Edward. "Radiation Dosimetry," *Science*, vol. 213 (August 7, 1981).

Radomski, J. L. "Evaluating the Role of Environmental Chemicals in Human Cancer," in Myron A. Mehlman, Raymond E. Shapiro, and Herbert Blumenthal, eds., *Advances in Modern Toxicology*, vol. 1, *New Concepts in Safety Evaluation*. New York: Halsted Press, 1979.

Rai, Kamta, and John Van Ryzin. "Risk Assessment of Toxic Environmental Substances Using a Generalized Multi-Hit Dose Response Model," in Norman E. Breslow and Alice S. Whittemore, eds., *Energy and Health*. Philadelphia: Society for Industrial and Applied Mathematics, 1979.

Rall, D. P. "Species Differences in Carcinogenesis Testing," in H. H. Hiatt and others, eds., *Origins of Human Cancer: Book C. Human Risk Assessment*. Cold Spring Harbor Laboratory, 1977.

Redmond, Carol K., and others. "Long-Term Mortality Study of Steelworkers: VI. Mortality from Malignant Neoplasms among Coke Oven Workers," *Journal of Occupational Medicine*, vol. 14 (August 1972).

———, B. R. Strobino, and R. H. Cypess. "Cancer Experience Among Coke By-product Workers," in U. Sofiotti and J. K. Wagoner, eds., *Carcinogenesis Annals of the New York Academy of Sciences*, vol. 217. New York Academy of Sciences, 1976.

Reid, D. D., and Carol Buck. "Cancer in Coking Plant Workers," *British Journal of Industrial Medicine*, vol. 13 (1956).

Rosenkranz, Herbert S., and Lionel A. Poirier. "Evaluation of the Mutagenicity and DNA-Modifying Activity of Carcinogens and Noncarcinogens in Microbial Systems," *Journal of the National Cancer Institute*, vol. 62 (April 1979).

Russell, J. L., and F. L. Galpin. "Comparison of Techniques for Calculating Doses to the Whole Body and to the Lungs from Radioactive Noble Gases." Paper presented to the mid-year topical symposium of the Health Physics Society, Richland, Wash., November 1971.

Saffiotti, V., F. Cefis, and L. Kobb. "A Method for Experimental Induction of Bronchogenic Carcinoma," *Cancer Research*, vol. 28 (1968).

Sagan, L. A. "Human Costs of Nuclear Power," *Science*, vol. 177 (August 11, 1972).

Salsburg, David S. "Use of Statistics When Examining Lifetime Studies in Rodents to Detect Carcinogenicity," *Journal of Toxicology and Human Health*, vol. 3 (1977).

Savin, W., and W. Adams. "Effects of Ozone Inhalation on Work Performance and VO_2 Max," *Journal of Applied Physiology*, vol. 46 (1979).

Scherer, E., and P. Emmelot. "Multihit Kinetics of Tumor Cell Formation and Risk Assessment of Low Doses of Carcinogen," in A. Clarke Griffin and Charles R. Shaw, eds., *Carcinogens: Identification and Mechanisms of Action*. New York: Raven Press, 1979.

Schoettlin, C. E., and E. Landau. "Air Pollution and Asthmatic Attacks in the Los Angeles Area," *Public Health Reports*, vol. 76 (1961).

Schoneich, Jorg. "Safety Evaluation Based on Microbial Assay Procedures," *Mutation Research*, vol. 41 (1976).

Selikoff, Irving J., E. Cuyler Hammond, and Jacob Churq. "Asbestos Exposure, Smoking, and Neoplasia," *Journal of the American Medical Association*, vol. 204 (April 8, 1968).

Shank, R. C., and Paul M. Newberne. "Dose-Response Study of Carcinogenicity of Dietary Sodium Nitrite Morpholine in Rats and Hamsters," *Food and Cosmetic Toxicology*, vol. 14 (January 1976).

Sidorenko, G. I., and M. A. Pinigin. "Concentration-Time Relationship for Various Regimens of Inhalation of Organic Compounds," *Environmental Health Perspectives,* vol. 13 (February 1976).

Simmon, Vincent F. "In Vitro Mutagenicity Assays of Chemical Carcinogens and Related Compounds with *Salmonella typhimurium,*" *Journal of the National Cancer Institute,* vol. 62 (April 1979a).

———, and others. "Mutagenic Activity of Chemical Carcinogens and Related Compounds in the Intraperitoneal Host-Mediated Assay," *Journal of the National Cancer Institute,* vol. 62 (April 1979b).

Snyder, R., and J. J. Kocsis. "Current Concepts of Benzene Toxicity," *CRC Critical Reviews in Toxicology* (June 1978).

Snyder, W. S., and others. "Estimates of Absorbed Fractions for Monoenergetic Photon Sources Uniformly Distributed in Various Organs of a Heterogeneous Phantom," Medical Internal Radiation Dose Committee, *Journal of Nuclear Medicine,* Supplement 3, Pamphlet 5 (August 1969).

Society of Toxicology ED_{01} Task Force. "Reexamination of the ED_{01} Study—Risk Assessment Using Time," *Fundamental and Applied Toxicology,* vol. 1 (1981).

Spengler, J. D. "Atmospheric Dispersion Modeling—A Critical Review, Discussion Papers—Comments," *Journal of the Air Pollution Control Association,* vol. 29 (September 1979).

Staffa, Jeffrey A., and Myron A. Mehlman, eds. *Innovations in Cancer Risk Assessment (ED_{01}* Study), Journal of Environmental Pathology and Toxicology, Special Issue, vol. 3 (1980).

Stallones, R. A. "Report on Mortality from Leukemia." Shell Oil Co., 1977.

Sterling, Theodor D. "A Critical Reassessment of the Evidence Bearing on Smoking as the Cause of Lung Cancer," *American Journal of Public Health,* vol. 65 (September 1975).

———. "Additional Comments on the Critical Assessment of the Evidence Bearing on Smoking as the Cause of Lung Cancer," *American Journal of Public Health,* vol. 66 (February 1976).

Stokinger, H. E. "Effects of Air Pollution on Animals," in A. C. Stern, ed., *Air Pollution,* vol. 1. New York: Academic Press, 1962.

Sundquist, James L. "The Crisis of Competence in Government," in Joseph A. Pechman, ed., *Setting National Priorities: Agenda for the 1980s.* Washington, D.C.: Brookings Institution, 1980.

Sutherland, J. V., and J. C. Bailar, III. "Multihit Models: Assumptions and Generalizations," in *Carcinogenesis.* Proceedings of the Twelfth International Cancer Congress, vol. 1. Oxford: Pergamon Press, 1979.

Sweet, F., K. Ming-Shian Kao, and S. D. Lee. "Ozone Selectively Inhibits Growth of Human Cancer Cell," *Science,* vol. 209 (August 22, 1980).

Tabershaw, I. "Mortality Study Among Refinery Workers," American Petroleum Institute, research no. EA-740247P. Washington, D.C.: API, 1974.

———, and S. Lamm. "Letter," *Lancet,* no. 2 (1977).

Tannenbaum, Steven R., and others. "Nitrite and Nitrate Are Formed by Endogenous Synthesis in the Human Intestine," *Science,* vol. 200 (June 30, 1978).

Tareeff, E. M., and others. "Benzene Leukemias," *Acta Unio Internationalis Contra Cancrum,* vol. 19 (1963).

Task Group on Lung Dynamics of the ICRP Committee II. "Deposition and Retention Models for Internal Dosimetry of the Human Respiratory Tract," *Health Physics,* vol. 12 (1966).

Taylor, Lauriston S. "The Development of Radiation Protection Standards." Public Comments on the Work Group Reports: Interagency Task Force on the Health Effects of Ionizing Radiation. U.S. Department of Health, Education and Welfare, June 1979.

Thorpe, J. J. "Epidemiological Survey of Leukemia in Persons Potentially Exposed to Benzene," *Journal of Occupational Medicine,* vol. 16 (1974).

Tomatis, L. "The Predictive Value of Rodent Carcinogenicity Tests in the Evaluation of Human Risks," *Annual Review of Pharmacological Toxicology,* vol. 19 (1979).

Tough, I. M., and W. Court-Brown. "Chromosome Aberrations and Exposure to Ambient Benzene," *Lancet,* no. 1 (1965).

Tough, I. M., and others. "Chromosome Studies on Workers Exposed to Atmospheric Benzene," *European Journal of Cancer,* vol. 6 (1970).

Turner, D. Bruce. *Workbook of Atmospheric Dispersion Estimates,* Office of Air Programs Publication no. AP-26. U.S. Environmental Protection Agency, 1970.

———. "Atmospheric Dispersion Modeling—A Critical Review," *Journal of the Air Pollution Control Association,* vol. 29 (May 1979).

Ullrich, R. L., and J. B. Storer. "Influence of Gamma Ray Irradiation on the Development of Neoplastic Disease in Mice: I. Reticular Tissue Tumors," *Radiation Research,* vol. 80 (1979).

United Nations Scientific Committee on the Effects of Atomic Radiation. *Ionizing Radiation: Levels and Effects,* vol. 2: *Effects*. New York: United Nations, 1972.

———. *Sources and Effects of Ionizing Radiation*. New York: United Nations, 1977.

U.S. Atomic Energy Commission. *Environmental Survey of the Nuclear Fuel Cycle*. WASH-1248. Directorate of Licensing, Fuels, and Materials. AEC, November 1972.

———. *Draft Environmental Statement Concerning Proposed Rulemaking Action: Numerical Guides for Design Objectives and Limiting Conditions for Operation to Meet the Criterion "As Low as Possible" for Radioactive Material on High Water-Cooled Nuclear Power Reactor Effluents*. Prepared by the Directorate of Regulatory Standards, U.S. Atomic Energy Commission, January 1973.

U.S. Congress. House. Committee on Governmental Operations. Subcommittee on Manpower and Housing. *Performance of the Occupational Safety and Health Administration*. Hearings. 95 Cong. 1 sess. Washington, D.C.: Government Printing Office, 1977.

———. Senate. Committee on Agriculture, Nutrition and Forestry. Subcommittee on Agricultural Research and General Legislation. *Food Safety and*

Quality: Nitrites. Hearings. 95 Cong. 2 sess. Washington, D.C.: Government Printing Office, 1978.

U.S. Consumer Product Safety Commission. "Review and Analysis of the Literature Pertaining to the Reproductive Effects of Exposure to Benzene." CPSC, 1980.

U.S. Department of Health, Education and Welfare. *Report of the Secretary's Commission on Common Pesticides and Their Relation to Environmental Health*. HEW, 1969.

U.S. Department of Health and Human Services. Food and Drug Administration. "Assessment of Estimated Risk Resulting from Aflatoxin in Consumer Peanut Products and Other Food Contaminants." FDA, January 1978a.

———. ———. *Report of the Interagency Working Group on Nitrite Research*. HHS, 1980a.

———. ———. *Re-evaluation of the Pathology Findings of Studies on Nitrite and Cancer: Histologic Lesions in Sprague-Dawley Rats*. Final Report to the Department of Health and Human Services. HHS, 1980b.

———, ——— and the U.S. Department of Agriculture. "FDA's and USDA's Action Regarding Nitrite." Draft Report, August 1978b.

U.S. Department of Labor. Occupational Safety and Health Administration. "Inflation Impact and Analysis of the Proposed Standard for Coke Oven Emissions," February 27, 1976.

———. ———. *Transcript of Proceedings, Informal Hearings on Proposed Standard for Exposure to Benzene*. OSHA, 1977a.

———. ———. *Economic Impact Statement: Benzene* (2 vols.). OSHA, May 1977b.

U.S. Environmental Protection Agency. *Environmental Radiation Protection Requirements for Normal Operations of Activities in the Uranium Fuel Cycle*. Final Environmental Statement for 40 C.F.R. 190, vol. 1. EPA, November 1, 1976.

———. *A Summary Statement from the Advisory Panel on Health Effects of Photochemical Oxidants*. EPA, June 1977a.

———. "Human Population Exposures to Coke-Ovens Atmospheric Emissions." Center for Resource and Environmental Systems Studies. Report no. 27. EPA, November 1977b.

———. *Assessment of Human Exposures to Atmospheric Benzene*. EPA, 1978a.

———. *Assessment of Health Effects of Benzene Germane to Low-Level Exposure*. EPA, September 1978b.

———. *Proposed Revisions to the National Ambient Air Quality Standard for Photochemical Oxidants: Report of the Regulatory Analysis Review Group*. EPA, October 1978c.

———. "Short-Term Tests for Carcinogens, Mutagens and Other Genotoxic Agents." Cincinnati, Ohio: Environmental Research Information Center, July 1979a.

———. "Review of a Method of Assessing the Health Risks Associated with Alternative Air Quality Standards for Ozone." Report of the Subcommittee on Health Risk Assessment. EPA, September 1979b.

———. Carcinogen Assessment Group. "Evaluation of the Carcinogenicity of Chlorobenzilate." EPA, 1978a.

———. Carcinogen Assessment Group. "Preliminary Report on Population Risk to Ambient Coke Oven Exposures." EPA, March 1978b.

———. Carcinogen Assessment Group. "Final Report on Population Risk from Ambient Benzene Exposure." EPA, 1979.

———. Office of Air Quality Planning and Standards. *A Method for Assessing the Health Risks Associated with Alternate Air Quality Standards for Ozone*. EPA, July 1978.

———. Office of Radiation Programs. *An Environmental Analysis of the Uranium Fuel Cycle*. Part I: *Fuel Supply;* Part II: *Nuclear Power Reactors;* Part III: *Nuclear Fuel Reprocessing*. EPA, 1973.

———. Office of Radiation Programs. *Environmental Radiation Dose Commitment—An Application to the Nuclear Power Industry*. EPA, February 1974.

———. Office of Research and Development. "An Assessment of the Health Effects of Coke Oven Emissions." EPA, April 1978.

———. Special Pesticide Review Division. "Chlorobenzilate: Position Document 3." EPA, 1978.

U.S. Federal Radiation Council. *Background Material for the Development of Radiation Protection Standards,* Report no. 1. Washington, D.C.: Government Printing Office, May 13, 1960.

U.S. National Institute for Occupational Safety and Health. "Criteria for a Recommended Standard: Occupational Exposure to Coke Oven Emissions," HEW, 1973.

———. *Occupational Exposure to Benzene*. NIOSH, 1974.

U.S. Nuclear Regulatory Commission. "Regulatory Guide 1-109—Calculation of Annual Doses to Man from Routine Releases of Reactor Effluents for the Purposes of Evaluating Compliance with 10 C.F.R. Part 50, Appendix I, Revision 12," October 1977.

———. "Summary of NCRC Staff Review of Radioecological Assessment of the NYHL Nuclear Power Plant," University of Heidelberg, June 1980.

U.S. Office of Science and Technology Policy. "Identification, Characterization, and Control of Potential Human Carcinogens: A Framework for Federal Decision-making." Staff Paper. OSTP, February 1, 1979.

U.S. Office of Technology Assessment. *Assessment of Technologies for Determining Cancer Risks from the Environment*. OTA, June 1981.

U.S. Regulatory Council. "Regulation of Chemical Carcinogens." September 1979.

Vigliani, E. C. "Benzene and Leukemia," *Environmental Research,* vol. 11 (1976a).

———. "Leukemia Associated with Benzene Exposure," *Annals of the New York Academy of Science,* vol. 271 (1976b).

———. "Occupational Animal Factors," Proceedings of the Eleventh International Congress on Cancer, 1976c.

Vogel, F., and A. G. Motulsky. *Human Genetics: Problems and Approaches*. Berlin: Springer-Verlag, 1979.

Von Nieding, A. "Studies of the Combined Effects of Nitrogen Dioxide, Sulfur Oxide, and Oxygen on Human Lung Function." Paper presented at Conference on Pollutants and High Risk Groups, University of Massachusetts, June 5–6, 1978.

Wade, L. "Observations on Skin Cancer Among Refinery Workers," *Archives of Environmental Health,* vol. 6 (1963).

Wald, N. "Radiation Injury," in Paul B. Beeson and Walsh McDermott, eds., *Textbook of Medicine,* 14th ed. Philadelphia: W. B. Saunders, 1975.

Watanabe, G. I., and S. Yoshida. "The Teratogenic Effect of Benzene in Pregnant Mice," *Acta Medica et Biologica,* vol. 17 (1970).

Weidenbaum, Murray L. *Costs of Regulation and Benefits of Reform*. Center for the Study of American Business, publication no. 35. St. Louis: Washington University, 1980.

Weinstein, Milton C. "Decision Making for Toxic Substances Control: Cost-Effective Information Development for the Control of Environmental Carcinogens," *Public Policy,* vol. 27 (Summer 1979).

Werthamer, S., L. H. Schwartz, and L. Soskind. "Bronchial Epithelial Alterations and Pulmonary Neoplasia Induced by Ozone," *Pathologia et Microbiologia,* vol. 35 (1970).

White, Lawrence. *Reforming Regulation: Processes and Problems*. Englewood Cliffs, N.J.: Prentice-Hall, 1981.

Whittemore, Alice S. "The Age Distribution of Human Cancer for Carcinogenic Exposures of Varying Intensity," *American Journal of Epidemiology,* vol. 106 (1977).

———, and Joseph B. Keller. "Quantitative Theories of Carcinogenesis," *SIAM Review,* vol. 20 (January 1978).

———, and E. Korn. "Asthma and Air Pollution in the Los Angeles Area," *American Journal of Public Health,* vol. 70 (1980).

Wolfe, S. M. "Standards for Carcinogens: Science Affronted by Politics" in H. H. Hiatt and others, eds. *Origins of Human Cancer: Book C. Human Risk Assessment*. Cold Spring Harbor Laboratory, 1977.

Wolman, Sandra R. "Cytologic and Cytogenetic Effects of Benzene," in S. Laskin and B. D. Goldstein, eds. *Benzene Toxicity: A Critical Evaluation, Journal of Toxicology and Environmental Health,* Supplement 2 (1977).

Woodard Research Corporation. "Chlorobenzilate Safety Evaluation by Dietary Feeding to Rats for 104 Weeks: Final Report, Geigy Chemical Corporation." Yonkers, N.Y., 1966.

Zeckhauser, Richard, and Albert Nichols. "The Occupational Safety and Health Administration—An Overview," *Study on Federal Regulation, Appendix to Vol. VI*. Senate. Committee on Governmental Affairs. 96 Cong. 1 sess. Washington, D.C.: Government Printing Office, 1978.

Zelac, R. E., and others. "Inhaled Ozone as a Mutagen. I. Chromosome Aberrations Induced in Chinese Hamster Lymphocytes," *Environmental Research,* vol. 4 (1971).

B. Subject Listing

Air pollution (*See also* **Ozone**)
Health effects
Amdur (1977)
Hammer and others (1974)
Lave (1978)
Lave and Seskin (1977)
Lave and Omenn (1981)
Schoettlin and Landau (1961)
Stokinger (1962)
Regulation
Lave and Omenn (1981)
U.S. Environmental Protection Agency (1977a)
——— (1978)
———, Office of Air Quality Planning and Standards (1978c)

Benzene
General
Goldstein (1977)
Laskin and Goldstein (1977)
Luken and Miller (1981)
National Academy of Sciences (1976)
U.S. Consumer Product Safety Commission (1980)
U.S. Environmental Protection Agency (1978a)
——— (1978b)
———, Carcinogen Assessment Group (1979)
Epidemiological studies
Aksoy (1974)
——— (1977)
——— (1978)
——— and others (1971)
——— and others (1972a)
——— and others (1972b)
——— and others (1974)
———, Erdem, and Dincol (1976)
——— and Erdem (1978)
Forni, Pacifico, and Limonta (1971)
Forni and others (1971)
Girard, Tolot, and Bourret (1970)
Goldstein (1977)
Infante (1977)
——— and others (1977)
McMichael and others (1975)
Ott and others (1978)
Pagnotto and others (1980)
Snyder and Kocsis (1978)
Stallones (1977)
Tabershaw (1974)
Tareef and others (1963)
Thorpe (1974)
Tough and others (1970)
Vigliani (1976a)
——— (1976b)
Laboratory studies
Chang (1972)
Deichmann, MacDonald, and Bernal (1963)
Gofmekler (1968)
Green and others (1978)
Hartwich and Schwanitz (1972)
Jenkins, Jones, and Siegel (1970)
Kissling and Speck (1972)
Leong (1977)
Maltoni and Scarnato (1979)
Murray and others (1979)
Nawrot and Staples (1979)
Picciano (1979)
Snyder and others (1969)
Tough and Court-Brown (1965)
U.S. Consumer Product Safety Commission (1980)
Watanabe and Yoshida (1970)
Wolman (1977)
Regulation
Chang (1972)
Luken and Miller (1981)
U.S. Department of Labor (1977a)
——— (1977b)

Carcinogenicity
General
Boice and Land (1982)
Gori (1980)
Interagency Regulatory Liaison Group (1979)
International Commission on Radiological Protection (1966)
Kellerer and Rossi (1978)
Kraybill (1977)
Laskin, Kuschner, and Drew (1970)
Lassiter (1977)
Maugh (1978)
Radford (1981)
Radomski (1979)
Society of Toxicology ED_{01} Task Force (1981)
U.S. Regulatory Council (1979)
Wald (1975)
Whittemore and Keller (1978)
Wolfe (1977)
Models
Armitage and Doll (1961)
Cornfield (1977)

Crump and others (1976)
Crump, Guess, and Deal (1977)
Druckrey (1967)
Gaylor and Shapiro (1979)
Guess, Crump, and Peto (1977)
Jones and Grendon (1975)
Kellerer and Rossi (1978)
Land (1980)
Mantel and Bryan (1960)
Mantel and others (1975)
National Academy of Sciences (1972)
——— (1980)
Radford (1981)
Rai and Van Ryzin (1979)
Scherer and Emmelot (1979)
Society of Toxicology ED_{01} Task Force (1981)
Sutherland and Bailar (1979)

Short-term tests
Ashby and Styles (1978)
Bartsch and others (1979)
Brown and others (1979)
de Serres and Ashby (1981)
Harnden (1978)
Lave and others (in press)
McCann and Ames (1976)
——— (1977)
Poirier and de Serres (1979)
Purchase and others (1976)
Rosenkranz and Poirier (1979)
Schoneich (1976)
Simmon (1979a)
——— (1979b)
U.S. Environmental Protection Agency (1979a)

Tier testing
Bora (1976)
Bridges (1976a)
——— (1976b)

Chlorobenzilate (*See also* **Pesticides**)
General
National Academy of Sciences (1980)
National Cancer Institute (1978)
U.S. Environmental Protection Agency, Carcinogen Assessment Group (1978a)
———, Special Pesticide Review Division (1978)

Laboratory studies
Horn, Bruce, and Paynter (1955)
Innes and others (1969)
Woodard Research Corporation (1966)

Coke oven gases
General
Fannick, Gonshor, and Shockley (1972)
Land (1976)
U.S. Environmental Protection Agency (1977b)
———, Carcinogen Assessment Group (1978b)
———, Office of Research and Development (1978)
U.S. National Institute for Occupational Safety and Health (1973)

Epidemiological studies
Brussgaard (1969)
Doll and others (1965)
Christian (1962)
Kawai, Amanoto, and Harada (1967)
Kennaway and Kennaway (1947)
Land (1976)
Lloyd and others (1971)
Mazumdar and others (1975)
Redmond and others (1972)
———, Strobino, and Cypess (1976)
Reid and Buck (1956)
Wade (1963)

Regulation
U.S. Department of Labor (1976)
U.S. National Institute for Occupational Safety and Health (1971)

Diethylstilbestrol (*See also* **Food additives**)
Antonioli, Burke, and Friedman (1980)
Bibbo and others (1977)
Herbst (1976)
Lave (1981b)

Economic methods
Graham and Vaupel (1980)
Lave (1981b)
Lave and Weber (1970)

Environmental dispersion
Basta and Bower (1982)
Chapman, Fisher, and Pratt (1968)
Freke (1967)
Hamburg (1979)
Hoffman and Baes (1979)
Holzworth (1972)
Kimm, Kuzmack, and Schnare (1981)
Loevinger (1969)
Martin, Nelson, and Cuny (1976)
Mirabella (1979)
Oak Ridge National Laboratory (1977)
Spengler (1979)
Turner (1970)
——— (1979)

Epidemiological methods
Breslow (1982)
Hill (1965)

MacMahon, Pugh, and Ipsen (1960)
Sterling (1975)
——— (1976)

Food additives and contaminants
General
Grumbly (1980)
Lave (1981b)
Merrill (1978)
——— (1982)
Health effects
Herbst (1976)
Lave (1981b)
Newberne (1978)
——— (1979)
——— and Shank (1973)
Shank and Newberne (1976)
Regulation
Food Safety Council (1978)
Grumbly (1980)
Lave (1981b)

Genetic effects (mutagenicity)
Court-Brown (1967)
Omenn and Friedman (n.d.)
Vogel and Motulsky (1979)

Ionizing radiation
(*See also* **Carcinogenicity**)
General
Altshuler, Nelson, and Kuschner (1964)
Beebe (1980)
Boice and Land (1982)
Brodsky (1979)
Brown (1976)
Carnegie-Mellon University (1979)
Cohen (1971)
Decker (1978)
Fletcher and Dotson (1971)
Garner (1967)
——— and Russell (1966)
International Commission on Radiological Protection (1959)
——— (1966)
——— (1972)
——— (1975)
Kellerer and Rossi (1978)
Kennedy and Little (1978)
Land (1980)
Lave and Freeburg (1973)
Loevinger (1969)
Morgan and Turner (1967)
Myers and Nucombe (1979)
National Academy of Sciences (1972)
——— (1980)
National Cancer Advisory Board (1979)
Raab, Book, and Parks (1980)
Radford (1981)
Russell and Galpin (1971)
Saffioti, Cefis, and Kobb (1968)
Sagan (1972)
Task Group on Lung Dynamics of the ICRP Committee II (1966)
Taylor (1979)
Ullrich and Storer (1979)
United Nations Scientific Committee on the Effects of Atomic Radiation (1972)
——— (1977)
U.S. Atomic Energy Commission (1972)
——— (1973)
U.S. Environmental Protection Agency (1976)
———, Office of Radiation Programs (1973)
———, ——— (1974)
U.S. Federal Radiation Council (1960)
U.S. Nuclear Regulatory Commission (1977)
——— (1980)
Wald (1975)
Dose estimation
Diel (1978)
Ellett and Humes (1971)
Loewe and Mendelsohn (1981)
Marshall (1981)
Epidemiological studies
International Commission on Radiological Protection (1959)
——— (1966)
——— (1972)
——— (1975)
Loewe and Mendelsohn (1981)
Marshall (1981)
National Academy of Sciences (1972)
——— (1980)
Radford (1981)
United Nations Scientific Committee on the Effects of Atomic Radiation (1972)
——— (1977)
Laboratory studies
International Commission on Radiological Protection (1959)
——— (1966)
——— (1972)
——— (1975)
Mays, Spiess, and Gerapach (1978)
Ullrich and Storer (1979)
Regulation
Brodsky (1979)
Carnegie-Mellon University (1979)
Cohen (1971)
Morgan and Turner (1967)
Myers and Nucombe (1979)

National Academy of Sciences (1977)
Taylor (1979)
U.S. Atomic Energy Commission (1972)
——— (1973)
U.S. Environmental Protection Agency (1976)
———, Office of Radiation Programs (1973)
———, ——— (1974)
U.S. Federal Radiation Council (1960)
U.S. Nuclear Regulatory Commission (1977)

Nitrosamines (*See also* **Food additives**)
Fine and others (1975)
Harvey and others (1976)
Lave (1981b)
Newberne (1978)
——— (1979)
——— and Shank (1973)
Shank and Newberne (1976)
Tannenbaum and others (1978)
U.S. Congress (1978)
U.S. Department of Health and Human Services, Food and Drug Administration (1980a)
———, ——— (1980b)
———, ———, and U.S. Department of Agriculture (1978b)

Ozone (*See also* **Air pollution**)
General
American Petroleum Institute (1978)
Burton and others (1976)
Corvalis Environmental Research Laboratory (1978)
Goldstein (1980)
Lave and Omenn (1981)
Miller (1980)
U.S. Environmental Protection Agency (1977a)
——— (1978c)
——— (1979b)
———, Office of Air Quality Planning and Standards (1978)
Epidemiological studies
Bell and others (1977)
Carroll (1977)
Gittelsohn (1977)
Kagawa and Toyoma (1975)
——— and Nakaza (1976)
Schoettlin and Landau (1961)
Whittemore and Korn (1980)
Laboratory studies
Bartlett, Faulkner, and Cook (1974)
Buckley and others (1975)
Coffin and Bloomer (1970)
DeLucia and Adams (1977)
Frank, Hackner, and Mueller (1977)
Goldstein (1977)
Hackney and others (1975a)
——— (1975b)
——— (1975c)
——— (1978)
——— and Linn (1980)
Hammer and others (1974)
Hazucha and others (1973)
Hazucha and Bates (1975)
Last (1980)
Linn and others (1977)
——— (1978)
——— (1979)
——— (1980)
Menzel and others (1975)
Mustafa (1975)
Savin and Adams (1979)
Sweet, Kao, and Lee (1980)
Von Nieding (1978)
Werthamer, Schwartz, and Soskind (1970)
Zelac and others (1971)
Regulation
American Petroleum Institute (1978)
U.S. Environmental Protection Agency (1978c)

Pesticides (*See also* **Chlorobenzilate**)
Carson (1962)
Innes and others (1969)
National Academy of Sciences (1980)
U.S. Department of Health, Education and Welfare (1969)

Regulation
Albert and Altshuler (1972)
Business Roundtable (1979)
Crandall and Lave (1981)
Doniger (1978)
Gori (1980)
Grumbly (1980)
Kimm, Kuzmack, and Schnare (1981)
Lave (1980)
——— (1981b)
——— and Weber (1970)
Luken and Miller (1981)
Merrill (1978)
——— (1980)
——— (1982)
Morgan (1978)
———, Hendrion, and Morris (1979)
Sundquist (1980)
U.S. Congress (1977)
Weidenbaum (1980)
Weinstein (1979)

White (1981)
Wolfe (1977)
Zeckhauser and Nichols (1978)

Risk assessment methods

General

American Petroleum Institute (1978)
Cornfield (1977)
Crump and others (1976)
Crump, Guess, and Deal (1977)
Food Safety Council (1978)
Interagency Regulatory Liaison Group (1979)
International Commission on Radiological Protection (1966)
Jones and Grendon (1975)
Kuhn (1970)
National Academy of Sciences (1972)
——— (1980)
National Cancer Advisory Board (1979)
Society of Toxicology ED_{01} Task Force (1981)
Staffa and Mehlman (1980)

Disease onset related to dose rate

Albert and Altshuler (1972)
Druckrey (1967)
Jones and Grendon (1975)
Raab, Book, and Parks (1980)
Sidorenko and Pinigin (1976)
Whittemore (1977)

Extrapolation (high to low doses)

Brown (1976)
Cornfield (1977)
Crump (1976)
Gaylor and Shapiro (1979)
Gittelsohn (1977)
Guess, Crump, and Peto (1977)
Interagency Regulatory Liaison Group (1979)
Jones and Grendon (1975)
Mantel and Bryan (1960)
Mantel and others (1975)
National Academy of Sciences (1972)
——— (1980)
National Cancer Advisory Board (1979)
Nelson (1978)
Pochin (1978)
Rai and Van Ryzin (1979)
Scherer and Emmelot (1979)
Society of Toxicology ED_{01} Task Force (1981)
Sutherland and Bailar (1979)

Extrapolation (rodents to humans)

Crump, Guess, and Deal (1977)
Dixon (1976)
Food Safety Council (1978)
Gaylor and Shapiro (1979)
Interagency Regulatory Liaison Group (1979)
Rall (1977)
Tomatis (1979)

Statistical models

Armitage and Doll (1961)
Cornfield (1977)
Crump and others (1976)
Crump, Guess, and Deal (1977)
Druckrey (1967)
Gaylor and Shapiro (1979)
Gehring, Watanabe, and Park (1978)
Mantel and Bryan (1960)
Mantel and others (1975)
Rai and Van Ryzin (1979)
Sutherland and Bailar (1979)
Whittemore (1977)
——— and Keller (1978)

Toxicological methods

Louis and Weinstein (1982)
National Cancer Institute (1976)
Salsburg (1977)
Society of Toxicology ED_{01} Task Force (1981)

Conference Participants

with their affiliations at the time of the conference

Roy E. Albert *New York University*

Elizabeth L. Anderson *Environmental Protection Agency*

Michael Baram *Bracken and Baram*

Nathaniel F. Barr *U.S. Department of Energy*

Thomas R. Bartman *University of Virginia*

Martha A. Beauchamp *American Petroleum Institute*

Martha A. Bradford *American Petroleum Institute*

Paul E. Brubaker *Exxon Corporation*

Kenneth T. Bogen *Congressional Research Service*

Edward Burger *Georgetown University*

William Capp *Gulf Science and Technology Company*

Salvatore J. Casamassima *Exxon Company*

Jerry L. Chandler *National Institute for Occupational Safety and Health*

J. B. Cordero *Food Safety Council*

Morton Corn *Johns Hopkins University*

William V. Corr *House Subcommittee on Health and the Environment*

Vincent T. Covello *National Science Foundation*

Robert W. Crandall *Brookings Institution*

Robert Cummings *Oak Ridge National Laboratories*

Robert J. Cynkar *Senate Subcommittee on Regulatory Reform*

Paul F. Deisler, Jr. *Shell Oil Company*

James V. DeLong *Administrative Conference of the United States*

C. J. Di Perna *Mobil Oil Corporation*

Ronald F. Docksai *Senate Committee on Labor and Human Resources*

R. E. Farrell *Standard Oil Company*

JoAnne Glisson *Senate Committee on Labor and Human Resources*

Bernard D. Goldstein *Rutgers University*

Michael Gough *Office of Technology Assessment*

Walter M. Gawlak *American Petroleum Institute*

Thomas P. Grumbly *House Subcommittee on Oversight and Investigations*

Leonard J. Guarraia *Synthetic Organic Chemical Manufacturers Association*

Ronald Hart *National Center for Toxicological Research*

David Hawkins *Natural Resources Defense Council*

David G. Hoel *National Institute of Environmental Health Sciences*

Fred D. Hoerger *Dow Chemical Company*

Thomas Hopkins *Council on Wage and Price Stability*

David Hughes *Procter and Gamble Corporation*

Steven Jellinek *Environmental Protection Agency*

Marvin H. Kosters *American Enterprise Institute for Public Policy Research*

David A. Kuhn *Continental Oil Company*

A. W. Kusch *Atlantic Richfield Company*

Lester B. Lave *Brookings Institution*

William Lowrance *Rockefeller University*

Ronald J. Marnicio *Carnegie-Mellon University*

Christopher H. Marraro *Carnegie-Mellon University*

Richard A. Merrill *University of Virginia*

Sanford Miller *Food and Drug Administration*

Laurence I. Moss *Energy/Environmental Design and Policy Analysis*

Thomas Orm *Consultant*

F. M. Parker *Tenneco, Inc.*

George T. Patton *American Petroleum Institute*

D. B. Rathbun *American Petroleum Institute*

R. D. Ridley *Occidental International*

Howard Runion *Gulf Science and Technology Company*

C. B. Scott *Union Oil Company of California*

Elliot A. Segal *House Subcommittee on Oversight and Investigations*

William T. Shepherd *Texaco, Inc.*

Robert Sielken, Jr. *Texas A&M University*

Max Singer *Hudson Institute*

M. Bruce Slomka *Shell Oil Company*

O. M. Slye *Mobil Oil Company*

Miller Spangler *Nuclear Regulatory Commission*

J. A. Sullivan *Standard Oil Company*

Steven M. Swanson *American Petroleum Institute*

Gail Updegraff *U.S. Department of Agriculture*

Arnold G. Voress *Union Carbide*

D. C. Wobster *Union Carbide*

Grover C. Wrenn *Clement Associates, Inc.*

Rudolph C. Yaksick *National Academy of Sciences*

Richard J. Zeckhauser *Harvard University*

Index